SPEECHES BY TONY BENN

Speeches
by
Tony Benn

SPOKESMAN BOOKS

1974

Published by the Bertrand Russell Peace Foundation Ltd.
Bertrand Russell House, Gamble Street, Nottingham
for *Spokesman Books*.

Printed by the Russell Press Ltd., Nottingham (TU)

Editor's Note

This selection of speeches, articles, letters and memoranda (many pre-viously not published) was chosen from the period 1951 to 1974 and within this period mainly from the last six years. The principle of choice has been to show Tony Benn's main political position and its develop-ment. I deliberately say 'position' because the speeches are reactions to actual political situations in relation to which his political philosophy emerges.

A central and unifying theme, it seemed to me, has emerged more strongly in the past few years: this is his consistent fight as a socialist to bring people into active involvement in all spheres from which they have been excluded.

The brief introductory comments to my selection of items were written by Tony Benn in August 1974.

Joan Bodington,
August 1974.

Acknowledgements

We wish to acknowledge permission to reprint articles from the following journals and newspapers.

Tribune for permission to reprint "The Great Debate" (14th June 1968), "After the Success of the Clyde Work-in" (6th June 1971), "Conference Democracy" (19th January 1973), "Labour Party Democracy" (15th June 1973).

Labour Weekly for permission to reprint "The Thoughts of Chairman Benn" (15th October 1971).

New Scientist for permission to reprint "Politics in a Technological Age" (6th and 13th June 1968), "Technology Assessment" (24th May 1973).

Business Administration for permission to reprint "Will you need a Visa to Visit Fords?" (May 1971).

Encounter for permission to reprint "Going into Europe" (1962).

Journal of the Royal Society of Arts for permission to reprint "Lecture on the Work of the Ministry of Technology" (18th November 1968).

Melody Maker for permission to reprint "Listening to the New Generation" (24th October 1970).

The Daily Mirror for permission to reprint "The Pentonville Five" (3rd August 1972).

The Times for permission to reprint "A Little Light in Dark Corners" (11th July 1973), "Misunderstood Champions of Democracy" (7th December 1973).

The Sunday Times for permission to reprint "Liberating the Lobby" (6th September 1970).

The Guardian for permission to reprint "Report on Manchester University Symposium on Broadcasting Policy" (9th February 1972).

Contents

FOREWORD by Tony Benn (August 1974)   9

I   INDUSTRIAL DEMOCRACY AND WORKERS' CONTROL
    1.   Industrial Democracy (1968)   11
    2.   Thinking About Workers' Control (1971)   16
    3.   Success at Upper Clyde (1971)   25
    4.   Public Enterprise and Workers' Control (1971)   29
    5.   Tolpuddle Revisited (1972)   35
    6.   The Pentonville Five (1972)   36

II. INDUSTRIAL POLICY
    1.   Reforming the Post Office (1966)   41
    2.   Government, Industry and Technology (1967)   43
    3.   Modernisation in Industry and Government (1968)   46
    4.   Government and Technology (1968)   48
    5.   Technology and the Quality of Life (1970)   52
    6.   Technology Assessment and Political Power (1973)   62
    7.   A Visa to Visit Fords? (1971)   67
    8.   Multinationals (1972)   70
    9.   Labour's Programme (1973)   76
    10. A Policy for Change (1973)   84
    11. Why New Politics are Needed (1973)   89

III. THE COMMON MARKET
    1.   Not Going into Europe (1963)   93
    2.   Technology and Politics in Europe (1968)   94
    3.   The Case for a Referendum (1970)   95
    4.   Referendum Campaign (1971)   100
    5.   The People Must Decide (1971)   103
    6.   A Grave Breach of the Constitution (1972)   113
    7.   Why Labour Opposed Entry (1972)   117
    8.   We Must Have that Referendum (1972)   119
    9.   Boycott European Institutions (1972)   130
    10. Renegotiation (1973)   133

IV. THE MASS MEDIA
    1.   Broadcasting and Democracy (1968)   135
    2.   Direct Access for Unions (1971)   143
    3.   A Voice for the People (1972)   145

V.   CIVIL LIBERTIES
    1.   The Case of Dr. Joseph Cort (1954)   153
    2.   Security Vetting (1956)   160
    3.   Computers and Freedom (1970)   162
    4.   Law and Order (1972)   164

VI.   BRISTOL
    1.   Against Hereditary Peerage (1961)   177
    2.   The New Bristol Group (1963)   179
    3.   The New Bristol Group in Action (1964)   180
    4.   The New Bristol Group Concludes its Work (1966)   181
    5.   The Index for Community Action (1973)   183

VII.   WOMEN AND YOUTH TODAY
    1.   Listening to the New Generation (1970)   185
    2.   Woman's Place (1971)   188

VIII.   THE HONOURS SYSTEM (1964)   197

IX.   OPEN GOVERNMENT
    1.   Developing a Participating Democracy (1968)   201
    2.   Politics in a Technological Age (1968)   207
    3.   The Barrier of Secrecy (1968)   215
    4.   Liberating the Lobby (1970)   218
    5.   The Politician Today (1970)   221
    6.   Controlling Science (1971)   224
    7.   The Civil Service and Political Advisers (1973)   232

X.   THE FUEL CRISIS AND THE THREE-DAY WEEK
    1.   The Energy Crisis (1973)   235
    2.   Monitoring the Crisis (1973)   243
    3.   Why the Three-day Week? (1974)   246
    4.   Challenging the Class Structure (1974)   254

XI.   LABOUR PARTY DEMOCRACY
    1.   The Labour Government and the Labour Party (1968)   259
    2.   A New Style of Politics (1968)   264
    3.   Developing the Party's Objectives (1971)   272
    4.   Democratic Politics (1971)   275
    5.   Unity with the Unions (1972)   289
    6.   Closing the Conference (1972)   292
    7.   Conference Democracy (1973)   294
    8.   Secrecy and the National Executive (1973)   298

INDEX   303

Foreword

Political speeches delivered at public meetings are in the oldest tradition of democratic debate; and they have retained their importance in the labour movement.

They are a part of the process of mutual education by which the people discuss and learn from their own experience.

These speeches, together with some articles and memoranda written over the years, record at least as much about what I have learned as about what I have tried to expound.

Some of the views expressed do not stand up so well to the test of time. Many are now widely accepted in the movement and outside.

Political arguments tend to be most sterile when they are confined within the limits of conventional wisdom and rotate around the personalities involved in them. The most fruitful are those parallel, analytical debates, rooted in our daily experience, which offer alternative explanations of that experience and open up different perspectives for the future.

Many of the speeches reproduced in this volume were intended to be part of that broader socialist debate.

Tony Benn
London, August 1974.

I
Industrial Democracy
and
Workers' Control

Industrial Democracy*

This speech referred to the solution mainly in terms of better communications and participation.

At that stage the Labour Party itself had got no further than a proposal for single-channel bargaining.

It was the experience of the GEC work-in in Liverpool in September 1969 and the later developments at UCS and elsewhere which clarified the real issues involved in workers' control.

If democracy means anything it means the establishment of institutions through which an individual can influence his own destiny by having some share of control over his material and human environment.

If we were to plot a graph of human fulfilment we should find it bore some relationship to the extent to which this power to influence our own lives existed.

Today a wide gap has opened up between man as a citizen enjoying full civil rights, enjoying greater freedom to think and move and act according to his wishes, and man as a wage-earner who at his place of work enjoys few of these rights.

When a man enters the factory gates in the morning, he sheds much of his dignity, with his overcoat, leaving both on a peg in the locker room. In the workshop he is part of an authoritarian type of society which differs sharply from his normal existence.

The extent of this authoritarianism varies according to the work he does and according to the degree of skill and imagination displayed by the management and to the strength of the Trade Unions in the plant. But great as these variations are, and they are enormous, man is a lesser creature than in his home or in his community.

There is another gap that is opened up too. However great his educational qualifications may be, if he works for a big firm the decision-making processes in that firm will be immensely complex

*Speech given at Industrial Society lunch, November 21, 1968.

involving considerations that cannot of their very nature be known to the individual. He thus finds his life at work conditioned by decisions that may be increasingly unintelligible to him. He does not know why these decisions are taken and yet he is expected to accept them. The case for a greater availability of company information is extremely strong.

The office worker's first introduction to automation may come when he sees the computers being delivered and installed. He hears the factory is to expand, or close or be moved. Technological change has brought a new type of uncertainty into life. If the very worst happens, technological change can strip him not only of his job, but through the obsolescence of his skill, of his self-respect too. Even the need for closer consultation on redundancies, and the provision of lump sum redundancy payment and an earnings-related pension scheme, vital as these are, do not go to the heart of the problem for those whose expertize has been rendered unnecessary.

Looking a few years ahead this process could go a great deal further. If that same man is, by then, working for a huge international corporation with world-wide outlets and a global strategy he will be a much smaller cog in the machine. Today there are men working in isolated factories who cannot fully understand or influence what the top brass in headquarters in Manchester or London are doing. How much less then will they understand or shape the decisions reached by the Boards of international companies run from Detroit, Milan or even Tokyo.

The rush of industrial mergers, many of which Mintech has helped to bring about, is now going on at such a pace, that the balance will, unless it is corrected, inevitably tilt against the man at work, in relation to his employer. Indeed one of the problems we have to face involves a much deeper analysis of the rights of those affected by mergers. Many international companies are already established in Britain. This is a problem with which we already have to contend.

The growth of large companies through mergers has gone on far more rapidly than Union mergers or the creation of supranational political institutions. The crucial role of Trade Unions, which would now have to be invented if they did not exist, is still not fully recognized.

The motor car industry provides a perfect example. Here we have three American-owned international companies, and one British-owned company, dominating the industry. There are over twenty Trades Unions representing the workers in the industry and the balance of power has moved heavily in favour of management.

The three international motor corporations operate across international frontiers with apparent ease. By contrast, the writ of

Governments still stops dead at the customs post. There is no political superstructure operating on a scale that, in any way, matches the scale of the international companies.

Thus for the individual worker in one of the international motor companies his membership of his trade union gives him a part-say in one-seventeenth of the total trade union voice in respect of the British component of that company which may itself have other components, within its command, that are 10 times as big as the British one. Similarly his vote in an election will only help to elect an MP in one parliament, sustaining one Government, which in relation to the international corporations, is just one Government among the many with which the corporation deals.

No wonder so many people are beginning to wonder whether they count as individuals at all. Could it be that, at any rate, some unofficial strikes are started because they are the easiest way of saying audibly "something is wrong and I want it put right".

We shall have to tackle these problems at a political level too. That is the heart of the argument about British entry into EEC. That is the case for far larger, far stronger, and perhaps internationally organised, trade unions.

But even if we had a United States of Europe with its own continental economic planning structure and further legislation on company law requiring disclosure of more information and even if we had a European General Workers Union, we should not automatically escape from the problems of remoteness. In fact, we should have to contend with new problems: remoteness affecting individual members of massive trade unions; and individual citizens in massive political communities, with all the communications difficulties involved. Nor incidentally, would the nationalisation of the British component of an international company necessarily help us solve this particular problem, if that component were only a part of a bigger whole.

But if all these things were right, the problems of man in his working environment remain to be tackled. This is what we mainly mean when we talk about industrial democracy. But we cannot really separate it from other discussions about the role of the trade unions, the decision-making process in industry about productivity and about consultation. The most important thing we have to try to do is to break through the water-tight compartments into which all these things had hitherto been confined.

Industrial democracy, in the past, has tended to rotate around too limited a range of arguments for, or against, nationalisation, workers' control, co-ownership and the placing of worker-directors on the board of management.

The role of the trades unions has too often been similarly confined

13

into arguments about wage negotiations, unofficial strikes, ballots and cooling-off periods and prices and incomes legislation.

Productivity has often been presented as if it just meant shorter tea breaks, longer hours, and a struggle against potential Luddites.

Consultation has often been spoken about as if it just meant a formal talk *after* decisions have been reached, or has involved prior discussion about such trifling matters as the colour in which the canteen is to be painted, or the car parking arrangements for the workers.

We shall never make any progress if we limit our discussions to such narrow confines as these.

We have got to start from scratch, to consider the role of people in their working environment, and see what they need to allow them to give their best and get the most out of what they do. If you can find a formula for doing that and it must include a role in management decision-making then almost everything else falls into place. People will become people again, and just because they are treated as such, productivity will rise and so will wages, and the task of management will be easier, as the democracy of the workshop develops more naturally. But if we go on behaving as if we believe that workers are only interested in wages, we must not be surprised if that is how they react. What is needed is a new dimension which recognizes the need for a fuller satisfaction from work and makes it possible.

I am not suggesting it is going to be easy to do that. But I am suggesting that many of the barriers that prevent us from finding a solution, are barriers that exist in our own minds.

If you start with the man, at his place of work, you will reduce the whole problem to more manageable proportions. He is then Joe Smith who works in the new factory at Stevenage along with a lot of other people. He is interested in his work including the decisions which affect it, his pay packet, his conditions, his prospects, his relations with his fellow workers and his security. His immediate working life is decided in the plant and it is there that communication must begin. A worker wants to be able to participate in decisions that affect him in the round, and not find that his working life is handled in bits and pieces by different people, on different occasions, none of whom are concerned with him as a person.

Thus he wants his wages, and his conditions, and his productivity and his promotion chances discussed and decided together. The present division into wage negotiation and consultation is completely destructive of that process of unification, and a single channel for both has great advantages.

He has got to get through, to management, that management itself, productivity, automation, wages, working conditions, human relations, and industrial training, are all different aspects of the same environment.

The worker may well discover, in the process, that he will acquire a far higher degree of respect for the professional skills involved in management. And similarly management will need to learn a far higher respect for the dignity and skill of the workers who work with him. It is the task of management to organise better communications and it is the mutual acceptance of a greater degree of respect and responsibility reflected in the relations between them that really matters. This will involve at least as great changes on the part of management at all levels as it does on the part of workers and their representatives.

This task is an urgent one. If we were to leave out of account human reactions and feelings there is no knowing how it might all end. And, equally important, if we try to solve this country's fundamental economic problems simply by demand management, secret board-room decisions, directives from the works manager, exhortations in newspaper leading articles, and a barrage of T.V. investigations we shall miss the whole point of what it is all about. It is about human beings and how and why they work. If Government-by-consent is the basic formula that makes our political system effective, it is at least as true that work-by-consent will be needed to make our industrial structure successful. And it may well be that in the experience of representative government at the national and local level there are lessons to be learned by industry.

If there is any valid parallel between our political system, and our industrial system, then we may find some part of the answer in improved communications. The whole parliamentary system has rested for centuries upon the experience we have had of the creative power of talk. This is not to blur the basic conflicts of interest that do exist, but to seek to resolve them.

It seems to me that we need much more talking at the factory and office level about industrial democracy.

Britain is still so hagridden by old ideas, and still so hopelessly divided by a hierarchical inheritance, that we have almost lost our capacity to look at old problems with the same freshness that comes so naturally to new countries.

The idea of an occasional mass meeting in a factory canteen in the lunch hour with the chairman, directors and shop stewards sitting on a table (as if they were Parliamentary candidates during an election campaign) speaking, listening and answering questions may seem quite ludicrous. Yet it is only at the plant level in tripartite discussions that the three functions of industry: efficient and profitable operation, service to the community and the achievement of fulfilment through properly rewarded work can be ventilated and reconciled.

15

Of this I am absolutely sure. We shall never make progress towards industrial democracy unless we set it in its widest context, begin thinking of people as people again right in the place where they work, talk about it together, right there and make a conscious effort to learn from the experience of others. We should naturally look to the public sector to give a lead here.

The exact machinery we evolve to make industrial democracy effective is very important and a number of concrete proposals have emerged in recent months. In addition we have to aim at the creation of a new mood and atmosphere in industry to make the new machinery work, based on mutual respect. Codification and statutory backing, though necessary will not work without it.

If we can do that we may find that we have solved a lot of other problems too including the basic economic problems that beset us. And if we cannot do the one I doubt if we can do the other either.

Thinking about Workers' Control*

This speech at the Annual Delegate meeting of the AUEW Foundry Section pointed to the need for a joint policy to be agreed between the Labour Party and the TUC.

It explored the idea of 100% workers' control on the municipal model, linked to an income-ratio of 10-1 within one firm. It also suggested a start in the nationalised industries, called for an extension of public ownership in shipbuilding and aircraft and a new policy to extend the public sector systematically in place of subsidies to private industry. In this respect it foreshadowed Labour's 1974 manifesto.

A great deal of policy thinking is now going on inside the Labour Party and we reviewed it at our weekend conference between the National Executive Committee and the Shadow Cabinet just 10 days ago. I want, today, to think aloud, in a purely personal capacity, about some aspects of industrial policy with which I have been, and still am, most concerned. We are agreed that it is essential to plan our future policy in close conjunction with the T.U.C. and our affiliated Trade Unions. There is no point in concealing the fact that the last Labour Government and the Trade Union Movement were disagreed on some important items of policy including our proposals on industrial

*Speech given at the Annual Delegate Meeting of the Amalgamated Union of Engineering Workers, Foundry Section, at the Winter Gardens, Morecambe, May 27, 1971.

relations and the statutory prices and incomes policies which we adopted.

Having been a member of that Government I willingly accept my full share of responsibility for what we did and I was proud to serve in a Government whose work will be treated more generously by future historians than it was at the time even by some of our friends.

But having said that it would be very foolish for any of us either to adopt a posture of total self-justification or to rake over the embers of past controversies just for the sake of it. We have got to start afresh in a situation that is radically changed.

First we must take account of the fact that unemployment has now emerged as a major national problem for the first time since the war.

Unemployment was too high under the Labour Government — especially in Scotland, Wales and the English regions. But at least we devoted hundreds of millions of pounds to get it down and to bring new industries into the development areas. When thousands of men became redundant due to the closure of a firm we didn't jump with joy at the death of a "lame duck" as happens now. Nor did we threaten to cut tariffs to bring in a flood of foreign imports, to make unemployment higher and weaken the power of the unions. Nor did we see the dole queue as a weapon to cut prices.

We must, therefore, begin our talks with the Trade Union Movement on future policy on a new basis. And for a start we must have a determined campaign to tackle rising unemployment which is now a blot on our country, imposes hardship on millions and destroys their self-respect.

Unemployment is the right point of entry for joint policy-making within the Labour Movement. In this way we can re-examine together the management of the economy and consider how to solve the problem of inflation which could threaten to undermine our living standards. We must get the spirit of this policy-making right. It would be fatal to think about it in the old terms. We are *not* now looking for a new Labour version of industrial relations legislation in some way to cater for the same needs that Mr. Carr saw in drafting his present odious Bill. Nor are we talking about going back to all the old ideas about prices and incomes.

We have got to broaden the argument and see our economic problems in human and political terms. One of the mistakes of the Labour Party has been its tendency to think that economic management and budgetary policy alone could get us the growth we want, or that legislation could solve the immensely complicated human relations that really determine the atmosphere in industry.

I feel this particularly strongly as a result of my experience as Minister of Technology over the four years that I spent there. We did a

17

great deal that was useful in encouraging the re-organisation of industry, in shipbuilding and engineering and by assisting the spread of new techniques that would help us to earn our living with less sweat and unnecessary effort.

But in one sense I became convinced that operating at Ministerial level on problems of industrial organisation could be a sort of technocratic dead end. There is a limit to what you can do by mergers and public money and encouraging better management even when you are dealing as humanely, as we tried to do, with the problems say of Upper Clyde shipbuilding.

What we are really looking for surely is a new approach to industrial policy that takes account of the human factor and makes our policy fit the people it is intended to help instead of doing it the other way round. The old idea of management from the top has got to be looked at again.

It isn't only the old family business where the grandson of the founder has inherited power that he is quite unfitted to wield. The new grey flannel brigade with their degrees in business studies, familiar with the language of accountancy and computers, and their shiny offices away from the dirt and noise of the factory floor are still often too remote, and claim too much power that they haven't the experience or knowledge to exercise properly.

I am strongly in favour of educating people in the complicated problems of organisation that have to be dealt with by upper management. There are plans to be made and long-term investment decisions that have to be got right and big marketing operations to be mounted and a host of administrative problems to be sorted out. Without expertise in these areas a firm can easily run into difficulties or even go bankrupt.

But it is also true that the man who actually has to do a job of work on the factory floor, or in a foundry, or in a shop or office is the best person to know how his or her work should be organised. There is nothing that creates more ill-will in industry than when people are denied the elementary authority they need to plan and guide the work they are qualified to do.

One of the most horrifying experiences of my Ministerial life was to walk round factories with management that obviously didn't know what was going on, or who was doing what, and yet quite happily assumed that the right to manage on behalf of the shareholders included the right to tell everybody what to do, and when things went wrong to try and find a remedy without consulting the men and women on whose work and effort the whole future of the firm depended.

I believe that there is more seething discontent in industry as a result of this situation than anyone is ready to admit. Indeed I think that many of the industrial disputes which we read about in the papers are merely triggered off by wage claims, and really reflect the deep feelings of workers who are fed up with being treated as if they were half-wits only fit to be told what to do and never asked for their advice or given the power to do things for themselves. They are consistently under-estimated and their intelligence is insulted because the structure of power in industry has failed to take account of the vastly improved educational advances of recent years; and the fact that the mass media – with all their faults on which I have strong views – have created a far more intelligent community than any country ever had in the whole of its history.

If we are going to talk about industrial policy let's start with the people. Let's forget about legislation for a moment and start talking about industrial democracy. And I mean industrial democracy and not just better communications, or more personnel managers, or consultations, or participation or company News Sheets. Least of all am I talking about putting one "tame" worker on the board of a company or trying to pretend that a few shares for the workers will make them all into little capitalists and iron out real conflicts of interest.

I am talking about democracy. And democracy means that the people ultimately control their managers. Just that, no less and no more. It's time we asked ourselves some fundamental questions about the management of industry.

For example why should the people who own a firm control it? We abandoned that principle years ago in the political arena. For centuries the people who owned the land in Britain ran Parliament. It took a hundred years of struggle to give the people the power to choose and remove their political managers – M.P.'s and Ministers. If we can trust the country to democracy why on earth can't we trust individual firms to the people who work in them?

This is not a particularly revolutionary doctrine in all conscience. No one is suggesting – at least I am not – that you do it by throwing petrol bombs or starting a guerilla movement in Morecambe. You could just as easily do it by peaceful industrial bargaining and by removing the obstacles to it by legislation.

I have always thought it was a great pity that working people in Britain set their sights so low. A wage claim to offset rising prices and improve real living standards is very important for workers and their families. But if the employer passes it on by raising his prices, which the workers have to pay back to him through the shops, the gain is not always as good as it looks. Worse still, it doesn't alter the power relationship between the worker and his employer at all. Indeed if the higher prices lead to higher profits and higher dividends it can actually widen the gap between rich and poor and thus prop up the very system that we ought now deliberately to be trying to replace.

The Trade Union Movement — in both the private and public sector — ought now to develop a conscious long-term policy of negotiating itself into a position of real power in industry. Nobody can doubt the negotiating strength of the Trade Union Movement in a modern industrial society. Indeed the Government is now underlining that power by attacking management for giving way so easily to wage claims. But why do management give way? Because they have no option. The dislocation that a prolonged strike will cause can sometimes be far more costly to the firm than paying the claim in full.

If the Trade Union Movement were to bargain as strongly for industrial power as it does for higher wages the management would also be ready to concede. Because then the alternative would be the high financial cost of a strike or the relatively low cost of sharing their power with the workers in their own firm.

No-one could expect to achieve everything in the first year. But if the Trade Union Movement set itself the target of negotiating for the workers power in each firm to acquire greater control of that firm, by agreement with the present management, over a five-year period — in my opinion it would succeed.

Moreover this could be done even with the present Government in power since no legislation would be needed. It might be that later a Labour Government would have to legislate to make it possible to finish the job by giving the workers the explicit right to do this.

After all, the present Industrial Relations Bill provides the most elaborate system of ballots to enforce the Tory view of trade union democracy and provide for the recognition of agency shops and the like. What could be easier than for a Labour Government to legislate, to carry it a stage further, so that the Boards of Directors of all companies were subjected to the same procedures for ballots when they were nominated by the shareholders and could be recalled, or replaced, if they did not measure up to the job.

It we did that, many of the problems of communication in industry would settle themselves. A Board of Directors which depended for their continuation in office on the consent of their work force would bend over backwards to communicate with them and consult them and let them participate and allow them to run their own work. They would have to.

Of course such a solution would not be without difficulties. A firm managed by consent would not find any of its problems solved by magic. It would still have to attract investment by getting a return on its capital. It would still have to find markets for its goods and produce the right products for those markets. It would still be liable to price itself out of the market by paying those who worked in it more than the market could bear. It would still need the best management it could possibly get, including the graduates in business studies. But with this one difference. They would be working, as workers, for the other workers and not for the shareholders alone.

Some Trade Unionists of the old school might object to this for another reason. They might fear that it would impose too great a responsibility on them and weaken their power to bargain for higher wages. But it would certainly not affect their bargaining role. They would still have to bargain about wages and conditions with the management the workers had chosen just as they now have to bargain with the managers that the shareholders have imposed on them. After all the electors still bargain with a Government even when they have elected it.

But it is true that this bargaining would be done under conditions in which the workers had to share the responsibility for the consequences of the increased wages they were asking and everything else they did.

Indeed one of the most powerful arguments for adopting the policies that I am discussing is exactly that *responsibility* would be placed upon workers in industry who already have *massive* power but are now denied the responsibility that should go with it. The third industrial revolution has transferred this bargaining power to the workshop, but the legal structure of our companies has not been adapted in such a way as to allow this responsibility to go with this new power.

For the community as a whole a policy for industrial democracy could help to combat inflation and increase productivity. Wage claims that might really bankrupt the firm would obviously not be pressed in a firm where self-management had placed the ultimate responsibility on the workers. And if the workers in a firm could be given the power to plan their own work, to take account of their own skills, productivity might increase more rapidly than could ever be achieved by hiring hordes of management consultants, to tell the managers, to tell the workers what to do in the interests of the shareholders.

But this alone would not be enough. It might – and I believe it would – provide the outline of a practicable sensible alternative to the shortsighted and reactionary Industrial Relations Bill now before Parliament.

But what it would not do would be to solve another equally difficult problem of the unacceptable differential between the highest paid directors in any company and the really low paid workers whose incomes are an affront to a society that pretends to be civilised.

It is true that the problems of differentials would certainly be discussed in any firm that had adopted self-management. But the percentage system by definition continually increases differentials again. 10% of £15 a week is very different from 10% of £20,000 a year and nothing that we have yet thought up, by way of national machinery, or ministerial intervention, offers us an answer to that problem.

It may well be that we have been looking at the problem from the wrong angle. It might be better to re-examine it from the point of view of the firm itself, since it is the firm which earns the income for everybody who draws his salaries or wages from that common pool. It is clear that if those at the top draw too much out of that pool there will be less for those at the bottom. The moral responsibility for seeing that those at the bottom get an adequate income must surely rest squarely and fairly on those others who draw a bigger income from the same pool.

If this is so then it is the ratio between the top salaries and the bottom wages in each firm that ought to interest us. Suppose just for example we set this ratio at 10-1. To take one case: suppose we laid it down that if the lowest wages in a firm were £15 a week – or £750 a year – then the highest salary paid should not exceed £7,500 a year. 10-1 is a very wide ratio but there are thousands of firms – if not the overwhelming majority – where the lowest paid do get £15 a week and the directors get £10,000, £20,000 or more which is not ten times as much, but twenty or thirty times as much.

If you were to work on the ratio of 10-1 how would you enforce this? Fortunately it would be relatively easy. The tax authorities would not accept as a tax deductible business expense any payment to a director, or anyone else, that was more than ten times as much as the lowest paid worker in that firm. If the firm paid him more it would have to come out of profits, and the shareholders would have to decide whether it was worth forking out money (that would otherwise come to them in dividends) to pay their top management. It would be the shareholders under the present system. But if the proposals that I have made for industrial democracy were accepted, then the workers would have to approve it too. It is possible that to recruit, or hold, really brilliant managers, both shareholders and workers might think it worthwhile allowing the 10-1 ratio to be exceeded. But it would be a conscious and agreed decision. For the general run of directors they would get no more money unless they raised the wages of their lowest paid workers. For every £1 per week granted at the bottom they would be allowed to vote themselves £10 a week. It still sounds a lot of money and it is. But it would be taxable. If every firm which now pays its directors £20,000 a year was obliged to pay its lowest paid worker 1/10th of that – which is £40 a week – we should have less to worry about on behalf of the lower paid. We should have to find the production to pay for it.

I suppose you could call that an Incomes Policy. For it deals with incomes. But it deals with incomes in a rather different way. It deals with the relationship between incomes, and it would iron out some of the gross inequalities that we now accept as normal but that ought to be regarded as unacceptable. Again it places responsibility where it ought to be — namely among the various groups who work in a particular firm. And it has the advantage of being entirely self-policing. For it is policed by the tax inspectors as part of their normal job.

It would even deal, indirectly, with the problems of dividends. For if the workers knew that the profits were high enough, they could either negotiate more of it by way of incomes more fairly distributed, or they could press their management for price cuts to expand their market and make their jobs more secure. Similarly if the profits were too low to attract investment, they would have to moderate their claims so as to attract the money needed for re-equipment and expansion.

So far I have not dealt with public enterprise. I have concentrated on the objectives of industrial democracy and a fairer distribution of wealth which public enterprise was invented to secure. I have emphasized that part of Clause 4 of the Labour Party Constitution which talks about "the best obtainable system of popular administration and control of each industry or service".

It is a sad reflection on the way in which we have set up our nationalised industries that even in those industries we have got nowhere near real industrial democracy nor achieved any fairer distribution or incomes between the board members and the lowest paid. So if the policies which I have been discussing were only applied in the public sector it would do more to change their social purposes and working environment than the act of nationalisation itself.

But there is no reason why we should not get exactly the same benefits even in firms that are privately owned. The shareholders could be contained into their more limited role, as investors, free to move their money in and out but deprived of their present insupportable and unenforcable claim to be the sole arbiter of the fate of the workers in the firms they own, or the sole authority to whom the management should be responsible.

What then is the case for the extension of public ownership? Clearly if by industrial democracy, and an egalitarian incomes policy we could drive capitalism back into a more limited role, as a form of investment deprived of the power that has historically gone with it, the argument about public ownership changes its character. But that is not to say it loses its force.

Quite the reverse. One thing should certainly be clear from our experience of the last Labour Government — and perhaps nobody is better qualified to say it than I am because I was responsible for administering the policy. Never again should a Labour Government pour money into private industry without claiming, and acquiring, the

23

same rights as any other private investor in exactly the same proportion as the total public investment stands to the private investment.

If we had done that in the last Labour Government many of the firms that we helped — certainly in shipbuilding and in the aircraft industry — would have automatically moved into the public sector simply by virtue of the grants and loans we made available. It would have been better to have done it that way. Next time we should see this as a conscious and constructive approach to the extension of public ownership.

After the Tories have first bankrupted, and then nationalised, and then subsidised Rolls Royce, we would certainly have nothing to fear from their opposition to such a policy in a general election campaign. Indeed I think the whole public attitude to public ownership has undergone a fundamental change and there is far more widespread support for it than there was even a few years ago.

And if nationalised industries were seen to be democratically run; and to be distributing incomes more fairly as well as being accountable to the public for the major decisions they make, we could take a massive step towards democratic socialism. And we could do it by the traditional means of common sense and public consent which lie at the hearts of the traditions of parliamentary democracy and the British Labour Movement.

Mr. Chairman, you will appreciate that I have just been thinking aloud. I am *not* speaking for the Shadow Cabinet of which I am a member *nor* for the Labour Party of which I am Vice-Chairman. I am hoping to start a great new debate within our Movement. We are democratic socialists operating in a free society and grappling with the problems of the third industrial revolution at a time when the most re-actionary and old fashioned and dictatorial policies for industry are in control in Whitehall and 10 Downing Street.

I am not seeking to deny responsibility for what the last Labour Government did nor engage in self-justification. That is now a past history and we should only study it to learn lessons for the future and to do better next time. The arguments of the past should be buried unless they can help us to avoid past mistakes and improve on our performance.

If I were to search for a keynote phrase to sum up what I have been trying to say it would be hard to do better than repeat a phrase that is already familiar to you: "More power to people". For that reflects exactly what the Labour Movement must stand for. It must mean believing in people and their capacity. It must mean sharing responsibility more generously and through a juster and fairer distribution of income giving more economic power to people who now experience unemployment or poverty so they can enjoy the fruits of their own labour and of the labour of us all.

This is the heart of our socialist belief. I am sure that unless we present it firmly, and believe in it, and argue for it, and keep at it until we have persuaded people to accept it we shall never be able to defeat the philosophy of the Government that is now in power.

But above all we must believe that it can be done. We must set our sights high. We must brush aside the pessimism of the ultra-right and the ultra-left both of whom tell us that we are destined to fail. Both are wrong. But only we, by our own efforts, can show the nation that there is another and better way.

Success at Upper Clyde*

This article in Tribune published on August 6, 1971 marked the end of the first stage in the UCS work-in, and pointed the way forward.

The public enquiry organised by the Scottish Trade Union Congress opened up many of the issues the Conservative Government wanted to conceal and the whole campaign gave a considerable impetus to the movement for workers' control.

After severe criticism in the Parliamentary Labour Party for supporting an illegal occupation the mood of the Party swung towards strong support for the shipyard workers and in the end their campaign was crowned with success.

However, as with all working-class achievements won by pressure from below, the establishment refused to recognise it.

The Government is clearly worried by the remarkable fight put up by the workers at Upper Clyde Shipbuilders in defence of their jobs and their future.

It is an historic event. These men have been tough, dignified and responsible in the defence of their own people.

The reaction of the establishment has been absolutely predictable. They have condemned the men as irresponsible. Now that the first ritual expressions of sympathy have been made, the campaign of vilification will begin in earnest.

Working people are "allowed" to be worried when they lose their jobs, but after that they are expected to go on the scrap-heap quietly, and be forgotten. The men of UCS are not reacting as they should in the Tory rulebook.

*Article in *Tribune*, August 6, 1971. Reprinted by kind permission of *Tribune*.

What about those of us who feel deeply committed to these men and want to identify with their fight? It would clearly be wrong to try to advise them what to do, because only they can make up their minds how best to handle a very difficult situation, just as they decided, without any outside advice, that they would begin the work-in.

No one supporting them in what they have already done, and who wants to stand with them should mislead them in any way.

If advice is out and leadership stays, as it should, in the yards, we can certainly analyse the situation in such a way as to help them to see their way through the very difficult decisions that lie ahead.

The initial work-in has dramatised the problem in a way that has won world-wide attention and admiration. The management — or most of it — has cooperated with the men. The STUC, local authorities and now the churches have expressed their support.

This first phase must be counted an unqualified success. But what of the next? There is clearly a very big decision lying ahead.

While it is obviously right to press for nationalisation, as we are doing in Parliament, or municipal ownership, as is being suggested in Glasgow, the Tory Cabinet must be expected to do everything it can to sabotage these efforts. Even so the campaign for these solutions must go on.

This leaves two ways forward. One is to carry on the working while it is legally possible and then, shift the campaign on to a wider industrial and political front.

The other is to choose the dead-end of a clash with the law. This has been clearly and rightly ruled out in all the statements made by the leaders of UCS. But, even so, it is worth considering in order to see its consequences in case anybody should urge it out of desperation.

First, it is exactly what the Government hopes will happen. If it could pin a charge of violence on the leaders of a peaceful campaign, it would dearly like to do so to destroy public sympathy.

Second, a deliberate Tory smear campaign of this kind, amplified by the mass media might appear to justify repressive measures. The "Angry Brigade" are in this sense working for Mr. Heath.

Direct action in a parliamentary democracy is an educational process requiring the most highly self-disciplined and controlled use of power and must be seen as such. That no doubt is why the shop stewards have emphasised that the workers will not allow hooliganism or vandalism.

But, if this course has been ruled out, there must be a clear alternative strategy that builds on the success of the first phase and then broadens, deepens and widens the campaign at exactly the right moment.

The first opportunity for doing this may come with the opening of the Scottish TUC public inquiry into UCS in the Clydebank Town

Council offices. This inquiry — the first of its kind ever held in Britain — represents an important extension of the same principles that inspire the work-in.

For what the inquiry will do is to lay claim, on behalf of the Scottish trade union movement, to the right to know the facts about UCS; how it was set up, what happened, what policy did successive governments adopt towards it, and what should be done next.

This inquiry is the trade union answer to the report of the Governments's advisory group which published no figures to justify its recommendations.

The STUC inquiry will be held in public and will provide an opportunity for the shop stewards and workers to have their say and for the cross-examination of all those — including myself — who come forward in response to any invitation to give evidence.

A record of these "hearings," together with supporting documents and any conclusions the inquiry may reach, will then obviously become the focal point for the next stage of the campaign.

This next stage will obviously involve the whole Scottish labour movement in demonstrations in support of the UCS workers' fight. With the spectre of rising unemployment this is everybody's fight.

It remains to be seen whether the Government intends to use the Industrial Relations Act to impose penalties on those who demonstrate against redundancies and in favour of men who want to work.

If so, its real purpose as an instrument of repression against the trade union movement will be revealed in a way that will mobilize even more people against the Tory Cabinet and its policy.

This in its turn will shift the campaign into even higher gear as part of a growing national campaign for an immediate General Election against the whole range of Government policies. If this campaign is taken up vigorously by Labour MPs in fighting the Government legislation throughout the new session the Cabinet could find itself in serious difficulties.

But this is not enough unless the Labour movement sees to it that the policies adopted in the next Manifesto are adequate to meet the situation revealed by the UCS crisis.

Public ownership of the shipbuilding industry must be adopted as Party policy at Conference, and intensive work has got to be done to produce a radical and workable system of industrial democracy as the centrepiece of Labour's alternative to the Tory Industrial Relations Bill, when it is repealed.

This latter point is of critical importance. Everybody wants responsibility in industry. But the Tory way of doing this by bringing the lawyers into the workshop is completely unacceptable and unworkable.

The only way to get responsibility is to give responsibility, and that means legislating for industrial democracy, self-management, greater workers' control, or whatever phrase you like to use to describe a major change in the balance of power over management in favour of workers and against the exclusive rights of shareholders.

This is not a Trotskyite dream, but a necessary and practical policy that is being advocated and tried by advanced schools of management thinkers. These ideas must be worked out in conjunction with the trade unions, which in the past have been deeply conservative in their attitude to them. And the next Labour Government must legislate to provide that the private sector as well as the nationalised industries moves forward to management by consent.

The formula which I used in the Bill presented to Parliament by the Opposition — which for that reason has no hope of enactment — contains a phrase, "The management pattern and structure of the company accepted by the management and workers as a whole." This was actually drafted in the shop stewards' room in John Brown's Yard. It is a good starting point for discussion within the Labour movement.

This five-point strategy: The work-in, leading to the STUC inquiry, trade union demonstrations against unemployment, the campaign for a General Election and a demand for industrial democracy *by Parliamentary means* introduced by the next Labour Government would give real meaning to the fight at UCS.

It may look a long and hard route, but it is the only way to a permanent change, which requires the destruction of the Tory Government, before it destroys us all.

Moreover, it is a practical strategy that does not raise false hopes. It looks to the UCS workers to give leadership in the process of achieving change from below in exactly the same way as the Chartists and the men of Tolpuddle changed the course of political history.

The victory that UCS is seeking is not a victory over the Liquidator as he attempts to enter the UCS HQ at Linthouse but a victory in the battle of ideas turning men's minds away from the barbarities of Tory philosophy, and towards a democratic socialist future for Britain.

Public Enterprise and Workers' Control*

The Public Enterprise Group was established after the 1970 Election to defend the Nationalised industries. It broadened out to cover a wider range of issues affecting public enterprise.

This speech delivered in October 1971 urged the extension of the public sector and called for a fundamental change in the power structure within the nationalised industries.

It attacked the idea of authoritarian management even when modified by clever public relations and made it clear that the leadership for change must come from shop-floor workers. The role of Parliament was defined as a maker of legal changes once a partnership between the industrial and political wings of the movement had created the demand for them.

Four years' experience as an industrial Minister dealing with both public and private enterprise is an excellent political education.

Anyone who has done that job is forced to re-examine his thinking and if he does so is driven to radical conclusions. In some industries which depend very heavily on the State for their continued existence, the term private enterprise cannot properly be applied.

For example, the aircraft industry would not exist without enormous subventions of public funds which have, in the past, been invested in the form of launching aid for particular projects, or research and development grants. These funds, had they gone in as equity, would have led to public ownership years ago. The same is true of shipbuilding.

Without massive public support, British shipbuilding would have been wiped out five years ago. Even today the so-called "private company" that the Government have now set up to take over the rump of UCS is dependent for its future on an outright gift of all the assets which will be "bought" from the liquidator, with millions of pounds of public money given by the Treasury.

The drug industry does not receive aid directly but as its profits stem from N.H.S., it is still all public money.

These special cases clearly call for an examination of private enterprise to bring the legal framework into line with reality. It is these and other facts that point so unmistakably towards an extension of the public sector and the accountability that goes with it.

There are, however, some very serious policy questions to be settled, as to how we carry out this extension.

*Speech given to Public Enterprise Group at the Metropole Hotel, London, October 5, 1971.

First there is the problem of compensation.

I am very uneasy at the thought of compensating firms on the basis of a market value inflated by the money the Government has already put in, in the form of orders, grants, or research assistance. We cannot accept it.

It was in part this problem that held us back from nationalising the aircraft industry in the last Government. When the Tories nationalised Rolls Royce, the doyen of successful private enterprise, there was no compensation problem because they first allowed the Company to go bankrupt; defaulting on its debts and making the sub-contractors and creditors carry the loss.

This particular method is, however, no substitute for a policy on compensation.

So we have got that problem to tackle.

But at least we can thank the Tories for having cleared up any final public misgivings about public ownership by nationalising what was regarded as the supreme example of successful private enterprise in the engineering industry.

After Rolls Royce not even the most nervous candidate need be shy of advocating nationalisation where it is decided upon as a conscious act of policy.

Moreover, the manifest success of management in the nationalised industries over the last twenty five years has been widely recognised, not only by industry, but by the public as well.

No-one using British Rail Inter-City Services, or flying BEA or BOAC, or reflecting on the wide range of services provided by the electricity and gas industries really believes that public enterprise is inefficient.

Quite the reverse.

And anyone who contrasts the tremendous social responsibility which the Coal Board demonstrated in handling the run down of the mining industry with the ghastly human tragedies in the shipbuilding industry, cannot fail to notice the achievement of public enterprise management.

It is against this background that we have to examine the Government's present proposals to cripple public enterprise and sell off its profitable parts.

These industries are huge public assets and they cannot possibly be treated like this.

"If it loses money close it down, if it makes money sell it off". That is the Government's policy. We will not have it. And when we return to power those who have tried to make quick money out of such a policy cannot expect to be compensated.

But this is not the end of the matter.

We must plan the defence of public enterprise and at the same time prepare to extend its frontiers.

But we must also ask ourselves some very fundamental questions about its future.

Public enterprise has proved its managerial efficiency and its social conscience, but it was not devised by socialists only for the sake of efficiency or to cushion the blow for workers it did not need. Socialists have always seen common ownership as a major instrument for changing our society. Unless we test it against our own political criterion we miss the whole point.

Put crudely, the substitution of Lord Robens for a bunch of private coal owners is not the same as socialism.

Nationalisation does not, of itself, shift the balance of power in society, democratise industry, nor entrench new values in work which will automatically enrich the lives of those in nationalised concerns. In short, our own criterion for judging public enterprise has to be a lot harsher than the Tory criterion.

It is perfectly logical that we should, on the one hand brush away, as irrelevant and inaccurate, all the criticisms levelled by opponents against public ownership, and simultaneously be even more critical on different grounds.

Our real criticism must necessarily be centred on the question of industrial democracy.

Although there have been some modest attempts in nationalised industries to improve consultation and broaden the range of people eligible for Board appointments, their inner power structure still reflects the power structure of private industry.

It is this that has disappointed the hopes of so many socialists and workers in nationalised industries who believed that a change of ownership would automatically change the power structure. Why is this? It is that *ownership* ought not to be the sole source of *management authority* in public or private enterprise.

The key word here is ownership.

Why should owners — whether private or public — claim that their ownership of the shares or assets conveys an absolute right to manage undemocratically?

It is a very fundamental question.

The answer can only be found in a re-examination of industry in terms of power.

Private industry claims that because it is privately owned the Government has no right to interfere with its business; and the workers being employed "by courtesy" of the owners, have no right to interfere either. This doctrine is politically unacceptable, and explains why private ownership has already been hedged around by statutory limitations on the crude exercise of its power.

But when you get rid of the arrogance of claims by private owners to unfettered freedom of action, and substitute common ownership you have only begun to tackle the problem of power.

In one respect we have succeeded in dealing with the power question in the public sector.

The investment programmes of nationalised industries which affect the whole economy are now accountable to elected governments.

The return on capital of new investment is laid down as an act of Government policy, and other socially important programmes are judged against national needs before they are approved.

In this way those decisions that have a national impact are shared with the nation's political representatives. Similarly, we have recognised that there are other internal decisions that the management of nationalised industries have to take themselves, and on which governments ought not to try to interfere.

This is a sensible division of responsibility and despite occasional conflicts it has worked well – at least until recent Government interference began in earnest.

But we have made practically no progress in achieving accountability within public enterprise in spelling out the area of power which properly belongs to those who work in the industry as a whole.

Indeed, Lord Robens' "Human Engineering" is a classical text book of authoritarian management that could as well have been written to guide the chairman of any privately owned corporation. In it he spells out a philosophy of thinly-veiled authoritarianism.

His only secret is to lubricate an authoritarian system by public relations techniques that allow people to think they matter so long as they don't lay claim to share in any important management decision.

No socialist can accept Dale Carnegie's "How to Win Friends And Influence People" as a political text to be read along with the works of Robert Owen and Karl Marx, as a guide to industrial democracy.

To do so would be to betray the serious political process of changing the nature of our society for which common ownership is only, at best, a mere instrument or technique to be judged by a political test.

The central question that remains to be settled is therefore the democratisation of public enterprise from the bottom up. We must find an answer by building upon the inalienable rights of those who work in nationalised concerns to shape those decisions that affect their lives.

This battle has hardly begun.

It means reopening questions of industrial democracy that have been bypassed for too long.

In its most extreme form it is argued that industrial democracy must model itself on political democracy, with workers electing their managers and then being free to replace them if they fail – in exactly the same way as the electors elect their Members of Parliament who then come up for re-election to be judged by their record.

Put more modestly, this claim expresses itself in general appeals for more participation through a single channel combining traditional trade union bargaining issues with those issues which are now the subject of consultation. Hundreds of schemes have been put forward and hundreds of experiments undertaken, not only in Britain but all over the world, which are worth studying.

What is lacking, is not blue prints or policies prepared by little study groups of sociologists, working for the National Executive of the Labour Party, but the will to demand a fundamental change in the balance of power by workers themselves. For this reason the events at UCS this summer have been more important than all the policy papers written on the subject over the last ten years.

There, on the Clyde, Scottish workers, not for the first time in the history of the Labour Movement, have given effective coherent and responsible leadership to a movement towards industrial democracy that will rank with the events at Tolpuddle when the history of British Socialism comes to be written.

They have been clear minded, incredibly tough, immensely dignified, good humoured and persistent.

They have said, in effect, "shipbuilding is our life and our future and we do not intend to be excluded from playing a decisive part in all those decisions which affect us whether they are taken by management or government".

For the political leadership of the Labour Party our task is to support the men, draw up the general lessons that come from that specific experience, and encourage others to see that unless they make similar demands the balance of power cannot be shifted.

Of course, in the end, adjusting to this new reality will require statutory changes and amendments to the law, which Parliament, when it has a Labour majority again, will have to pass.

But because there is a Parliamentary job to be done later, is not to say that it is principally a Parliamentary battle, or that Parliament alone could conceivably make this change effective except in response to an impetus of popular pressure to make it work.

History is full of examples of people winning their freedom, but there are no examples of freedom being given to people who had not demanded it, and did not seem to want it.

In the fight for industrial democracy, the shock troops must be the work-people themselves.

In their campaigns, which will be long and difficult, they will be engaged in educating themselves politically through their own experiences and generating their own style of leadership which will not only carry them through to success, but must be strong enough in the end to exercise the power that they have won.

But just as Parliament cannot do it alone without them, workers cannot do it alone without Parliament — at least not in a society that enjoys the benefits and possibilities of Parliamentary democracy and has not been driven by despair along the road of violent revolution.

A real partnership between an active and determined Labour movement in industry, and a Socialist Parliamentary leadership is a precondition of success.

Historically, all progress in Britain has been made this way. That is how we won the battle for the vote, free trade unions, the welfare state, the health service and the environment.

In each of these cases the pressure built up underneath, guided and encouraged by far sighted political leaders. Parliament only made the changes once the battle in people's minds had been won.

One final footnote.

I have been talking about the next stage in public enterprise, but the same battle must also be fought, in parallel, by workers in the private sector.

Although another Labour Government will certainly extend the frontiers of public ownership, a private sector will remain in some form or another.

Those firms must be made more accountable for their major decisions by future Governments.

But the battle to enlarge the area of industrial democracy within them will equally have to be fought by the workers who work in them.

These are some of the tasks that lie ahead for the Labour Movement during its years in opposition and when it returns to power.

Fortunately, change from below does not depend entirely upon the existence of a Labour Government.

It can be fought for just as hard when we are in opposition. Indeed, the fight begins now. We will not only create 'the climate of opinion necessary to bring us back to power, but also, more important even than that, a body of support strong enough to sustain us as we carry through the changes we must make.

Tolpuddle Revisited*

This statement was in support of the five dockers sent to Pentonville by Sir John Donaldson in July 1972. Three days later the TUC General Council called for a General Strike if the men were not released; and the National Executive Committee unanimously supported the TUC in its stand.

The men were undoubtedly released because of the scale and volume of the protests. This was in some ways the turning point in the politicisation of the trade union movement, during the years of the Heath Government.

On the eve of the Annual Tolpuddle Martyrs' Demonstration and Rally at Dorchester, I issued a message which was reported in the Sunday Times *under the heading: "Millions will respect the men who have gone to jail". The paper went on to report:*

Mr. Anthony Wedgwood Benn, the Chairman of the Labour Pary, in a message issued yesterday on the eve of the annual Tolpuddle Martyrs' demonstration and rally at Dorchester, likened the plight of the dockers who have been sent to jail to the spirit of the six Dorset men who were transported to Australia in 1834 for attempting to form a trade union. He said:

Millions of people in Britain, whatever they may think of the rights and wrongs of the dockers' actions, will in their hearts respect men who would rather go to jail than betray what they believe to be their duty to their fellow-workers and the principles which they hold.

For centuries Britain's democratic liberties have been won and upheld with the help of men and women who stood up for their beliefs and took the consequences. The right to worship freely, to organise trade unions, to vote – for men and women – in Britain were all won against powerful people who sought to maintain their privileges by stirring public fears about anarchy whenever anyone challenged these privileges. That is what the Government are now trying to do.

The British people are the most law-abiding people in the world. It would be quite wrong for anyone to tell others to break the law. But we cannot forget that, in the end, each man is answerable to his own conviction as to what is right and wrong. If a man's conscience lands him in jail the bars that keep him there also imprison part of all our freedoms.

The law which has put these men [the dockers] in prison is an evil law, drawn up by a Government which hates the trade unions and is being enforced by lawyers who have no experience of the problems of working people and their families.

The British people must, before disaster overtakes us, be given a chance in a general election, to decide how they want these problems to be handled. Do they want them dealt with by a judge and tipstaff and prison officers? Or by repealing the Act and seeking the way of reconciliation based on fair play and concern and a respect for our traditional human values?

It is these values, and not the Statute Book which are the real bedrock of consent on which all our democratic institutions ultimately rest. It is these human values that we must all now rally to defend.

The Pentonville Five*

Hugh Cudlipp offered me the centre pages of the Daily Mirror *on August 3, 1972 to make the dockers' case.*

Readers were then invited to write in with their views. Over 1,100 did so, running 8-1 in favour.

Something very important has happened in the last ten days.

Is it the beginning of anarchy? Revolution? Is Vic Feather planning to seize power? Was Pentonville the British Bastille? Of course not.

But something very important did happen. And it matters a lot that we do try to understand exactly what it was.

According to the Prime Minister, Britain has been taken to the brink of anarchy because five dockers disobeyed the law.

If that was true the situation would be serious. But it is not true.

No five men could undermine our country. What has really frightened the Cabinet is that millions of people who did *not* break the law expressed their sympathy and support for the dockers. One of them was me.

The Pentonville five are a symbol of the injustice which the dockers have had to suffer over the years and most recently as a result of containerisation.

Twenty thousand of them have lost their jobs already, and yet the owners of the docks aren't suffering. They sell the wharves where the dockers used to work and transfer their money elsewhere.

Hardly anyone seems to speak up for the dockers. They are always being abused. But they are passionately loyal to each other.

Like the miners they won't dump the old and the weak. They have come to believe that their best way to get justice – and publicity for their grievances – is by industrial action.

*Article in the *Daily Mirror*, August 3, 1972. Reprinted by kind permission of the *Daily Mirror Newspapers Limited, London.

For them the Industrial Relations Act is a political attempt to take away that power. When five of their elected leaders were jailed the dockers wouldn't have it. And a lot of people agreed.

No one should tell anyone else to break the law. I have never done so. But I hope I should have the courage to go to jail if I thought a law was absolutely unjust and contrary to my conscience and was forcing me to betray my friends.

Our history is full of men and women who have.

A few years ago two journalists went to jail for refusing to reveal their sources of information to a judge in court. Their livelihood and their honour were at stake.

Fleet Street made them into public heroes. No one goes to jail for fun, or risks life-long black-listing which may be an even graver sentence.

The dockers aren't the only ones demanding "the right to work".

Last summer the Upper Clyde Shipyard workers all faced the dole queue. The Government bankrupted their firm and planned to throw thousands of them on the scrapheap in what would have become a new ghost town called Clydebank.

They wouldn't have it. They took over the yards. It may not have been strictly legal. It didn't lead to anarchy. But they would not have got justice without the "work-in."

The miners had lost jobs, too and their wages were a disgrace. The Government thought they could beat the miners. But they didn't know them or their wives and families.

The miners didn't win because they held the nation to ransom. They won because the public, in their hearts, thought their cause was just. It didn't lead to a revolution.

Next were the railwaymen. Why were we never told that British Railways couldn't work unless the railwaymen gave up Sundays and their rest days? The men stayed together and won — quietly and peacefully.

We've got four BBC radio programmes and three TV channels. But it seems to take a strike — or at least a demonstration — before ordinary people are allowed to get near the camera and microphone to explain what's wrong. And even then they are often shown as though they were bully boys or reds.

Now the Industrial Relations Act makes it easier to brand them as anarchists or revolutionaries as well.

You can't go on treating decent people with real grievances like that. If you do they won't feel they're being properly represented.

A lot of people feel that way: lower-paid workers without big unions, women workers, minority groups, pensioners and students who have got real battles to fight feel left out.

There still isn't a single television programme that lets people talk to the people straight — before the pressure builds up — without some clever men asking tricky questions or hogging the camera with their own views, whether they know anything about it or not.

Even the Labour Party occasionally forgets that it is more than a bunch of ex-ministers and would-be future ministers.

Carefully worked out alternative policies are important.

But political leadership is more than offering alternative management. It must mean, for us, speaking for the people who put us there.

This is even more important now that Heath has gone back to hard-faced Tory policies. He is no national father figure like the war-time Churchill nor is he a middle-of-the-road Conservative like Macmillan.

He acts like the Managing Director of Great Britain Limited. He works for the shareholders — literally.

He doesn't seem to know or understand what the rest of us think, or care very much anyway. Perhaps that is why he is bitterly opposed to a referendum on the Common Market.

The best of our history has been change from below, led by the Chartists, the Tolpuddle Martyrs, Mrs. Pankhurst, the suffragette leader, and hundreds and thousands of nameless people who stood up against authority, suffered and won. They gave us democracy — not the kings and queens.

None of these people were revolutionaries thirsting for blood. The British tradition of political change rests on countless individuals with obstinate consciences who would not put up with unfair laws and pushed until Parliament changed them.

It is all happening again.

A great new movement for reform is building up — peaceful but determined and coming from below, and the leaders of it are tough and self-confident and irreverent.

Top people despise the public. No wonder the public despise them.

The so-called credibility problem in politics is not so much that people don't trust individual politicians.

It means they are learning from the shipworkers and the students and the miners and the women, the railwaymen and the dockers that if you want to get things changed you've got to do something about it yourself.

This is a rebirth of our national self-confidence.

Only we can solve our own problems, including inflation and industrial relations. If we want a fair society we must build it ourselves.

The people are only looking to Parliament to make it easier to solve these problems.

They want the right to work.

They want decent schools for their kids that don't just fatten them up for unskilled jobs at sixteen and the sack at fifty as unemployable.

They know you can't freeze prices but they want Governments to try and control them.

They want the old people to have real dignity in retirement and are quite prepared to pay for it.

They want a lot more equality than we have got so far.

They want a new different and fairer balance of power and wealth and income and responsibility.

Above all they want to run more of their own affairs; where they work; and where they live in England, Scotland and Wales.

They want those huge companies especially the international ones to to be answerable to somebody for those big decisions that can land you in the dole queue with virtually no notice.

They want trade unions that are strong. But they expect to be consulted by the trade union leaders they themselves have elected.

They want Members of Parliament to represent them — not to speak as if the ballot box had given them some divine right to do what they want regardless of public opinion.

Many members of the Labour party share that feeling.

They wish party leaders would sometimes admit that they had made mistakes.

It's time our leaders started listening more carefully to what is being said to them.

For these demands are quite modest when you add them up. There isn't a Lenin lurking in the wings. The Angry Brigade couldn't pick up a hundred votes in any constituency.

The thing that makes this country — with all its injustices and imperfections — such a law-abiding place is not the fact that we've got police and courts with judges in long wigs.

It is that we are basically decent, generous, compassionate, hardworking and fair-minded people.

Those qualities and not the statute book, are our copper-bottomed guarantee against anarchy — so long as we play it fair amongst ourselves.

People are fed up with being treated as if they were ignorant and irresponsible.

A tiny minority always will be. The overwhelming majority are not.

If we could only get this message across and people believed we meant it Britain could release enough energy to set us all doing things — together — for ourselves.

There's really nothing that we can't do if we set our minds to it.

39

II

Industrial Policy

Reforming the Post Office*

This brief report on eighteen months' work as Postmaster General was included in a speech at the Association of Post Office Controlling Officers' Conference in May, 1966.

.... the Chancellor has authorised a programme on a scale commensurate with our needs and I must be the first Postmaster General in history whose expansion programme is not held back by Treasury policy but by the practical difficulties of turning capital authorisation into urgently needed new plant and equipment on both postal and telecommunications sides.

Just twelve months ago these preliminary tasks were completed and the more fundamental job begun.

In order to undertake it, it was necessary to create new machinery and a great deal of our work in the last year has been directed to that end.

Perhaps the most important has been the establishment of an Economic Development Committee for the Post Office which will be responsible for looking at the long-term prospects for our services within the targets provided for in the National Plan. It brings together both management and staff sides under an independent chairman with other independent members. This is the first little E.D.C. in the public sector and it is up to us to make it a success.

My next task was to try to improve the lines of communication between the staff associations and myself and I shall be saying more about that later on.

After that came the creation of the Post Office Users' Council to focus more sharply the interests of those whom we exist to serve. This Council replaced the old Post Office Advisory Committee which had ceased to function effectively. The new Council is representative and completely independent in character and promises to be a formidable watchdog for the public interest.

In addition we brought into the Office a major firm of management

*Extract from a speech to the Association of Post Office Controlling Officers' Conference, Bournemouth, May 16, 1966.

41

consultants with terms of reference sufficiently wide to allow them an opportunity to advise us on some pretty intractable problems of productivity and organisation. They were not commissioned to look at us, write a report and go away. They are working with us in a number of important ways and have proved their value.

Finally we have submitted ourselves — voluntarily and indeed with enthusiasm — to the close scrutiny of the House of Commons Select Committee on Nationalised Industries — the first time that that Committee has ever looked at a Government Department.

All this has involved us in a great deal of work and, I hope, has created an atmosphere favourable to the development of new thinking at every level.

It has certainly not been used as an excuse for inactivity within the Department itself. No decisions that should have been taken have been delayed on the grounds that we were waiting for what others were going to say about us.

During this period we have launched into many new ventures. The most notable have been the Investment Accounts for the Savings Bank which start next month, and the Giro which will begin in two years. Together these two enterprises represent the biggest development in popular banking since Mr. Gladstone founded the Savings Bank in 1865.

We have pressed on with mechanisation and postal coding and fixed the date for the introduction of standard-sized envelopes. We have established a long range study group to look at the future pattern of the postal services and are trying to anticipate the degree of concentration that mechanisation will make necessary. We have turned our minds to the need to conserve manpower — a critically short factor — and have reached useful productivity arrangements. We have begun experiments and pilot schemes, which if they are successful, will diversify our activities still further.

But it is true that some really major decisions cannot be made without more information than is, at this moment, available. It is tempting to rush into them. But nothing would be worse than acting on a hunch in an age when scientific management and carefully considered judgements are really needed.

So I must ask you to be patient for a little longer and give us a chance to complete the work we have started. The modernization of the Post Office was long overdue and when we do it we want to do it right.

I now turn to a matter of great mutual concern to us both — the role of the Trade Unions in the Post Office.

I must affirm, at the outset, my belief in the necessity for strong Trade Unions in an industry that is changing as rapidly as our own.

Technical change will have such an impact upon the lives of all of us that, by itself, it constitutes a most powerful case for strong Trade Unions. Indeed if the Trade Unions did not exist they would have now to be invented.

This is not only because of the function of the Unions – to uphold the interests of their members and to negotiate wages and conditions of service – it is also because they are necessary to provide the focus for continuing consultation between staff and management so that the whole work and development of our industry can be jointly reviewed and human factors can be given the weight appropriate to their importance.

In the Post Office we have a fine record in this field and I should like to pay tribute to those on the staff side who have made it possible.

But having said that may I now invite you to consider again the way in which the representation of the staff is actually organised.

There are no fewer than 20 staff associations representing Post Office workers. I have with me the full list. It is a formidable one.

Most of these associations have a long history of representation and are all served by dedicated officers and officials. I have no doubt that each is inspired by high ideals and is genuinely anxious not only to represent their members but also to help the Post Office to do its job successfully.

But is this really the best arrangement? Do we really need 20 entirely separate organisations to represent the workers in one industry? . . . .

Government, Industry and Technology*

This speech was delivered at the American Chamber of Commerce in February, 1967, a few months after my appointment as Minister of Technology.

. . . Government wants to cure the chronic weaknesses of our economy. It has to face a revolution of rising expectations just as great as that which exists in developing countries – indeed probably more so since advertising is much more effective in stimulating consumer desires here than it is in Africa or Asia. Government needs more and more money to finance the public expenditure that technology demands: roads for cars: new schools and universities; more hospitals and better

*Extract from speech given to the American Chamber of Commerce, London, February 8, 1967.

pension schemes; and it knows that this can only come from the wealth created by industry.

The challenge posed by technology to both industry and Government has, in fact, created a strong common interest between them. Not everyone yet recognizes it. Not everyone would welcome it even if they did. But I believe it is the most important political and industrial consequence of the technological age, and that when we do understand it it will transform our society. Please do not conclude from this that I am suggesting that we can look forward to a future unmarred by any conflict of economic interest or that we shall all be suffocated in a mushy and meaningless cloud of goodwill that ends all controversy.

I see many arguments ahead. Let me mention some of them.

(1) Arguments arising from the rival claims of public and private enterprise to control certain sectors of the economy.

(2) Arguments arising from disagreements as to the distribution of profits between the shareholders, workers and consumers; of which the discussions of prices and incomes policies are a current example.

(3) Arguments arising over the amount of our national wealth that ought to go to private consumption as against public expenditure.

(4) Arguments arising over the exact nature and scope of Government influence in industry.

(5) Arguments about the accountability of all those who exercise power whether private or public and how it should be secured.

(6) Arguments about the role of workers in industry and the extent of their right to participation.

These arguments — and there are many more of them lying ahead — are going to be hard fought and hard to resolve.

All I am saying is that Technology challenges Governments, whether Capitalist, Communist or Socialist; and industry whether publicly or privately owned in such a direct fashion that the common interest uniting them is far stronger and more important than the disagreements that divide them.

Every society will seek to express this common interest in its own way and in the light of its own history.

Here in Britain we start with a mixed economy, and we shall have one as far ahead as I can see.

We must therefore make a mixed economy work. Make it successful; make it competitive; look to it to create the wealth we need to do the things we want to do. We must also believe in its capacity to succeed at least as much as other nations believe in their own systems.

I suspect that the mixed economy may well turn out to be the system to which the whole world is moving. If that is so the more we can refine and develop it here the better for us.

I also suspect that the success of all economies will depend above all on the rapid application of science to the problems of industry and that that may of itself be easier in a mixed economy where Government and public enterprise have a part to play.

For Britain I am sure that its application of technology in our mixed economy offers us a way out of our past difficulties and can secure for us the social objectivies that I want, as a citizen, to see achieved. I also think it is likely to do more to restore our national self-confidence than any other single factor.

All that I have been saying so far has been intended solely as an introduction to the work of my department, and to make its purposes seem credible.

The Ministry of Technology was set up to do one important part of the very job that I have described. It was founded in the belief that if we wanted to develop a successful and technologically advanced mixed economy some people had better be given the specific job of trying to help it forward. That idea gave birth to Mintech.

(1) Its purpose is simple: work for industrial success through technology.

(2) Its composition reflects its new and different role. It is manned by scientists, engineers, and those with industrial experience as well as by administrators, economists and politicians.

(3) Its methods are based upon co-operation. In general this involves working jointly with the engineering industries which it sponsors to evolve strategies that will strengthen them technologically.

(4) Its resources are enormous: consisting of 9,000 qualified scientists and engineers working in Government research establishments.

(5) Its main instrument is communication: transmitting information from those who have it to those who can use it.

(6) Its aim is clear: pick likely winners and back them to the hilt, with everything that is available including money.

I have only had this job for eight months. But in that time I have become utterly convinced of the importance of co-operation between

Government and industry and of the possibilities that exist for making a reality of it.

One thing ought to be apparent right now. This Government is solemnly committed to the strengthening of our economy and our industry, and is ready to innovate by trying out new instruments for this purpose.

I hope that those who are watching Britain as it goes through this great and exciting period of change will not forget one characteristic of ours that is peculiarly useful at this moment. I am thinking of our realism and adaptability.

These qualities are often written off as inconsistency or written down as weakness. Do not be deceived. Britain's trick of survival and its continuing social stability derive from the same qualities that have given her her strength in the past and promise to offer her a way through the present technological revolution: Realism and adaptability.

Realism and adaptability will also lubricate the relations between Government and industry upon which our whole future depends. These, Mr. Chairman, are my grounds for optimism about the future of Britain . . . .

Modernisation in Industry and Government*

This speech delivered in January, 1968 at a Labour meeting in Hampstead reveals the managerial view of industrial policy. It was re-thinking all this later that led on to the new industrial policy that emerged in the 1974 manifesto.

If we look to the present and the future we can see another historical trend that has received far too little attention. It is the period of Reconstruction and Reform that began in 1964. Here again we may well be too close to it to see its shape with the clarity that future historians will command. Let us look more closely at the future of a Britain that now stands alone.

After a century of near neglect, industrial reconstruction is now well under way. The managers of British Industry are now engaged in a massive programme of modernisation. The fragmented pattern of industrial organisation is beginning to give way to large undertakings that have it within their power to compete successfully against their foreign rivals. British Leyland, to take the most recent example, will be

*Extract from speech given to Labour Party Meeting, Netherall Gardens, N.W.3., January 24, 1968.

a world giant in automotive manufacture — able to increase productivity and exports dramatically. Rolls Royce, strengthened by its merger with Bristol Siddeley, is another such company. Soon we may see similar developments in computers. Shipbuilding is now reorganising itself into a small number of highly competitive units that can face and beat Japanese competition. GEC and AEI together, will be far stronger than the sum of their component parts. We shall soon have a re-organized Nuclear Power Industry to convert our unrivalled lead in atomic technology into a powerful export effort. Public industry too is reorganising. The Electricity industry is growing fast. Gas is preparing to build on the North Sea bonanza. The new Post Office Corporation free from the leading strings of Whitehall will develop telecommunications, mechanised Postal Services, the Giro and Data Processing Services that will provide the infrastructure of communications that industry needs.

Underlying all these changes is a reconstruction in Management that is already working its way through to the top and reflecting itself in a new professionalism and competence of a kind Britain has never known before. The British version of a mixed economy could prove a powerful force for us, and since the world may converge towards such a system, we must make it work.

Government is now fast reorganising itself to work constructively with industry to help it do its job. But Government cannot do this unless it makes a far greater effort to understand how industry works and what it needs. Entirely new institutional arrangements are necessary for this purpose. That is why new public agencies like NRDC, NEDC, DEA, Mintech, the NBPI and IRC were set up. They were not established just so that Government could shout louder at industry, but in part to allow it to listen to, learn from and help industry. They approach industry not with a megaphone but with a microphone — to pick up information and make Government planning decisions affecting industry more scientific and intelligent. No one would claim that the new arrangements are perfect. But at least Government knows that a productive, technologically-advanced and successful British industry is going to form the economic foundation for future developments. It is our only way of ending Stop-Go, stagnation and endless crises.

The new role of public enterprise is to stimulate and guide and start in this growth. The Industrial Expansion Bill will provide some of the machinery for doing this. . . .

Government and Technology*

In 1968 I delivered the Cantor lecture at the Royal Society of Arts and spoke on the work of the Minister of Technology. This begins with a factual report and moves on at the end to the social implications.

As the task of strengthening our industrial structure has proceeded, our task of research management in relation to our own establishments has become much clearer. The problems of transfer of technology from a government establishment into industry can be enormously difficult. Historically the government acquired its large block of research facilities partly because industry, protected by the soft colonial market, had not organized itself on a scale to enable it to undertake these research responsibilities itself. Having inherited the finest complex of research facilities available anywhere in the Western world, it has been my object to try to bring about four distinct shifts of emphasis.

First a shift from the almost exclusive concentration of government support on defence research to more general support for civil industry. Although it has always hitherto been the case, there is no reason why defence needs should exclusively pioneer new technology. Next year, for the first time in our history, we shall spend more money on education than on defence. There is no reason why in education or some other field of civil expenditure there should not be a similar stimulation by means of public procurement in technologies associated with areas other than defence. No doubt for many years to come defence research will also produce and develop new technologies as it has done in the past.

The next shift of emphasis I have tried to achieve has been to get away from the idea that it is only in the aerospace and nuclear fields that government has any role at all in relation to the support of the engineering industry. This also arose because government was concerned simply with defence matters. But if you look and see what you are up against in terms of foreign competition, if you look at the enormous spending of the Americans on civil space research, it is obvious that much of this money has been filtering through into the non-aero-space, non-nuclear industries of the United States. Since we cannot afford to emulate their methods of supporting their general engineering industries, we have got to develop more direct forms of support for our key industries.

The third shift of emphasis I have tried to achieve has been this. Where there is an absolutely equal choice between intra-mural and extra-mural research we are trying to get more of the research done in

*Extract from Cantor lecture to Royal Society of Arts, subsequently published in the *Journal of the Royal Society of Arts,* February, 1969.

industry, where the transfer problems are less and where the opportunities for rapid exploitation under commercial management can be more directly related to marketing and especially exports.

Last but by no means least, we are trying to get away from the idea that a scientist must necessarily confine his efforts to the research end of the business, rather than to work at the later stages of development, manufacture, sale, and after-sales service. This refocusing of our research effort has been made possible by redefining our role in more commercial terms.

After industrial policy and research management I want to turn to an aspect of our work that may seem less glamorous than some of the other things we do – the development of productivity services. We see this now in a very different light from the way in which government saw its attitude in relation to industry in the past. We have progressed way beyond the time when Ministers used to say 'Exporting is fun', or to urge higher productivity as a moral imperative. We regard the function of the productivity services, in modern terms, as being part of the machinery by which technological information is disseminated to those who can profit by using it. To this extent I hope I shall be in line with what Sir Paul Chambers is going to say in his last lecture. Take the Production Engineering Advisory Service, or the new numerical control advisory and demonstration service for machine tools, or the high-speed photography unit which happens to be based at Farnborough, or any other aspect of our productivity work. These productivity services are mainly designed for very small firms which will never merge into giant groups. In this way they can get access to new technology, not by any means on the frontiers of knowledge, but of real value to them in their struggle to compete.

Mintech's approach to industrial structure, to research management and the productivity services has, I believe, in its turn, made some contribution to some of the other problems in which we have inevitably become involved. One is the problem of the brain drain. There are many factors contributing to it. There is the attraction – the 'pull' – of working in laboratories abroad for those who specialize in a certain field. You won't change that. Those men will go and some will come back, all the better for having done so. It is reducing the 'push' element in the brain drain that really matters: that is to say, eliminating the frustration that drives people to emigration by providing better opportunities for satisfying work in industry in Britain. This improvement of opportunity is closely linked with the development of our industrial policy, and the restructuring of our industry. If it leads to better management (which is one of the major objectives) it will open up for the young engineer a better opportunity of finding a good career prospect at home.

Our interest has spread, by way of our interest in the status of engineers which is of critical importance, to the whole area of education. It is in a myriad of school rooms, up and down the country, at the age of about thirteen or fourteen that the basic decisions are taken affecting a child's future, where girls are driven in droves from even thinking about work in engineering or industry, and where young men who have the potential talents in this direction are in some ways discouraged by teachers, parents and others who may not know at all what engineering and industry could offer. Through our advisory board on relations with the universities under Vice-Chancellor Curran of Strathclyde, we are gradually building up closer relations between universities and industry, and in this way working with new forces in universities which are trying to correct old trends so that we do not continue as victims of nineteenth-century values.

The Ministry of Technology has, by building up technological collaboration with the Russians and other Eastern European countries, made a serious attempt, through technological links, to open up markets for our goods which promise to develop still further.

Finally I must draw attention to our developing interest in the relevance of procurement practice in introducing modern technology and improving industrial performance. It is not a question of bullying firms into doing what government procurement agents want but of lifting some of the barriers which have in the past prevented export development from going ahead as rapidly as it should. Our work in standardization and metrication, for example, has I think helped, and will help still more, to meet our single-minded objective of helping industry to profit through the use of modern technology.

The techniques that we have used have been various. We have developed pre-production orders as a means of backing success and allowing new developments to come into production before they otherwise would have done and linked them to free trial period schemes. We have passed an Industrial Expansion Act which has initiated government support beyond research and development, including where necessary the whole development of the productive process.

All this has made possible a closer relationship between government and industry. With government looking at its own return on its own investment, using D.C.F. calculations, and sophisticated criteria for the evaluation of projects that come up and providing high risk support for industry, its thinking and that of board members of large companies have come closer together. I wonder for how long more we ought to argue about relations between government and industry in purely ideological terms.

We have a public sector which in recent years has moved more speedily towards a commercial approach to its task. When I was in the Post Office I succeeded in getting it agreed that this should cease to be a government department and become a nationalized industry, with the object of lifting from a large industry in the fast-growing communications business the restraint of serving under a Minister. Look at the way in which the railways, under new arrangements, are to balance their books, and if the government wants them to do something uneconomic the government will be ready to pay for it on a subsidy basis. All this is an attempt to make public enterprise use its own resources and take its economic decisions on a more rational basis. By contrast, if you look at private industry you will find that some major firms are finding it impossible to carry the enormous risk of launching products in the advanced technology field without some help from government. Add to this a number of, what are effectively, mixed enterprise arrangements − created so that government can make its support effective. That is why we took a shareholding in I.C.L. and why, following the Fairfields operation, we have an equity participation in Upper Clyde Shipbuilders. In the atomic field we are blending public and private enterprise together to produce a stronger industrial unit.

When all these things are taken together it becomes clearer how we are developing our mixed economy in this country. I believe it has great advantages over the more *laisser-faire* approach of the Americans, or the rigidly centralized Marxist approach in the Soviet Union. One important difference between the Russians and the Americans on the one hand and ourselves on the other is that they each believe in their separate systems whereas we don't seem to believe in ours. When the Americans describe what they have done they almost always ascribe it to private enterprise; similarly the Russians describe their own successes as examples of socialist power working through industry. I don't really believe either of these explanations. But what I do believe is that both of them believe in what they are doing and benefit from doing so, and that belief in your own mythology has some bearing on whether the system works or not. In Britain we are working a mixed system within which the frontiers of public and private enterprise will change and will be the subject of argument. It would be wrong to try to blur the conflict of interest which will arise between the different participants in industry. But we have a system which very few people want to see fundamentally changed in one direction or the other. There is some merit in seeing the advantages of it, and in seeing whether you cannot make it work better as a result of believing in it.

I do not want to finish on a departmental note and least of all upon a controversial one. May I therefore turn for a moment on to some of the social implications of the changes which we are observing. If you look at the world in which we live it seems to me that the great pressure for revolutionary change does not come from the students in Paris or Chicago or London. It is the engineers and technologists who are changing our society. They are the people who are destroying our old society simply by finding better ways of doing things. Every revolution begins by destroying. The constructive part of the revolution starts later. In so far as the engineers are finding better ways of doing what we now do they are in effect destroying what we now do. The consequences of this for all of us present us all with a number of dangers that we shall have to face.

One is the danger of continuing amateurism, by which I mean a failure to keep abreast of advancing technology. One of the most vivid examples of this danger was described in a speech delivered by Buckminster Fuller at an Architects' Congress some years ago in Mexico City. He reminded his audience that from the beginning of time the architect had been concerned with the human environment, with protecting man from heat and cold, providing him with basic services. But that when man came to construct his first ever total environment, the space capsule, the ultimate in self-contained houses, nobody had thought it worth calling in architects to ask them how it should be designed, because over the years architects had allowed themselves to become separated from developing technology and thus had nothing to offer. . .

Technology and the Quality of Life*

This lecture, delivered at the Manchester Technology Association's annual meeting at the Royal Society, gave an opportunity of linking the problems of technology with broader themes of democratic control.

This speech was strongly disapproved of by some officials in the Ministry of Technology, who felt it went far too far in urging political control of industrial decisions. Looking back on it in 1974, it seems very mild.

The 'sixties saw a greatly quickened public interest in Technology. More and more people have come to see how the rapid application of scientific methods could improve their performance and help to raise the standard of living. Mintech has been encouraging the idea that technology can and ought to be put into service in industry and society more quickly and the growing acceptance of it is most welcome. We have had to give economic growth a high priority.

*Lecture given to the Manchester Technology Association in London at the Royal Society, February 25, 1970.

At the same time public awareness about the broader effects of technology on human beings has also been growing. As economic standards rise, there is an increasing fear that technology is being misused, that we are pursuing increased production of goods and services too singlemindedly and without regard for the general quality of life. People are becoming increasingly concerned that this general quality of life will be damaged because the wider effects of technological change are either not thought about or disregarded.

In its most extreme form this reaction sometimes seems to be in danger of becoming a campaign against technology. To read some of the wilder comments made one would imagine that technology had produced a steady reduction in the quality of life over the last 50 years; and that we were all being actively poisoned to the point where the immediate survival of the species was now in question. This of course is a ludicrous overstatement of the nature of the problem. And it leaves out of account the fact that it is only by the application of technology that we can cope with the consequences of technological change that has already occurred. In fact, the application of technology has noticeably raised not only the standard and quality of life, but the length of life as well.

For example, the generation of electricity by nuclear or hydro power is immensely cleaner than any previous method of providing light and heat. Domestic technology has liberated millions of women from hideous drudgery. Communications technology has given us all a wider range of experience, either by extending our capacity to move freely or to enjoy a fuller range of experience from our own home.

Medical technology – in the form of drugs and appliances, surgical and other equipment – has not only lengthened the expectation of life but is making life itself more tolerable for the old, the sick and the disabled.

Computer technology, too, has opened up possibilities of managing complex systems without which we could not hope to control the power we have created.

No-one wants to turn their back on all this. But what is now, quite rightly, under direct challenge is the tendency for an unthinking acceptance of everything that is scientifically exciting and technically within our capability; regardless of its social consequences.

Technology, like all power, is neutral and the question is how do we use it. It is the decision-making process that we are concerned with and how it can be improved. This is indeed one reason why the Ministry of Technology itself was set up.

What people want is a better method of decision-making that takes into account wider considerations that have in the past been left out of account.

They are dissatisfied with narrow assessments that do not take sufficient account of the wider social and human consequences which may, in the end, turn out to be more important than any immediate short-term and purely economic analysis could reveal.

They also want the information and the time necessary to allow these wider factors to be publicly discussed before final decisions are made.

The time scale of technological development is so long and the costs so high that, if there is no discussion during the formative stage, people may wake up one day and find that major technological changes are well advanced and it is too late to stop them because so much money and effort has already been committed.

This, more than almost anything else, gives people the feeling that their views count for nothing and drives them to the extremes of obscurantist opposition against technology itself, or worse still, against scientists and engineers in general. It is therefore to the decision-making process that we must look for improvements. In fact the position is not as bad as it may sound. A great deal of progress has been made, but there is a great deal more to be done.

First as far as Government is concerned the process of analysis must be widened at the very outset. Everyone working on or promoting new projects or processes must be actively encouraged to think much more widely about the social implications of what they are doing while they are actually engaged in their work, and so must all those in responsible positions in industry and society, who are concerned with the advocacy of technological change.

Secondly, these wider considerations must be independently examined by some interdisciplinary groups to be composed of those with a wider range of human experience: and who can identify those people who are most likely to be affected.

Thirdly, this whole exercise of initial proposition, evaluation and assessment must be made public so that everyone can join in, before the final decision is made.

Though these proposals sound quite mild when simply stated they may require further fundamental changes in our decision-making machinery. All this must apply increasingly in industry as well.

The wider responsibilities which need to be opened up for managers, engineers and scientists could help to liberate them from the restrictions which may have hitherto limited their scope. Most of them are highly qualified, with a deep knowledge of and concentration upon, their field of work or responsibility. No one wants to restrict the specialist. Quite the reverse.

What we want is what Dr. Paine, the NASA administrator, calls T shaped men. The vertical stem of the T reflects the deep knowledge of a special subject in which a man may study and work throughout his life. The horizontal cross-bar at the top of the T symbolizes his wide and general interest over the whole range of human activities.

We shall have to devise some more comprehensive interrogation to which we can subject new industrial processes, new methods or new projects as they emerge from Government and industry. In recent years propositions of this kind have been subjected to increasingly sophisticated analysis, covering economic costs and benefits.

In addition to that we shall now have to push some fairly basic questions down the line and require them to be answered at the point of initiation, by the initiators. In this way, we may hope to establish an early warning system, which will widen the discussion at the outset. The sort of questions we might want to ask in the case of major development could include the following:

1. Would your project — if carried through — promise benefits to the community, and if so what are these benefits, how will they be distributed and to whom and when would they accrue?

2. What disadvantages would you expect might flow from your work; who would experience them; what, if any, remedies would correct them; and is the technology for correcting them sufficiently advanced for the remedies to be available when the disadvantages began to accrue?

3. What demands would the development of your project make upon our resources of skilled manpower, and are these resources likely to be available?

4. Is there a cheaper, simpler and less sophisticated way of achieving at least a part of the objective that you have in mind; and if so what would it be and what proportion of your total objective would have to be sacrificed if we adopted it?

5. What new skills would have to be acquired by people who would be called upon to use the product or project which you are recommending, and how could these skills in application be created?

6. What skills would be rendered obsolete by the development you propose and how serious a problem would the obsolescence of these skills create for the people who had them?

7. Is the work upon which you are engaged being done, or has it been done, or has it been started and stopped, in other parts of the world and what experience is available from abroad that might help us to assess your own proposal?

8. If what you propose is not done what disadvantages or penalties do you believe will accrue to the community and what alternative projects might be considered?

9. If your proposition is accepted what other work in the form of supporting systems should be set in hand simultaneously, either to cope with the consequences of it, or to prepare for the next stage and what would that next stage be?

10. If an initial decision to proceed is made, for how long will the option to stop remain open and how reversible will this decision be at progressive stages beyond that?

These questions are very general, and no doubt could be refined and improved.

The real value of such an interrogation would be in the fact that in order to answer the questions the whole research team, Board of Management, or sponsoring agency would have to engage in an intense discussion of a kind that does not always now take place.

At least it doesn't take place in the widest context, even though in better managed organisations the implications for that organisation will be debated.

I am now considering whether such a procedure could be introduced into the process of evaluation within the Ministry of Technology itself, with a view to providing that major submissions, whether they come from outside the department or inside, should include an annexe containing answers to these or similar questions.

But this of course will not be sufficient by itself. The answers provided would have in major cases to be considered by a wider inter-disciplinary group including those whose special knowledge will allow them to consider the implications in greater detail.

They may require more information than has been furnished or identify greater benefits or more far-reaching side effects than have been pin-pointed by the originators in their initial answers. They would also have the task of identifying all those groups or interests which should be specifically consulted.

They may find it necessary to have further studies done and recommend that these be set in hand either before the project is approved or in parallel with its development.

This group would not be a 'think tank' upon whom to off-load the full responsibility for assessment. What is wrong to-day is that too few people are encouraged to think for themselves outside their own field. To seek to correct that by establishing 'think tanks' as new centres of specialisation could have the effect of encouraging even more people to believe that they didn't have to think because thinking had been made the responsibility of others.

The assessment group, to be effective, has got, therefore to be made up of people who are themselves also regularly engaged in their own work and who have been drawn out of it part-time to work with others for the purpose of the assessment. What we want is sabbatical groups, made up of people who take part in the problems of inter-relationships without losing their contact with reality. It should be a changing group, whose membership is selected according to the problem that is to be thrown to it, always changing while maintaining its fundamental inter-disciplinary character.

I am now considering how best we might organise studies into major projects that are now beginning to come forward.

But these two stages of interrogation and independent assessment are not enough.

There is a third essential process — the process of public discussion.

Without full public discussion decision-making would still be dependent on an entirely internal process.

People today are just not prepared to accept their own exclusion from the process of assessment. They do not accept that anyone should be able to secure the commitment of large chunks of scarce resources of qualified people and money without a public debate. And they are absolutely right.

For this whole process that I have been describing has, in fact, a much wider significance than may at first appear. It represents the demand by an ever-growing number of thinking people that the power of technology, whoever exercises it, be brought more effectively into the arena of public affairs and made subject to democratic decision.

Just as in earlier centuries the power of kings and feudal landowners was made subject to the crude and imperfect popular will as expressed in our primitive parliamentary system; and just as the new power created by the Industrial Revolution was tamed and shaped by the public which demanded universal franchise, so now the choices we make as between the alternatives opened up by technology have got to be exposed to far greater public scrutiny and subjected more completely to public decision, especially by those whose interests are most intimately affected. The case can best be demonstrated by considering the effect of choosing the opposite course.

If Parliament and the electorate were solemnly to decide that decisions involving technological judgments were so intrinsically complicated and specialised that it would be best to leave them to people who understood these subjects, we could reduce democracy to the discussion of those matters with which it has hitherto been preoccupied — namely the election of M.P.s and their work in economic and social fields where the choices are thought to be within the range of understanding of ordinary simple people.

If we were to do that we could throw away in a single decade all the gains that generations of people have struggled to achieve for public accountability.

But if this is not to happen the discussion process must be stimulated and made more real.

The development of the Ministry of Technology which has brought most industrial sponsorship and the control of many public research resources together under a single minister accountable to Parliament represents a significant shift in the right direction.

The establishment of a Select Committee on Science and Technology in the House of Commons in recent years marked an important step forward and it has significantly altered the balance of power in favour of elected M.P.s and it has quite properly kept my own department's work under close examination.

It has helped to educate Parliament in the new problems that confront us all and has brought the House of Commons more directly into contact with the decision-making processes in this field.

Another important development has been the innovation of Green Papers through which the Government now shares its thinking with the public before it commits itself to a firm policy decision.

The recent Green Paper on Industrial Research is a perfect example of this completely new approach to the role of the public in our national policy for technology.

The Government is actually inviting people to give their views, and inviting Parliament — whether through the Select Committee or not — to participate in policy making.

If this development is to be carried further there are two obstacles to be overcome.

The first will be from those who believe that the decisions that have to be made require such specialist and expert knowledge that it would be foolish, dangerous and wrong to allow ordinary people to have a say in them.

They will argue that it would be disastrous if a nation, the majority of whom, by definition, have, as it were, 'failed the 11 plus' should be allowed to decide things which can only be understood by Ph.D.'s or the chairmen of big corporations or ministers, together with their highly qualified teams of economists and technologists.

However superficially persuasive this argument may seem, it is in fact exactly the same argument as was used in the last century — and in this — against both universal suffrage and votes for women.

For our policy towards technology is now the stuff of government and that is either to be under democratic control or not. There is no middle course.

To argue for the exclusion of these issues from popular control is not only fundamentally undemocratic but is also completely impracticable.

As the implications of scientific and technological decisions become more and more the subject of public interest, people will insist upon having a greater say in these decisions. If you were to try to shut them out from participation, public dissatisfaction could reach the same explosive proportions as it would have done if the vote had not been given to everyone.

But there is another reason too.

The doctrine of limiting democratic control is based upon a complete under-estimation of the general level of public intelligence and knowledge.

Even with all its present, and unacceptable defects, the educational system and the mass media have enormously raised the level of public education and understanding in the course of a single generation.

The genie of human genius has got out of the bottle and it cannot ever be put back in again and the cork replaced.

The next obstacle — and it is a far more formidable one — lies in the minds of people themselves.

Far too many ordinary people themselves still believe that they have not got the knowledge to make independent judgments on these matters or that if they tried to do so, their efforts would be doomed to failure, because nobody really cares what they think.

This combination of lack of self-confidence and defeatism — both self-generated — must be overcome.

You may have to be a brilliant surgeon before you can do a heart transplant but you don't have to have any scientific qualifications at all to be able to reach a view as to whether the largest sums of money and the medical research teams involved would do more good by transplanting a few hearts each year or by establishing say more health centres, or developing a better industrial health service to cut down the thousands of preventable deaths and disabilities that occur each year.

You may have to be a brilliant aerodynamicist to design a space capsule that will land on the moon, but you don't have to have any qualifications before you express the view that some of the money spent in space research might be better employed in improving the quality of public transport and the development of quicker, quieter, cleaner and more comfortable bus services or commuter trains.

Judgments of this kind may be difficult to reach, but if sufficient information about alternative strategies is more available the choice between objectives can be made by anyone.

Anyone is perfectly qualified and fully entitled to contribute his opinion as to the purposes that technology should serve, even though he may know nothing about the first law of thermo-dynamics, nor be able to mend a blown fuse in his own house.

But if we are able to persuade people that they ought to be able to influence decisions and are qualified to do so we still face the much more difficult job of overcoming their suspicion that, even if they were to make the attempt, it would be bound to fail because nobody cares two hoots what they think.

This defeatism is borne out of past frustration, before the wider assessments were made, or public discussion was encouraged as now is beginning.

As people realise the significance of what has been done public confidence in their ability to have an influence will slowly return.

Of course, there will always be people who genuinely don't want to participate, either because the issues don't interest them or because they don't feel strongly enough.

The right to opt out, like the right to abstain in an election, is a fundamental human right and if persuasion fails to change that view no one should be compelled to join in. But if the right to decide is exercised it carries with it the duty to become informed and study the evidence.

If people who want to join in effective discussion and decision-making are not able to do so then they either become apathetic or they are driven into a frenzy of protest.

Protest and apathy, apathy and protest, are both evidence of alienation.

No society can be stable unless it provides the machinery for peaceful change and institutions capable of reflecting the desires of ordinary people.

In a democratic society like our own, the future must be shaped by the wishes of the community at large. Indeed to a remarkable extent it is.

The social values which we have developed and the national temperament and character which have built up over the years will offer to the serious student a far better and more accurate explanation of what we are, why we are, than can be obtained from the incessant scrutiny of the policies of those in authority.

This structure of values may be changed by political and public discussion bringing new objectives into the forefront to replace old objectives. The process by which people change their minds is at least as important as the shelf of printed statutes which record the legislative work of Parliament.

We would, I think, all see the future more clearly if we studied the way that community thought has developed rather than focusing exclusively on what scientists are capable of giving us, or what the big corporations have in their five-year plans, or even what Ministers and

Shadow Ministers are putting before us by way of proposals.

But the task must not be limited to the vetting of technological proposals submitted to the community. We have also got to identify the main problems facing society and find ways and means of converting these needs into real demands which can be met best by the use of technology.

There are already many thousands of human pressure groups or action groups now in existence with proposals to do just this. Unless we can provide better facilities for these people to have access to those who might be able to solve their problems we could miss one of the most important ways in which technology could be used for human benefit.

Indeed I suspect that the political leadership that has the most lasting effect exists not in the confrontations so beloved in Fleet Street, but in the stream of analysis, exploration, interpretation and argument that slowly but surely changes the collective will.

What I am really saying is not at all new.

It is no more than that the method we use to reach our decisions is at least as important, if not more important, as the decisions themselves and the expertise that lies behind them.

But this, of course, is exactly what the Parliamentary System is all about. It is based upon the belief that how you govern yourself — by argument, election and accountability instead of thought control, civil war and dictatorship — is what really matters.

I am, therefore, simply arguing that the methodology of self-government based on the concept of talking our way through to decisions must now be clearly extended to cover the whole area, at all levels of the development of technology which is in our century the source of all new power, just as ownership of the land or the ownership of early factories was in the nineteenth century.

If we don't succeed in doing this we shall run the risk of becoming robots.

It won't be the machines themselves that make us robots but the fact that we have subcontracted our future to huge organisations backed by their own resources of managerial, scientific or professional talent.

Whether we do this or not is, I believe one of the most important single issues in the whole area of public policy.

And before we can really make sense of it we need more of a national debate. Now, as we enter the '70's with great decisions lying ahead of us is the time when that debate should begin.

People want technology — but it must be *technology with a human face.*

Technology Assessment and Political Power*

In May 1973 this article on Technology Assessment appeared in the New Scientist. It assessed the role technology plays in building up industrial power and buttressing intellectual elites.

No country would now think of deciding to build a supersonic aircraft, start a massive space programme, or launch a new drug on to the market without assessing all its implications as carefully as possible. The Roskill Commission that studied the third London airport (even though its recommendations were set aside) and the studies that have been undertaken on the Channel tunnel are likely to be the norm from now on. The Americans have set up an Office of Technology Assessment and there is pressure to establish a similar office in the European Community. The Select Committee on Science and Technology at the House of Commons has opened up areas of policy that have until now been shrouded in secrecy.

Experts have begun to appear on the scene, led by multidisciplinary groups who are seeking to establish themselves in this field. But before we get submerged in this new jargon, and find ourselves worshipping ecologists and technological institutes stuffed full of double Ph.D.'s in civil engineering and psychology who are now busy thrusting the economists and cyberneticists (last season's heroes) into the background, it might be well to consider what technology assessment is all about.

It is about power, the power to make decisions that affect our lives. It is about the people who have that power; and how they got it; whose interests they serve in using it; and whom they hurt; and how we control or replace them; and to whom are they accountable. This is not a new problem, but about the oldest problem in the world. History is full of technological decisions which had a profound effect.

The significant thing about the decision of the Pharaohs to build the Pyramids was not the choice of projects, or the attempts made – if any – to forecast their value, but the light it throws on the absolutist power exercised by the kings of Egypt at that time. The impact of the discovery of effective methods of birth control was significant, not only for its immediate consequences but also – say – for the long-term side-effect it had in weakening the authority of the church over the faithful. The effect of dropping an atom bomb on Hiroshima and Nagasaki is not only measurable in terms of the appalling cost in human life, or even on the shortening of the last war. It has to be measured

*This article first appeared in *New Scientist*, London, the weekly review of Science and Technology, May 6, 1973 and is reprinted by kind permission of the publishers.

against its longer-term effect of making nuclear war unthinkable. The Industrial Revolution in the 19th century not only re-equipped mankind with a new set of tools but in doing so fundamentally altered the balance of power which has created multi-national companies and the powerful trade union movement together with a myriad of other community organisations now fighting in defence of human values.

The trade unions have always been concerned with technology assessment in that they were brought into being by the impact of technical change on workers' jobs, wages, status, and working conditions. If the ecologists are sometimes called Luddites, the Luddites should now be seen as the first ecologists, concerned with the quality of life long before polluted fishing rivers, congestion, and diesel fumes in Hampstead first engaged the interest of the middle class in the environment.

All technology assessments must take us straight on to a study of the structure of society and the political balance of power that determines its decisions. Karl Marx said it all when he wrote in *Das Kapital:*

"Technology discloses man's mode of dealing with nature, the process of production by which he sustains his life and thereby lays bare the mode of formation of his social relations and the mental conceptions that flow from them".

Since Marx wrote these words, we have witnessed a fantastic acceleration of technical change which has greatly increased the magnitude of the problem: and has polarised the struggle between the new centres of concentrated industrial and political power, and the decentralised groupings of people defending themselves against the abuse of power. Public attitudes have altered, and the mass media by instant communication of events, and the rapid spread of ideas, have shortened the cycle of social and political change. We are all deeply involved in any conflict between those with control over technical power and the rest of us.

There are, however, different ways of looking at technology assessment, according to whether we are on the issue in question, playing the role of managers, managed or government. For the manager, technology assessment is an aspect of his corporate planning. It involves studying future trends and forecasting how these will affect his business. A car manufacturer might expect to suffer, or a sewage contractor might benefit. Their attitude will depend on their own calculation as to how they can use the situation to their advantage — and preserve the corporate image of their companies upon which their standing with their customers depends.

Seen at the receiving end by people who will be affected by technical decisions, there are highly personal interests to be safe-guarded. Individuals will soon learn that to protect their interests

63

they must organise and campaign, inform other people and bring pressure to bear on those in power by direct action or the use of their industrial or political strength. These campaigns will throw up new leaders as the trade union and consumer movements have done, and these movements create communities of interest that may become of lasting importance.

Governments see it all rather differently. They are not looking for new problems and it may only be when these issues are forced to their attention that they are stirred into action. Even here, Ministers are divided in their interests, recognising the importance of industrial progress, which inclines them to side with industry; but also sensitive to the changing values of people and the electoral consequences of ignoring new and strong pulses of opinion. Ministers must act as representatives of the community and sternly interrogate those with projects to promote – in the interests of their constituents. The legislation in the 19th century to regulate factory conditions was an early response and the establishment of Britain's Ministry of Technology (with its programmes analysis unit) and the Department of the Environment were the most recent responses by successive British Governments to the need for political control.

The political decisions taken reflect differing national attitudes to these questions. The fact that the Germans were first to build the Autobahn, and that the British deliberately concentrated all their public sympathy on the people whose homes would be destroyed by the concrete motorways is one indication of how these very different values were reflected by two Governments. Every time a Frenchman hears a supersonic bang made by Concorde, he seems to be basking in the reflected glory of French achievement. In Britain such an event would more likely be seen as a monstrous invasion of privacy. These are important differences. The question is: how can we make sure that our technological decisions are made accountable to the people who will be affected by them? In 1970 I drew up a questionnaire[1] for use at Mintech to help determine this. It is a political problem, and the struggle is a struggle for democratic control against a new feudalism or the brainwashing methods of technological determinists who tell us that science has charted our future for us, and we have got to accept it.

The problems of technology assessment cannot be resolved by stuffing computers with specially commissioned economic, social, and psychological data. Even if every single factor could be fed in, and properly weighted – which is impossible – people would not accept the resultant decision, simply because they had played no direct part in reaching it. When we talk about participation, or "assessment done in the light of a wide range of studies," we are talking management

1. See pages 55-56 above.

language with all the dangers of human manipulation that this implies. This sort of "participation" is no substitute for democratic control.

To say this is to challenge the expert trying to impose political decisions on us, head on; to query his credentials and to encourage the same disrespect for him that good democrats have always shown to those who purport to dispense revealed truth. The language surrounding the decisions that have to be made may be complicated. The scientific factors or engineering problems may be complicated too. But unless the public insists upon deciding or approving the objectives which are to be striven after, it will abdicate all power over its own future.

There is no predetermined future that we have to accept, nor is there any specialist entitled to claim a monopoly of wisdom in telling us what it is. Nor is it true that, as scientific and technical skill increasingly reveals the laws of nature, and helps us to use them, that our freedom and happiness will automatically expand in proportion to our knowledge or our material power. The truth may prove to be the exact opposite. As technical power increases, mankind's apparent conquest of nature may produce new tyrannical organisations to organise that "conquest", and they then extend their domain over their fellow men. It is never machines that make us slaves. It is the men who own them, and control them, who are creating the new feudalism.

If we want to alter that balance of power, we have got to understand the nature of the power we are trying to shift. Much of this power is knowledge. The "private ownership of knowledge", and control over its use, is at least as important in developing and sustaining the new tyranny, as the private ownership of the means of production, distribution and exchange.

That is why secrecy surrounding the decisions made by industry and government is now a central political issue and no longer a marginal one. Secrecy allows those in power to reach their decisions without being forced to publish the facts available to them which might lead the public to prefer an absolutely different policy to be pursued. If the secrecy is complete enough, the public will not even learn about the decision until it is too late to change it. Many technological decisions are virtually irreversible once they have been reached, and until we strip away unjustifiable secrecy we can have no real democracy. For this reason, Daniel Ellsberg, who was charged with publishing the secret Pentagon papers, may well be honoured, by future generations, much as we honour Galileo who challenged the establishment of his time and their claim to a monopoly of wisdom revealed to them by divine power.

Educational reform is also the key to the democratic control of the private ownership of knowledge. If we allow the educational system to serve the great centres of industrial and political power by selecting the so-called "able" child from the so-called "less able" pupil, our school system will actually deepen a class system under which the minority are prepared for power, and its exercise, and the majority are branded as failures so as to make them pliable in later life when they are told what they have to accept. Self-confidence is the key to any attempt to control events and our present educational system sees that it is only installed in the selected few, and is denied to the rest.

The private ownership of knowledge also encourages over-specialisation. We artificially divide different sorts of knowledge, and compartmentalise it so completely that we forget that all babies are born multi-disciplinary, and if they are converted by our educational system into narrow specialists who cannot communicate with each other the system must be wrong.

Finally, the control of knowledge — who gets it, from whom and in what form and with what bias — leads us straight to the problems of the mass media, which play an enormously important part in conveying decisions downwards, and desires and demands upwards. No country in the world has yet learned how to make use of its media to extend democratic control of technology or other forms of political power. Dictatorships control the media centrally. Western parliamentary societies hand it over to commercial interests, or non-accountable public service bureaucracies, which feed audiences with filtered news and views, and filter back what they want to say to each other. This is why the mass media have moved into the centre of political debate. We cannot hope to control technology effectively until the technology of modern communication is made more generally available. Ordinary people must have access to it to get their needs and feelings across directly to their fellow men.

The control of technology is therefore now a central political question that cannot be separated from the old and continuing debate about the distribution of wealth and power in every country in the world. Technology assessments may involve complicated calculations but the final decisions must not be handed over to the new breed of self-appointed specialists living a monastic existence in the think tanks of the world. They must be seen as a part of man's unending struggle to control and shape his own future. If we cannot do that, technology assessment could even become a new mask behind which new men of power plan new ways of imposing their will on a new generation of new serfs.

Against that broad background there are four things that should be done at once.

First, the assessment work undertaken by government departments should be greatly strengthened, and the findings of all assessment units should be automatically made public before Ministerial decisions are reached.

Second, the specialist committees of the House of Commons, especially the Select Committee on Science and Technology should be expanded to extend their work over more government departments and should be equipped with the necessary permanent staff to carry their investigations forward more effectively.

Third, technology assessment units should be developed in universities and polytechnics and made available to do contract work for local authorities on their behalf, or on behalf of the people living in areas likely to be affected by major projects of all kinds.

Fourth, some research council funds should be specifically allocated to trades unions and other recognised community groups to allow them to sponsor relevant research into the best means of safeguarding the interests of their members.

These developments would help to bring technology assessment down to earth — which is where it ought to be.

A Visa to Visit Fords?*

This article written for Business Administration *in May 1971 carried the issue of multi-national corporations up to the point where we had taken it before the defeat of the Labour Government in 1970. The origins of the planning agreements are described but the role attributed to the EEC in controlling the international companies was over-stated.*

The warning is there in relation to the domination of the developing world by global business.

When Henry Ford fired his broadside against British workers and was promptly invited to lunch with the Prime Minister and his most senior colleagues at No. 10 Downing Street, it came as a bit of a shock to many people. Here was an American industrialist getting a V.I.P. treatment almost as if he was a head of state.

The fact is that Henry Ford is a head of state, and the turnover of his world-wide empire is of the same order in money terms as the whole National Budget of India, second most populous country in the world. In dealing with Mr. Ford, the British Government is dealing with someone who has the same resources — but possibly more personal power — than Mrs. Gandhi. Certainly, his capacity to influence the future of the countries in which there are Ford plants makes him a man to be reckoned with.

---

*Article in *Business Administration* May, 1971. Reprinted by kind permission of the publishers.

The power of Henry Ford, and of international companies generally has been growing steadily over the years. But the full realisation of their importance was very slow to come. Indeed, it is only in the last few years that the multi-national corporation or global company has been studied and described in any detail. Most of these descriptions have concentrated on the massive management task of corporate planning that faces these corporations. Their political significance is only now beginning to be apparent.

A comparison between the rates of growth of national G.N.P. and company turnover reveals a startling picture. The astonishing industrial growth of Japan is seen to be topped by even more rapid growth rates achieved by two global companies. Looking ahead 10 years or more it is clear that the relative position of the nation state in terms of power is likely to decline relative to the companies that operate world-wide.

Charles Wilson of General Motors is once reported as having said "What's good for General Motors is good for the United States". It is quite clear that statement has no automatic validity in countries which, like Britain, have a General Motors subsidiary (in our case Vauxhall Motors − operating in its home territory). General Motors plans its operations world-wide to maximise its own profit and it does not follow that its decisions will correspond with the national economic interests of all the host countries in which its plants are situated.

The position of I.B.M. reveals how these conflicts may arise when the company's money is flowing across national frontiers. These flows of money may be for payment in parts, for royalties, or in the form of central management fees. Profits too, can be transferred, and so can money for capital investment. Thus, I.B.M. of America may invest in a plant in Scotland to take advantage of investment incentives there and have its simple components manufactured with low labour costs in Portugal for assembly in Scotland and re-export back to the U.S. Again, theoretically, by adjusting internal payments, the profits can be transferred to where the level of the company taxation is lowest and thus the company strategy developed to maximise the return.

It is, therefore, quite possible for a major international company operating in the U.K. to be running a balance of payments deficit. In one case which came to my attention as a Minister, this was actually happening.

Some years ago, in Mintech, we began a serious study of the role of international companies and began to develop an active policy towards them.

I assembled a high-powered team of officials from various departments and we developed a series of questions to put to the corporation about their operations. These questions covered the corporate policy of the company in Britain including its expansion plans, its trans-national rationalisation and its export performance. We also cross-examined them on the constraints on their growth, including the lack of qualified man-power and capacity shortages. We were interested in their balance of payments position, and in their industrial relations policy.

For their part the companies asked us about Government policy in so far as it might affect them.

They were so anxious to be accepted by the Government on the same basis as British companies that they were ready to answer our questions fully, and, they came to see positive advantages in using these discussions to acquaint the Government with the nature of their operations as a guide to policy-making in Whitehall.

Of course those managers who were British were also anxious that the companies for which they worked should be helpful and not damaging to the national interest. Some of them were a bit schizophrenic, in the nicest possible way, as loyalties to country and company sometimes pulled them in opposite directions.

One of the risks is that the global corporations may play off one country against another. I discussed this problem with some of my opposite numbers who were Ministers in Europe and gradually the realisation is spreading but only common action can protect us against this danger. The oil-producing countries have already learned this lesson, and the recent tough negotiations with the world's oil companies are the most vivid example of this sort of cooperation at work.

In Washington last year I discussed these issues with the American administration and they are just waking up to the fact that the big American corporations have now reached such a size that their operations can be harmful to the United States too. If American know-how acquired as a result of their own massive educational expenditure and defence or space contracts can be transferred abroad and linked with low labour costs in factories built by American foreign investment leading to highly competitive goods re-entering the U.S.A. as imports, the American balance of payments can be hit twice. However much Government intervention in business may conflict with their capitalist philosophy it is likely to grow if the Americans think that the global corporation is pursuing policies that may damage the U.S.A.

It would be a mistake to suppose that the Iron Curtain serves to check the global company. Commercial and technological relations are getting closer and closer between the communist and non-communist worlds. The big companies are even beginning to invest in Eastern Europe. Although that is not yet permitted in the Soviet Union, joint ventures that stop short of equity investment already exist.

Developing countries too may well calculate that they would get a better return from encouraging international companies to develop their resources than by traditional forms of aid from the richer nations. But, being weaker, the risk of a political takeover is far greater and all the lessons from Latin America, where American business has been in control for years, offer a grim warning of what can happen if there is no effective political control.

The conflict between the advantages which international industrial operations can bring and the attendant dangers of political domination are not confined to any one country. Everybody is suffering from a great vacuum of policy, and the institutions to evolve and implement it. There is an urgent need for a really effective international industrial policy and we must now look to see how we can get it.

This may be one of the most important arguments for British entry into an expanded European Common Market. After years of ignoring industrial policy the commission has now begun to consider it. Admittedly, it is *laissez-faire* in its inspiration, but that could be changed. It is clear that without an agreed policy global corporations could play one nation against another and enforce their will that way.

Multinationals*

This lecture on the 'multi-nationals and world politics' delivered at a Conference of business leaders in Trinidad on January 14 1972, soon after a visit to China, developed the argument for the political control of global corporations a stage further.

It identified a number of international, national, trade union and political forces that would need to be deployed as a countervailing power to check the abuse of power by the multi-nationals. This was somewhat coolly received.

. . . The nation state at present offers the only scope for popular influence to be brought to bear on political and economic power of business.

During the sixties the growth of multi-nationals was in many cases more rapid than the growth of national budgets by which governmental power may be measured and, in the UK, the profits of the multi-nationals have been higher than those of purely domestic enterprises. This suggests that the power of the multi-national

*Extracts from a paper for the Business International Chief Executive Officers' Round Table on "Corporate Leadership for Survival in a Turbulent World" held in Trinidad, January 14, 1972.

companies are most likely to grow and to find themselves more and more the subject of political interest as the years go by. In particular trade union interest, expressed directly and indirectly through the political system is likely to be a bigger factor in shaping governmental responses.

Looked at globally the concentration of industrial technology in the north is now one of the major political factors in the world today, as may be seen by comparing the growth of production in the Northern hemisphere with the growth of population in the south. This distorted development pattern complicates the relations between the white and non-white races since it deepens the ethnic division of which we have become increasingly aware in recent years. And since the multi-nationals have played a part in that pattern of development and operate world-wide they are seen as a symbol of northern domination.

The first concern of governments in dealing with multi-national enterprise lies in the area of industrial and economic policy where the multi-national has built-in advantage deriving from its international status, permitting it to escape more easily from domestic legislation of all kinds by planning its own development in a way that best suits its own interest, undertaking new investment to take advantage of lower labour costs, lower taxation, easier labour relations and even to avoid domestic regulations governing pollution or measures to locate industry to meet the regional policy of national governments.

Although the differences of ideology between the capitalist and communist halves of the developed world have dominated political thinking since the cold war began, it is now apparent that this division may have less significance than the tension growing up between the developed world as a whole and a third world which sees itself challenged by both Capitalist and Communist superpowers spreading their influence southwards, by both military and industrial pressures.

The recent emergence of China has acquired greater significance just because its whole world strategy seeks to marshall the third world against — as she sees it — American Imperialism and Russian Social Imperialism, by spreading revolution.

It would be a mistake to think that the only effect of technological development has been to create very large organisations of which military establishments, multi-national companies and big Governments are the most obvious examples, and that all that needs to be done is to adjust people's attitudes to accept those developments and learn to live with them.

Higher living standards, better education, access to news information and a variety of cultural and ideological influences through the mass media have expanded the horizons of the world's population in a way that no one could have anticipated 50 years ago. This in its turn has

71

triggered off tremendous new movements by ordinary people to expand their scope and improve their opportunities and environment. The anti-colonial movements, political revolutions throughout the world, the struggle for racial equality and human rights, women's liberation, a cleaner environment and the revolt against materialism are all part of the same process that produced the global corporation. Moreover, in the process people have acquired far greater power to enforce their will because an inter-dependent economy and society is much more vulnerable to direct pressure. Strikes, hi-jacking and urban guerilla movements each in their own way illustrate the extent to which real power has been distributed downwards as well as upwards, by the process of technical change.

The effect of all these developments has been to outdate many of the political institutions that we have inherited from the past.

50 years ago all the effective political and economic decisions were taken within nation states which were only subject to occasional external military pressures.

Today the pattern of institutional development has begun to change radically. Some functions of the nation state we have attempted to transfer to the world level. Others are dealt with by regional organisations like the Common Market involving many nations.

Similarly most governments have devolved more powers from the centre downwards, and every political system is being subjected to growing pressure from underneath from people who want to have a greater say over their own future.

This new pattern of world institutions, now embryonic in character, could — if further developed — be made strong enough to contain and absorb the power of global corporations. We still lack a clear idea of how this framework will operate. But the need for it is becoming more apparent.

The necessary framework within which global corporations should operate will have to be constructed at various levels from the United Nations right down to plant level.

The internationalization of industrial technology has now proceeded so rapidly that it is not unreasonable to expect that the UN — set up to prevent the misuse of military technology by war — should extend its functions to take on board responsibility for supervising some aspects of the operations of global companies which are of international concern.

What may well be required is something approaching the diplomatic recognition of these companies, when they reach a certain size, holding them accountable directly to the UN for any decisions that they make, which affect international peace and security or human rights.

With all its imperfections the UN is the only international centre of political representation to which these international companies could in any way be made accountable. For example, it could be that the quickest way to bring sanctions to bear on a particular country would be by laying down an international embargo enforced through control of international companies.

The registration of the multi-nationals with the UN could carry with it the requirement to supply information about their activities on a regular basis, and might offer some measure of protection for their legitimate interests if these were improperly threatened.

There is also scope for the development of ground rules which will make possible an expansion of industrial operations between the Western and Communist world, and the developing world. We shall soon see more international companies operating within the communist world. There will also be joint ventures that will bring the big communist industrial organisations increasingly into the non-communist world which will require that they should be regulated too. The 1970's could well see Communist multi-nationals emerge in competition with those from the Capitalist countries.

The attitude of national governments towards multi-national companies necessarily reflects their interpretation of the national interest which they were elected to safeguard, taking account of all the external and internal influences to which they are subject.

The nation's economic performance, seen as a whole, is a major priority in all countries and global corporations will be judged by their contribution to it.

There may also be strategic considerations or matters of national pride which make it undesirable that the control of a key industry should fall into foreign hands.

Moreover the attitudes of the community towards business generally as reflected through trade union and other social pressures will reflect themselves through the democratic process in such a way as to influence governments in their policy making.

In Britain policy towards multi-nationals has evolved in recent years based on an understanding of their value in bringing inward investment, new technology, management skills and access to world marketing operations. In addition Britain herself has a number of large and important home-based multi-national corporations which are important export earners — both visible and invisible.

Perhaps the most important development of government policy has been the decision to engage in direct consultations with big companies seeking information on a reciprocal basis. Governments have wanted to know about the inward and outward flow of trade and investment, transfer pricing practice, the extent of access by British subsidiaries to export markets, managerial devolution, industrial relations practice, and research policy, and have sought to win the support of the multi-nationals for the location of new plant in areas of high unemployment. The multi-nationals have wanted information about all government policies that affect their operations or plans.

All this amounts to a form of diplomatic recognition followed by negotiation to identify the areas of common interest and the possible areas of conflict.

In these negotiations the balance of power between the two sides has been a subtle one. The global corporations are clearly dependent upon the maintenance of the goodwill of the host country, their own general reputation, the need to safeguard their own investment and even the importance of such non-economic factors as the national loyalty of their UK employees. The Government, for its part knows of the potential power of these companies to move elsewhere if the going gets too rough.

The trade unions operating nationally and internationally can bring pressure to bear on their governments and on international organisations to develop policies and procedures that will safeguard their interests.

The unions in Britain have underlined the need for a more systematic collection of information, for conformity with British industrial relations practice, for the need to develop increased consultation between the companies and the unions on corporate planning including manpower plans and research policies. These pressures have already reflected themselves in British Government policies and are likely to increase in the future.

There has also been a slow but steady development of international trade union links which may tend progressively to redress the balance — or at least part of it — between capital and labour.

But it may be that at the plant level we shall see the most significant changes over the years. Here there is a combination of pressures from management for the devolution of real responsibility and parallel pressures from workers for a far greater say in the control of their working lives.

These trends may be regarded as a part of the development of personnel policies designed to increase involvement or job enrichment. For workers' participation merges imperceptibly into a demand for industrial democracy. The pace of advance towards this objective and the extent to which it moves towards true worker self-management will depend partly on the attitude of management itself and partly on the development of political ideas in the working-class movement generally.

Companies faced with these demands will, in my judgment be bound to respond to them partly in the interest of efficient operation and partly because of their vulnerability to pressure from below. It was exactly by conceding to pressures from below that political, industrial and social advances were made throughout British political history and which explains the combination of change with stability of which Britain is most proud.

It will be clear from this line of argument that the future of the multi-nationals are inextricably bound up with the development of world politics, and cannot be isolated from main currents of political thought.

The mythology which the multi-nationals have sought to develop to justify their own existence is a mythology that is bound to come under challenge in the new era of world politics which we are just entering.

Most global corporations grew to their present strength at a time when the United States was the unchallenged and unchallengeable political and military power in the world, and when American business philosophy was enjoying a pre-eminence sustained by this political and military power.

But in the 'sixties this pattern of American pre-eminence has been challenged by the growth of alternative centres of power first in the USSR, then in Japan and Western Europe and now by the emergence of China.

It will no longer be possible for those who run the multi-nationals to avoid entering into political alliances with all the compromises that this may involve, if they are to survive.

But the more political that they become in order to survive and expand and advance, the more they must expect to find themselves subject to political pressures exerted upon them by nation states and international organisations.

In short, multi-national companies employing thousands of people, controlling great resources, with a vested interest in territorial development and with reserves of capital and know-how to protect, have become States and must expect to be treated as such.

Like all states, they will be subject to the demand for political and democratic control. If this is not successfully achieved, many of the advances that the West claims for political democracy, as compared to centralised bureaucracy or dictatorship, could be eroded until the main difference between the systems finally disappears.

This is the biggest political challenge facing man in his attempt to control his own environment. For having developed an engineering capability which allowed him to conquer nature he finds he has set up organisations that may in fact control him.

The single biggest political issue of the 'seventies, 'eighties and beyond is the need for democratisation of power.

In Communist countries this must necessarily mean gaining real popular control over the bureaucratic structure of the State and dismantling its most dictatorial features.

In the West, it must involve the democratisation of political bureaucracies, military machines and industrial power symbolised by the global companies.

In the developing world, it must mean a determination to shape their own individual destiny without falling under the military influence of the super powers or the economic control of multi-national companies.

To succeed, global industrial development must therefore recognise the inevitability that it too will have to adapt itself to accept democratisation. If it does not do so it is likely to go the way of all authoritarian systems.

Labour's Programme*

In June 1973, just before "Labour's Programme for Britain 1973" was published, I was invited to speak at a Financial Times *Conference in London, and thus had the opportunity of spelling out the background of events and experience against which that policy had been developed.*

My phrase 'a fundamental and irreversible shift in the balance of wealth and power in favour of working people and their families' was to be the first objective of the next Labour Government replacing the 1964-70 objectives of improved economic management and growth.

At that time the controversy over the twenty-five companies was very much in the news, but this speech made it clear that the issue was not one of numbers but of really substantial extensions of public ownership into manufacturing. The policy was adopted by Conference in 1973 and appeared in the manifesto in 1974.

On Friday morning the Labour Party publishes its 1973 Programme for Britain.

This policy statement is the product of three years of very hard work, involving hundreds of people and dozens of policy groups; supplemented by our Liaison Committee with the Trades Union Congress, and our agreement with them.

The National Executive Committee has now approved it for presentation to our October Conference, in Blackpool, for decision.

The manifesto on which the Labour Party will fight the next General

*Speech at a lunch at the London Hilton, as part of the conference on "The Future of the City of London" organised by the *Financial Times* and the *Investors Chronicle*, June 6, 1973.

Election will be drawn up, from this programme, by the National Executive and the Parliamentary Committee, sitting jointly for that purpose.

The next Labour Government, responsible to the House of Commons and the electorate, will then have the job of seeking to implement that policy during its term of office.

There is a debate — but no crisis.

The Public debate about that policy is therefore just beginning.

No-one should mistake this debate for a split or a leadership crisis. There is no split and no crisis. Of course there are disagreements but even the range of issues on which we are not yet all agreed is a very narrow one. We shall have no difficulty in finding common ground and the debate will help us do it.

We are proud of the fact that, unlike the Conservative Party, our policy is not handed down from above but is decided at every level by democratic decisions.

That is how we have always done it; and that is how we all mean to keep it.

It is odd that those who are always demanding 'Open Government' should not recognise it when it happens — as it always does within the Labour Party. Open Government means a public instead of private debate.

Labour exists to bring about a shift in the balance of power and wealth.

As a Labour Party, born out of the trade union movement, we represent, politically, the same people whom the unions represent industrially.

Our first and prime objective is therefore to bring about a fundamental and irreversible shift in the balance of power and wealth in favour of working people and their families.

We also intend to make economic power more fully accountable to the community, to workers and the consumer; so as to eliminate poverty; to achieve far greater economic equality and to meet urgent social needs.

This is not a new challenge but a very old one. As more people become dissatisfied with the obvious inequality that exists in Britain and the growing abuse of business power, the demand for fundamental reform will grow too. Unless it is met, the consent necessary to run our society will not be available.

Let me take some recent examples of the abuse of financial power.

First Lonrho. Lonrho is important — not as a glimpse of an untypical 'unacceptable face of capitalism' — but because it reveals, openly, patterns of inequality in personal remuneration and perks and tax avoidance, which are not uncommon.

Firms may be able to get away with the payment of £38,000 a year to a part-time chairman if no-one else knows about it.

But when it becomes public, and we know that the same chairman supports, as an MP, a statutory wages policy to keep hospital and other low-paid workers, earning less than £20 a week, down to an increase of £1 plus 4% it is intolerable.

Next the Hill Samuel/Slater-Walker merger[1] bringing together gross assets reported to amount to £1,500 million, has been allowed to take place without any reference to the Monopolies Commission for an independent scrutiny and a public report on the criteria adopted, even if only to safeguard the shareholders. Why was it not referred?

Hill Samuel and Slater-Walker have both contributed very substantial sums to the Conservative Party. Close relations between any Government and the City are inevitable. But where personal and political links like this exist, there is proper public anxiety, and the case for an independent examination becomes overwhelming.

The Poulson affair and the recent case of a Minister's holdings in oil shares, underline the great urgency of requiring a full disclosure by all Ministers and M.P.s and councillors — and possibly officials — of their business interests and connections of all kinds.

Let me list some other recent abuses of power:

* The gross overcharging by Roche for Health Service drugs.
* The initial refusal by the Distillers directors to compensate the thalidomide children properly.
* The scandal of land speculation, raising rents and agricultural land prices.
* The whole industry of tax avoidance, including the use of tax havens abroad.
* The high profits made from second mortgages.
* The unsolved cases of insider dealings.
* The casino-like atmosphere of the Stock Exchange.
* The collapse of Vehicle and General.
* The international scandal of IOS and what followed.

Millions of people who experience real poverty in Britain are gradually learning about all this on the radio, or television and from the press. Such things are a cynical affront to the struggle that ordinary people have to feed, clothe and house their families.

But the problem goes deeper than that. Workers have no legal rights to be consulted when the firms in which they work are taken over.

They are sold off like cattle when a firm changes hands, with no guarantee for the future.

1. In the event this merger did not take place.

78

The rapid growth of trade union membership among white collar workers and even managers indicates the strength of their feelings about that.

But it is not just the economic, but also the political power of big business, especially the multi-nationals which is now coming into the open.

In Chile, ITT plotted to overthrow an elected President.

Watergate revelations suggest that some big business funds were used in an attempt to corrupt the American democratic process.

In Britain we are now promised a massive political campaign also financed by big business, to oppose the Labour Party's programme for public ownership and to secure the re-election of the present Government.

Leaving aside the question of abuse, the sheer concentration of industrial and economic power is now a major political factor.

The spate of mergers in recent years in Britain alone — and their expected continuation — can be expressed like this.

In 1950 the top hundred companies in Britain produced about 20% of our national output.

Today, they produce about 50%.

By 1980 the top hundred companies will produce 66% — two thirds of our national output.

And many of them will be operating multi-nationally, exporting capital, and jobs, and siphoning-off profits to where the taxes are most favourable.

The banks, insurance companies and finance institutions are also immensely powerful.

I have been looking through those institutions represented here today at this lunch, in order to get some idea of the power of this very audience.

You will not be surprised to hear the result.

The banks represented here alone have total assets worth at least £65,000 million. Add the other financial institutions and the figures rises to about £95,000 million. This is about twice the Gross National Product of the United Kingdom and four or five times the total sum raised in taxation and spent by the British Government each year.

The Labour Party must ask what effect all this power will have on the nature of our democracy.

Britain is proud of its system of Parliamentary democracy, its local democracy and its free trade unions.

But today the Industrial Relations Act, designed to shackle the trade unions; and the Counter-Inflation Act which may make industrial disputes illegal and subject to legal penalties; and the Common Market legislation which strips our elected House of Commons of its control over some key economic decisions have all greatly weakened British democracy at a time when economic power is growing stronger.

I have spelled this out because it is the background against which we have been developing our policy proposals. We have also taken account of unrest in Britain.

Sometimes this discontent expresses itself in strikes, militant speeches or angry demonstrations outside the Parliamentary arena; sometimes in deep cynicism.

The Labour Party was created to express this discontent within Parliament, to produce alternative policies for fundamental reforms, to seek electoral support for those reforms and then to carry them through democratically.

You will be familiar with some of the things we have said we will do to make this power accountable.

We shall repeal the Industrial Relations Act immediately, completely and unconditionally and replace it by legislation, drawn up to entrench the rights of working people and to develop industrial democracy.

What we have in mind goes far beyond the window dressing of some European schemes.

We are thinking of say 50% of workers, elected through their trade union membership on to supervisory boards with real powers.

And we mean to carry this sort of reform through in the public sector, as well as in the private sector.

We shall carry through a real redistribution of income and wealth through radical changes in the tax system.

We shall retain permanent controls over key prices and profits and control food prices and be ready to subsidise essential foods.

We shall bring urban land for development into public ownership and repeal the Housing Finance Act.

We shall restore free collective bargaining and seek a wide-ranging agreement with the Trade Unions on the control of inflation and the economy.

We shall start renegotiating the terms of entry into the Common Market and the British people will be given the right to decide the matter, when these negotiations are over, through the ballot box.

Before I turn to public ownership which has tended to dominate the head-lines in the last few days I should like to deal with other elements in our Industrial Policy which are of equal importance, and on which we are absolutely agreed.

In the light of our own experience before 1970 and taking into account the far greater powers which this Government has taken over business, we believe it will be necessary for us to present a new Industry Bill to Parliament and ask them to approve it.

Our legislation must cover the following points:

The right to acquire adequate disclosure of information by companies.

The right of government to invest in private companies requiring support.

The provision for joint planning between Government and firms with reserve powers.

The right to acquire firms, if Parliament approves.

The right to protect firms from foreign takeovers.

The extension of the present insurance companies provisions for ministerial powers over board members.

The development of a more flexible system of Company Law.

The extension of the idea of Receivership to cover the defence of the interests of workers and the nation.

Safeguards against the abuse of power by global companies.

If we are to have a managed economy — and that seems to be accepted — the question is 'In whose interests is it to be managed?'

We intend to manage it in the interests of working people, and their families.

But we do not accept the present corporate structure of Government Boards, Commissions and Agents, working secretly and not accountable to Parliament.

The powers we want must be subject to House of Commons approval when they are exercised.

All these things that I have described are commonly agreed between us and they are very important.

May I now turn to the question of Public Ownership. If you will allow me to speak from my own personal experience as Minister for Industry — Technology as we called it — during the last four years of the Labour Government I should put the case to you like this.

We tried to work by the indirect method using a system of negative controls, and huge public subsidies to try to inject the national interest into boardroom thinking.

It was a great improvement on the old fashioned doctrine of 'laissez-faire' to which this Government returned during its first two-year 'lame duck' period.

That has now been abandoned and this Government has returned to many of the policies we evolved.

But our experience, and their experience, has convinced us that policies based on the carrot and the stick are not adequate.

Such policies cannot create new jobs in Scotland, Wales and the regions on a sufficient scale and at sufficient speed.

Such policies cannot handle the high risks of developing advanced technology.

Such policies cannot catch up with the chronic problem created by years of under-investment in Britain.

The catastrophic drop in investment during the first two years of this Government's life cycle, and the delayed upturn just beginning now may well yet be too little and too late to sustain the boom which they have tried to create by boosting consumer spending.

We should all now have learned the hard way that you cannot bully and bribe business men into pursuing policies to meet our regional employment needs, our investment needs and our national interests, against the interests of their shareholders. We have come to the end of that road.

This is why we are now discussing — and are very largely agreed — about the need for an extension of public ownership to some of the sector leaders in successful manufacturing industry; well beyond the basic industries or those which have obviously failed — like shipbuilding, which have been the only candidates for public ownership in the past.

We are not interested in ownership just for the sake of ownership. We *are* concerned with the power that ownership carries with it to shape our future.

What is at issue, in our much-publicised discussions, is not the precise number of firms which we might need during the next Parliament or the periods of Labour Government that might follow.

There never was any magic significance in 25 — although it might be noted in passing that if Slater Walker can acquire 29 companies in a single year — 1972 — a government target of 25 over a far longer period does not sound excessive.

It is not the number but the principle of really substantial extensions of public ownership into manufacturing that does matter. Put this way, as it should be, the case is very powerful indeed. I am sure that the next Labour Government will want to move forward on these lines.

Whatever the merits of these arguments may be some people assume automatically that if the Labour Party put them forward in the next election we would be heavily defeated.

I wonder.

Do the British people really want a society in which industrialists and bankers have more power over Britain's economic future that the Governments they elect?

How long will the housewife, trying to shop around to get a bargain, believe in competition when prices seem to be rigged against her.

Can we seriously expect workers to accept a real cut in living standards due to rising prices and rents and food costs while so many firms are making profits?

Can we ignore the fact that many workers — right up to management level — are also now more worried about takeover bids and asset stripping which are inseparable from private ownership.

Maybe if the choice was just between a concentration of power in public hands, or tens of thousands of genuinely competing, small, intimate businesses, the voter might think there was safety in numbers.

But that is not the choice.

The choice is between a growing concentration of private power, held in a very few — closely linked — hands, not accountable to the community; or greater accountability to workers, the consumers and to the people — from within the public sector.

Moreover as the debate about these alternatives develops we shall see big business come out of its corner and start fighting in earnest against these policies.

And when that happens the whole story will be rather different from the campaign of Mr. Cube a generation ago.

People will not be quite so ready to fall for that old line, now they know a bit more about the ugly face of capitalism.

The Labour Party has a very strong case and the public, once they hear the arguments openly discussed, may well find that our case is overwhelmingly in their own interests.

No wonder the Prime Minister wishes that that argument had not started. That may be why he is trying to shift it back to the safer ground of an imaginery leadership crisis within the Labour Party.

I doubt if he will succeed. But I am not a bit surprised that he is trying to see that the real issue doesn't get debated.

Now that the dust is settling, and the full text of the Labour policy statement is just about to come out, this debate will begin and it will go on up to, during, and well beyond the next general election.

The problems we have identified are real problems.

Economic power *is* getting too concentrated; *is* being abused; *is* threatening democracy, *is* preserving a pattern of power and privilege that is grand for the minority who enjoy it but not good for the rest.

All this is bound to lead to a public demand for fundamental reform.

We believe that in putting forward our policies we are speaking for a majority of the British people and when they hear us argue for them they will recognise the authentic statement of their case — exactly as they did in 1945.

A Policy for Change*

Labour's industrial policy was presented to Conference by Harold Wilson on October 2 1973 and in replying I had to summarise the debate and try to set our new objectives in perspective pointing out that "The crisis we inherit when we come to power will be the occasion for fundamental change and not the excuse for postponing it".

Our policy – the most radical presented by the Labour Party since 1945 – far from harming Labour's electoral chances provided a perspective of social, industrial and political transformation that had been absent in 1970 and contributed to the energy with which the movement threw itself into the election campaign in February 1974; and to its success in that campaign.

The industrial policy which we put before the Conference this year and which we have been debating today occupies a central place in meeting our central objective of bringing about the changes in taxation that were discussed and agreed yesterday. Even the radical Chelmsford national plan for the redistribution of wealth and income cannot itself achieve what we know has to be done unless we can bring about a great extension of public ownership.

Now, this debate on our programme, and the reception given to Harold in presenting it, proves that the three years' hard work that has been done within the movement as well as on the Executive and in the House of Commons has produced a policy that does more than meet the demands of the movement for an expansion of public ownership. It meets the deep needs of the people of this country as they turn to others for protection from the abuse of business power to which they are now exposed: and those who talk about public ownership as if in some way it represented a threat had better realise the truth which is that there are millions of workers, and I mean workers, right up to management level who are much more frightened today of the possibility that Slater Walker will take them over and sell their assets and close them down than of anything we may do.

Moreover the violence of the attacks upon our public ownership plans and on us for defending them launched by big business and by the media confirm our judgment that these plans are a serious threat, as they are intended to be, to the unaccountable power they wield and the unacceptable privileges that they defend with that power.

Now in all this the mention of 25 companies has played an interesting part. In choosing those figures we were seeking to give some numerical significance to a better-known phrase, 'the commanding heights of the economy', long accepted as the party's objective in its extension of public ownership. And I say this to a Conference that has

*Speech to the Labour Party Conference, October 1973.

84

discussed this and will decide it in the spirit that has been reflected this morning: that we have by our programme this year triggered off the first serious public debate about public ownership for a generation, and for that we must be very grateful.

If those of us who have joined in this comradely debate have acted as a lightning conductor for the attacks of our opponents, I must tell the Party that we have been getting a little batting practice for what will be happening over the whole range of our programme when people realise how radical it is.

Our policy on public ownership is based upon a serious analysis of the developing power structure in our society: fewer, larger companies, many of them multinational, growing larger and more powerful, and we know, and we must say that if we do not control or own them, they will control and own us, and that is the challenge that we face.

It is not just a matter of efficiency, it is not just a matter of investment, it is not just a matter of regional policy. It is a matter of political power, for as Michael Meacher rightly said, if this political expression of unaccountable economic power is allowed to continue, our political democracy too will be reduced to a fiction, and that is what matters about the programme we bring forward.

Comrades, the Executive recommends that the Conference accept Composite 35, moved by Brian Anderson, which endorses our programme. It recommends that the Conference accepts Composite 36, which was moved by Denis Howell and seconded in a very powerful speech by Sheffield Hallam. It recommends that we accept Composite 18 on industrial democracy, subject to our discussion continuing with the TUC with whom we aim and must necessarily reach full accord. We ask the Conference not to accept Composite 34. Nobody reading it can doubt that it is firmly based upon the ideas of Clause 4, and there is much within it with which we could all agree. Perhaps the mover of the resolution did not realise that the Industry Act is an enabling act subject to full parliamentary control. That is what it is, but it calls for 250 companies, and Brian Anderson said it, and I must repeat it, it is a composite that confuses strategy with tactics. Therefore, we ask the Conference not to accept it.

Now, reference was made at the end of his speech by Charles Loughlin to compensation. We are not, never have been and never will be, a party of confiscation. But we will not over-compensate in the acquisition of profitable manufacturing industries which we propose to bring into public ownership. On hiving off, our position is exactly as it was in 1971, when I had the responsibility for replying to the resolution moved by Sid Weighell of the NUR at that conference. Our warning words issued in that debate have not changed, indeed, they are somewhat confirmed by our experience since. Let me cite one case of effective hiving off in respect of Rolls-Royce Motors. In the case of Rolls-Royce, a company sustained by thousands of millions of pounds of taxpayers' money, when it went bankrupt, the shares dropped to one penny a share. They were described in the press as "collectors' items", but for people, speculators in New York, they seemed possibly to be more than collectors' items, and many tens of thousands of those one penny worthless shares were bought at that time, and each one of those speculators is now to receive 33 pennies for the shares. And where is that £7 million to come from but from the £25 million that has been acquired by selling off Rolls-Royce Motors? That is not a tolerable situation.

May I say something else to the movers of Composite 34? I believe that conference decisions must be taken seriously. That applies to the National Executive Committee; that applies to the Parliamentary Party. That must apply to the Shadow Cabinet, but is must also apply to Conference itself. We are not ready for Composite 34, and if Conference takes its own decisions seriously we ask it not to pass that resolution.

However, we are ready for the programme that we have put before you in our statement. When we are sent back to power, as I believe we surely shall be, we are ready to give instructions for the completion of the Industry Bill with the powers contained within it to establish the National Enterprise Board, not to be an ambulance for lame ducks, but to move into the area of profitable manufacturing industry which is at the heart of that proposal.

Why have we come forward with this proposal? Because we know, and we know with the benefit in my case of ministerial experience of struggling with these problems, we cannot get jobs in the regions, we cannot raise investment in new plant and equipment on which future employment prospects depend, without a radical extension of democratic ownership and control.

If I may say to the delegate from East Moors who raised the case of steel, and he was only one of many here today for whom the steel decision affects the community in which they live, not only are we challenging, as we are, the British Steel Corporation corporate plan, which we believe has been created in part by pressure from the Government, but we are determined that where areas are affected by decisions of that kind we as another Government will have the power to channel employment there without having to rely on bribing and bullying business men to do things they do not really wish to do.

We shall not change the power structure in our society solely by Conference resolutions, by Cabinet decisions, or by parliamentary legislation. Historically, all pressure for social change and improvement has begun outside Parliament, as indeed the history of the Labour movement itself proves. The trade unions, the Trades Union Congress, the Labour Representation Committee, Labour Members of Parliament, Labour Governments, Acts of Parliament, are the last and never the first stage in the process of political and economic reform.

Therefore, we must now carry the debate we are having today out to the people of this country and we must begin with the workers in industry, and particularly in discussions with the workers in the firms that we shall need to acquire. I cannot conceive of an extension of public ownership without the same active support and pressure from workers in the firms of which we are now speaking that we historically enjoyed from the miners, from the railwaymen, and from others who demanded public ownership and looked to us to give it to them.

What I am saying is that industrial democracy begins now. We do not have to wait for the legislation we intend to introduce to begin the process of debate and dialogue within industry about how the firms should be run and which of them should be acquired. Oonagh Macdonald, who spoke from South Gloucestershire, spoke of the work of the Bristol aircraft workers who for over a year twice a month have met to develop a plan for the control of their own industry based on the knowledge that we shall be bringing it into public ownership.

We reject as a party and a movement the idea that one worker on the board is industrial democracy. We reject co-ownership. We reject the phoney works councils not rooted in the strength and structure and traditions of the trade union movement.

All these are window dressing, designed to divert the demand for democratic control into utterly harmless challenge. We are talking about the transfer of power within industry and we will not accept the existing pattern of nationalisation as a form for the future.

We have had enough experience now surely to know that nationalisation plus Lord Robens does not add up to socialism, and that is the message we are sending out.

Some delegates, quite properly, today have asked us what is our strategy for victory, as well as our economic and industrial strategy, and to those who raise these proper questions I would put, as best I can, this answer: if we are only concerned to win the votes we shall never mobilise the strength we need to implement the policy. That is the question. If we win the argument then we shall win the election, but with the counting of the ballot papers on polling day will come the power from public mobilisation to implement what we put before the people. And I say further, if we win the argument now we can acquire much of the power even before the election, for the pressures that will emerge from the debate we want to see will operate even upon Mr. Heath.

We are offering much more than legislation, we are offering at this conference a perspective and a vision which will transform the political atmosphere of cynicism which has happened to develop so much in recent years. Without a vision people will turn to their immediate and narrow self-interests, with some sense that they are part of a change in our society we shall be able to draw much more from them.

We must mean what we say and say what we mean and not run for cover when Fleet Street turns upon us, because I must say this quite seriously to this conference that if it looks tough now it is as nothing to the roaring of attack that will descend upon us as we seek and mean to carry through this programme.

One delegate said that we shall inherit a crisis when we come to power. Everybody knows that and certainly the spending priorities will have to be determined in the light of what we can do. We cannot do anything about that, but the question we are answering today is a different and important question, in respect of our industrial policy, and let me spell it out clearly so that nobody is in any doubt whatsoever about what we are saying. We are saying at this conference that the crisis that we inherit when we come to power will be the occasion for fundamental change and not the excuse for postponing it; that is what we are saying in this debate today.

Now in the light of that, it is not the drafting but the will that matters. The moment of decision on this policy is today. We have debated it and discussed it in comradely ways and in ways, perhaps, less comradely on occasions in the years leading up to this conference, but it is for the conference today to decide its attitude to our policy. That does not mean that the debate ends today, for we in the Labour party are, and have always been, the Parliament of Labour, and this debate will continue and nothing we must do or say must indicate or suggest that we wish to end the debate or to prevent those who would like to go further or those who think we are going too far from continuing the process of peaceful persuasion.

But let us be quite clear that when, in a few minutes' time, the decision is taken, it becomes our programme, our policy, for our movement, to be put forward by our party under our undisputed leader in our campaign for a victory, not just for the Labour Party, but a victory for the British people against the attacks that are made upon them by those who exercise power, not in the interests of the people, but in the interests of their own special interests and privileges. And from this day and this week at this conference, our task is to go out, delegates, to organise and campaign for that victory and to start that campaign right now.

Why New Policies are Needed*

In December 1973 the Times *published this article by me in which the arguments for our new policy were set out against a background of failure by both parties in government since the war to solve the nation's underlying problems. The* Times *which had been campaigning energetically for over a year to promote a third party was still hopeful that Labour would be defeated as a result of adopting such an openly socialist policy, thus reviving its long-term aim of a re-alignment of British politics to isolate the Left.*

These hopes were dashed on February 28, 1974.

Since the war men of undoubted talent and integrity in both political parties have tried very hard to make the British economy work. They have been assisted by the Civil Service, advised by committed and able academics, and for much of the time have had the goodwill and active support of the public expressed through the ballot box.

During the whole of this period the leaders of management and labour have maintained a working relationship with successive governments and have agreed to cooperate constructively with their policies.

The national interest, first identified and reflected in the wartime coalition government, continued to be expressed afterwards within a framework of agreed objectives, which we termed consensus politics. These included an attempt to maintain full employment, the maintenance of a welfare state, together with policies designed to promote economic growth.

This was the social contract, and within it, the two parties developed their own different emphases and conducted their political arguments. Yet today after all that effort this country is fighting for its industrial survival. Even before the oil crisis our economic prospects had become grim. The energy problem has hit us at a time of weakness. At the same time the electors in their votes at by-elections have been expressing their disquiet and discontent.

In parallel with this, there has been a growing lack of confidence by much of the leadership of our society in the people, and in themselves. This has been charaterized most recently by wild charges of Marxism, militancy, fanaticism, mental instability and even madness.

All this is evidence of deep anxiety. But unfortunately it has also made a serious discussion of alternative policies difficult, if not, at times, almost impossible. Unless we are prepared to accept that most politicians are self-seeking liars, most workers are being cowed and

*Article in *The Times*, December 7, 1973. Reprinted by kind permission of Times Newspapers Limited.

dominated by irresponsible extremists and most members of the public are incurably selfish, and at times ungovernable something else must be wrong. And so it is.

There is, in fact, a growing agreement about what has gone wrong and it is worth stating. Industrial investment in the private sector has been consistently lower than everyone in management and labour has known to be necessary if Britain was to remain a major industrial power.

In recent years this private sector investment has dropped disastrously despite everything that this Government has done by adopting traditional measures of cutting company taxation and pledging itself to go all out for expansion. Even growing government intervention within a market economy has not produced this investment.

Essential social needs have also been neglected. The affluence, of which some boast, has never reached millions of our people who still experience real poverty, poor housing, low pay and nagging unemployment in Scotland, Wales and the regions. Our social investment has deteriorated and cannot now provide the services we need.

We have tolerated inequality in education, employment and retirement that offended against the common decencies of a society that claims to be civilized.

In industry, we have had continuing trench warfare deriving from low pay, and authoritarian and remote management made worse by continual lectures from well-paid directors, ministers, editors and others to workers to show restraint. Moreover as business and City power has grown, democratic rights through free trade unions have been steadily eroded by the Industrial Relations Act.

Those who champion these discontents in Parliament, which exists to mirror discontent and remedy grievances, are now pilloried as inciters of the discontent they articulate. This is the dead end of democratic politics.

Now the Lord Chancellor seeks to interpret these tensions as a challenge to law and order and a betrayal of patriotic duty.

It just will not do.

The real situation is very different. Accelerating inflation and higher unemployment caused by industrial dislocation, and a serious setback in world trade and our economy, confronts Britain with a political situation is has not had to face for over 40 years.

The sheer magnitude of the task of industrial transformation and renewal that the United Kingdom will have to undertake is difficult both to grasp and to convey.

We shall have to develop oil and coal and nuclear power as

indigenous fuels to keep our economy going. We shall need to build up rapidly an industrial capability to carry this through.

We must invest in fuel-saving equipment of all kinds, in building and transport and acquire the industrial capability for that as well. The whole economy will need to be reshaped around energy considerations. This task can no more be tackled by free enterprise, even with government intervention on the present scale, than we could undertake a big rearmament programme by shopping around from competing business firms.

During this period there will be hardship and difficulty for the British people. The only basis on which we can appeal to them for cooperation is by adopting policies of social justice and greater equality − not just equality of sacrifice but greater equality of rewards and top priority for those in greatest difficulty. If this is not done we cannot expect and shall not receive their consent for what has to be done.

It is against this background that the relevance of Labour's commitment to bring about a fundamental and irreversible shift in the balance of power and wealth in favour of working people and their families by democratic means can now be judged. Indeed, if growth is denied us, even more of our social provision must come from the redistribution of wealth and income.

Other policies to eliminate inequality − in education, for example − will also have to be carried through by reallocating what we have, without waiting for more money to lubricate the change.

Our structural changes, involving an extension of democratic accountability and public ownership in industry − which impose no strain on our resources − will soon be seen as essential if Britain is to get the investment in fuel and fuel saving and the industrial capability it must have.

Even our proposals for workers' control in industry can now be seen as the pre-requisite for converting the enormous defensive power of the trade union movement into the positive power we must be able to harness if we are to survive.

But our real hope lies in our capacity to preserve and extend democratic self-government as we go through this period. We must not be hypnotized by the magnitude of the crisis into believing that our democratic rights must be given up as part of the price of survival and that only dictatorial political leaders can save us.

The only way we can acquire the cellular strength necessary to survive this crisis is by freely debating the alternatives and jointly deciding on our course of action.

III

The Common Market

Not Going Into Europe*

The magazine Encounter *published a series of comments on Mr. Macmillan's first attempt to get Britain into the Common Market. I was one of those approached to give my views, here reproduced in full.*

The idea of Britain joining the Common Market is emotionally very attractive. To throw open our windows to new influences, to help shape the destiny of a new community, even to merge our sovereignty in a wider unit — these offer an exciting prospect. By contrast the xenophobic, parochial delusions of grandeur fostered by the Beaverbrook press appear petty, old-fashioned, and reactionary. But the issue must not be decided by either of these emotions. A political decision of this magnitude calls for a cold hard examination by each of us of what is involved. It seems to me:

First, that the Treaty of Rome which entrenches *laissez-faire* as its philosophy and chooses Bureaucracy as its administrative method will stultify effective national economic planning without creating the necessary supra-national planning mechanisms for growth and social justice under democratic control.

Second, that the political inspiration of EEC amounts to a belief in the institutionalisation of NATO which will harden the division of Europe, and encourage the emergence of a new nuclear super-power, thus worsening East-West relations and making disarmament more difficult.

Third, that the trading policy which the community will inevitably pursue will damage the exports of under-developed countries and increase the speed at which the gulf between rich and poor countries is widening.

Fourth, that on balance Britain would have far less influence on world events if she were inside than she could have if she remained outside.

Fifth, that experience shows that written constitutions entrenching certain interests and principles are virtually impossible to alter.

*Contribution to a series in *Encounter*, January, 1963. Reprinted by kind permission of *Encounter*.

93

Of course things will never be the same again. Remaining outside means making just as many radical changes in British economic, social and foreign policy as would be necessitated by going in. But we should be free to make them in the light of the wider needs of the world as we see them.

The Common Market as it now exists is inspired by narrow regionalism. Relevant internationalism today means accepting disarmament controls, following liberal tariff and trading policies, and working all-out through the UN to end the deadly contest between East and West and substitute a policy of co-operation based on our common interest in survival. Those are the causes that inspire the new generation.

Technology and Politics in Europe*

This lecture delivered in Bonn in February 1968 after the Labour Government had applied for membership justified that application in terms of "the inexorable logic of scale" imposed by technology. It accepts technological determinism and plays down political issues.

... My Department is becoming increasingly involved in the development of closer relationship with our fellow European countries.

Indeed it was partly through our analysis of the impact of technology upon industry that we came to the historic decision to apply for full membership of the European Economic Communities.

Britain may have been slow to see the importance of the European Communities. But I believe she was the first to see that technology imposes on us all its inexorable logic of scale.

And it is this inexorable logic that led the Prime Minister to speak about a European Technological Community as the industrial heart of an extended EEC.

Of course we are disappointed by current setbacks. But we are confident of the outcome, partly because of the inescapable logic of technological development. The political opposition to our membership will be ineffective because the nationalistic arguments upon which it is based are becoming increasingly irrelevant. Political argument must be relevant to be effective. Realism is the foundation of all political success. Thus it will be with the development of Europe.

*Extract from a speech given to the Deutsche Gesellschaft für Auswartige Politik in Bonn, February 20, 1968.

The full benefits of an integrated European technology can only be achieved when Britain is a member of the EEC. Meanwhile we must make what progress where and when we can. We must co-operate now and we must prepare for the day when the Community can be enlarged.

We have put forward important proposals for a European Institute or Centre of Technology.

We believe that what is required is a joint study by European industries of the way in which technology is likely to affect the market for advanced products over the next ten years. This mid-term technological demand forecasting is already being done by the large American corporations who plan to meet it with their own products.

We must, therefore, analyse this demand together, compare it with our present capability of meeting it, and then plan to rationalize, strengthen and develop that capability so that it can meet it. Perhaps in developing a European Institute or Centre of Technology some of the experience of the British Ministry of Technology may be helpful.

The Case for a Referendum*

This letter to my constituents in November 1970 set out the case for a referendum on British entry to the Common Market.

... The formal position of all major political parties in Britain is that if the terms that can be negotiated are not too onerous, and if Britain's basic interests can be safeguarded, we should sign the Treaty of Rome, and become full members in an enlarged Community. We are therefore waiting to find out what terms we can achieve.

So far this argument has been conducted almost entirely in economic terms. We have been considering what effect entry would have on the balance of payments and our cost of living, what contribution we would have to make to the Community budget, how we could cushion our Commonwealth trading partners, and what the long-term benefits might be. These are important questions that ought properly to be the subject of intense negotiations. But the terms may in fact tell us very little. We may be able to estimate the initial cost of going in, but we cannot possibly estimate with any accuracy either the long-term advantage of entry, or the long-term cost of not entering. That will depend on what we do if we enter and what we do if we don't. When the negotiations are over, we cannot feed the results into a computer and expect it to tell us whether or not we should enter. The idea that Britain's entry into the Common Market is solely, or even

*Extract from a letter to constituents of Bristol South-East, November 14, 1970.

mainly, an economic decision is to miss the whole point of what is happening. It is a major political decision we have to make, and it must be seen as such.

What is being created is not just a customs union, but a political unit. Slowly but surely the pressures are building up to create a federal political structure. If the talks now in progress led to a monetary union under which Europe would have the same currency, the major economic decisions, now taken by individual Ministers of Finance in their annual budgets, would be taken within the framework of a European financial policy worked out by the Commission in Brussels. If that happens the policies of every nation state would be subordinated to this supra-national policy.

Successive British Governments have so far been singularly quiet on the idea of political union. This was partly because no such structure has been agreed even amongst the Six. De Gaulle, being a strong French nationalist, was very much opposed to it, and Britain, being on the outside, played no part in the discussions that were going on. Some advocates of British entry thought that too much talk about federation would frighten off British opinion and thought it would be more tactful not to say too much about it. So the political implications of entry have been played down and anyone who asks questions about it is always told that it would have to be decided later and Britain would, by then, be a member of the Community, and would have a say in the decision.

But this really is to fudge the issue. It is inconceivable that Britain with its strong Parliamentary tradition would allow a bureaucratic Commission in Brussels to reach central decisions about economic policy without being subject to broad democratic control by an elected Assembly. Certainly no Socialist could accept anything less.

All this highlights the importance of thinking now about the policy which a British government would follow if Britain were to become a member of the Community. Although there is firm support for entry among members of all political parties in Britain, there would be sharp differences about the policies the two major parties would advocate if they were represented on the Council of Ministers. Conservatives see the Common Market as a way of widening the area of capitalist competition which they believe would have a bracing effect on the British economy. Inside the Community they would want the European "Government" to withdraw from industry in exactly the same way as they are now withdrawing from involvement in British industry. A Labour Government, by contrast, would obviously be arguing for a socialist European policy designed to control market forces, make economic power accountable and extend the area of public activity. It is therefore not good enough to argue that the only question is whether we join, without indicating what policy we would pursue if we were there.

The key question at this moment is how we are to decide whether we want to join. Up to now it has been assumed that, like every other Treaty, the decision would be reached by the Government after a Parliamentary vote. But this is not the same as any other Treaty. It is an irreversible decision which would transfer certain sovereign powers now exercised by the British Parliament to the EEC. Parliament would then be obliged to carry through those changes in its law that were necessary to implement Community policy and the Courts would have to uphold and enforce Community law in Britain. Thus a Government that signed the Treaty of Rome would be binding all succeeding Parliaments for all time and these decisions could not be changed even if that Government was later defeated in a General Election.

In short to sign the Treaty of Rome would be as significant for Britain as the Act of Union was for Scotland. We would be entering an organisation that could develop into a full United States of Europe even though we would enjoy far more independence than say Texas or California enjoy within the USA.

This being so it is inconceivable that we could accept a situation under which this decision was made after a vote in the present House of Commons. This would mean in effect that a bare majority of the Cabinet — 9 men out of 17 — could reach a decision, put the Whips on to force it through the House and commit the nation for all time. Even if there were a free vote, which the Prime Minister would not accept, this would still leave the matter to MPs, not one of whom was able to commit himself during the election on this issue, since the terms were not then known.

But would an election fought on the Common Market help very much? If both parties were in favour there would be no choice offered to the public. And if one party was opposed to it this would not be a good way of reaching such an important decision. In some constituencies there would be candidates from both main Parties who were personally in favour; and in others candidates who were personally opposed which would deny to many electors the right to make their voice heard.

Moreover it would be quite wrong to expect a life-long supporter of one party who deeply believed in its philosophy and policy to vote for the other party just because he or she agreed with them on the Common Market issue. No General Election could allow people to record a separate vote on the Common Market question.

This has not only to do with whether the terms are good or bad. There are both Labour and Conservative voters who on political grounds wouldn't want Britain to join the Common Market even if you could prove conclusively that they would be far better off financially if we did join. And there are also people who would still think it politically desirable even though it did mean higher prices and a lot of painful changes in the short run.

It is for these reasons that we have got to consider the use of a unique mechanism to help us reach a unique decision. The case for a referendum on the question of Britain's entry is, in my opinion, immensely powerful if not overwhelming. If people are not to participate in this decision, no one will ever take participation seriously again.

Consider first the arguments against it and see how valid they are.

First, it is said that there is no provision for a referendum in the British constitution. But neither is there any provision in the Constitution for Parliament to surrender part of its sovereignty to an international federation. Britain has allowed referenda in various colonial territories to permit them to decide – as in the case of Gibraltar – whether they wish to remain under British sovereignty or to be transferred to others – in that case Spain.

A Bill to allow a referendum on the Common Market could easily be introduced into Parliament and passed through in such a form as to provide the necessary machinery.

Secondly, it is said that if you had a referendum on this you would have to have a referendum on everything – including hanging and flogging and immigration. But each case must be argued out on its merits and in none of these other examples are the decisions permanent and irreversible. Entry into the Common Market is irreversible.

Thirdly, it is said that this issue is too complicated for people to understand. This is arrogant nonsense. People are perfectly able to make up their own minds for themselves. It is true that they may reach what will, to others, seem to be a wrong view. But that applies equally to giving them the vote. It is, if anything, more complicated to decide which party you wish to represent you than it is to decide on the question of Britain's entry into Europe.

Fourthly, it is said that people would not have enough information on which to make a decision. But the very best way of getting information out of Government on the long-term effects of entry is to have a referendum. Then the Government would have to release all it knew if it was going to persuade us to accept its view. If the Government know they don't have to bother about what the people think, they won't bother to put out the information and will hope to persuade us that they are the only people who really know enough to decide.

If Britain really is to play a useful part in Europe, and to accept the inevitably difficult process of transition, it must have decided consciously that it wants to enter. Nothing would be more likely to lead to trouble than the feeling that we had been led into Europe by leaders who didn't trust the public to make their views known on it.

Public opinion polls are no substitute. The last Election showed how unreliable they can be. It is one thing to ask a sample of people to give their opinions, but quite another to ask everyone to play a part in reaching the decision.

The Labour Party, at its Annual Conference in 1970, decided by a narrow majority to stand on its old position of supporting negotiations and suspend final judgment until the negotiations are complete. If possible and if necessary a special Labour Conference will be called to discuss this question before Parliament is asked to debate it. That is much better than nothing. But if the Labour Conference is to be given this opportunity to record its view, why should the British public not be allowed to give their view too?

In the post-war years I was very hostile to the idea of a Common Market. I did not like the strong anti-Russian cold war bias that lay behind it, since the reconciliation between the Communist world and the West seemed, and still seems, to me to be at least as important as the reconciliation between France and Germany. I was afraid that the EEC would be inward-looking with no interest in the developing world and would forever be dominated by Conservative forces. None of these fears now seem to be so justified. Willy Brandt's Eastern policy and rapprochement with the USSR is of great significance.

One other factor which changed my view was the enormous growth of international companies which are now, in many cases, bigger than nations and growing more rapidly. If man, as man, does not organise himself into bigger political units the international companies will run the world and we shall be like Parish Councillors in our Parliaments with little say in what happens. Big power requires big politics if little people are to be protected. The world is so small that Britain alone cannot separate itself from world influence nor prevent its destiny being affected by what happens abroad. Nor should we suppose that merely joining the EEC will solve all our problems for us. It will not.

Of course we can stay out and stand alone, but we will still find that European, American and Russian decisions will set the framework within which we would have to exercise our formal parliamentary sovereignty. If that is what the British people want we shall have to live with the consequences of it. It is true that many who are opposed to entry have urged a referendum because they believe that it will reveal a majority against entry. That is a matter for them. Those of us who feel that, given the right terms, the arguments for entry are strong should be the first to want to see that decision shared.

The whole history of British democracy has been about *how* you take decisions; and this has always been seen to be more important than what the decisions were. All political parties in Britain are prepared to accept electoral defeat because they believe the machinery represented by the ballot box is more important than the result it produces.

If the Common Market question is decided without consulting the people, it will split the country and both parties. Many of those who really want to go in will oppose entry just because they have been shut out from the decision. If there is a referendum the whole atmosphere could be transformed and we could face up to this decision at least agreed about how it should be reached.

We do not have to wait, therefore, until the terms have been negotiated. We can start the great debate now on the question of the referendum. It would involve a constitutional innovation which would raise many practical difficulties which would have to be sorted out, but we cannot accept arguments against it based on the false idea that people are too ignorant or apathetic or ill-informed to reach a view for themselves. It would be a very curious thing to try to take Britain into a new political unity with a huge potential for the future by a process that implied that the British public were unfit to see its historic importance for themselves.

Referendum Campaign*

In the summer of 1971 Bristol South-East Constituency Labour Party decided to launch a campaign to persuade the Labour Party to adopt the referendum as its official policy. Every constituency and trade union was circulated with the text of a Private Members' Bill showing how a referendum could be organised, which I had presented to the House of Commons.

The campaign was launched at a public meeting in Transport House, Bristol. This speech separated the question of the referendum from the Community and argued the case for renegotiation from inside the Community.

Those who advocate a referendum have often been accused of using it solely as a device to frustrate entry.

But I hope you will acquit me personally of any inconsistency in this matter, or of being a recent convert to this view.

Almost exactly ten years ago, we in Bristol South-East were involved in a much smaller — but still significant — constitutional issue arising from my expulsion from the House of Commons on the grounds

*Extracts from a speech at a public meeting organised by the Bristol South-East Labour Party in Bristol, July 2, 1971.

of peerage. This constituency re-elected me and sent me back in a by-election campaign fought on a single constitutional issue and thus asserted the right of the people to be represented by the candidate they had chosen.

The 1961 by-election was a Referendum in all but name. It was justified because of the constitutional importance of the issue. It was effective in that the House of Commons accepted the verdict and changed the law.

Shortly after the Labour Government applied for entry I made a speech in Llandudno – on May 8th 1968 to be exact – in which I said, and I quote, 'The five-yearly cross on the ballot paper is just not going to be enough. Inevitably we shall have to look again at the objections to the holding of referenda and see if they are still valid . . . If some real issues . . . were actually put out for a decision in principle by referendum, the situation would be transformed. This would involve real responsibility. We might not all like the result. But at any rate by sharing responsibility an interest in public policy would be stirred in every household.'

Immediately after the last election I specifically argued the case for a referendum on the Common Market and I have since presented a private Member's Bill in the House of Commons which would make this possible.

Nobody could therefore say – of me – that I have just thought this up to help the Labour Party over a difficult period by allowing it to get off the hook with the minimum of embarrassment.

It is a part of a deeply held personal conviction that modern democracy cannot survive unless it shares much more power with the people.

The Bill I have introduced provides that a referendum should be held no sooner than three months after both the White Paper containing the terms has been published *and* the arrangements for the Referendum embodied in a special Act of Parliament have been agreed.

The question on the ballot paper would be identical to the question that would be tabled by the Government in the House of Commons were no referendum to be held. It would thus allow each elector the same right as each MP would have, to record a clear answer, YES or NO.

The result of the Referendum, declared constituency by constituency, would be published and laid before Parliament so that each MP would know how his own constituents had voted and the total vote for and against in the country as a whole.

Only then would the same question be put in the House of Commons for the vote, which would be binding upon the Government. . . .

. . . Whether Conference reaches its final view in July or at the normal Conference in October, there can be no doubt that the Parliamentary Labour Party will share its view and will wish to be guided by its vote.

The Party Constitution which provides the policy shall be decided at Conference and its application determined by the P.L.P. could not possibly lead to any other conclusion on an issue as basic as this.

May I sum up my views like this.

First: I am wholly and fundamentally opposed to the présent Government's proposals for taking Britain into the E.E.C. without any consultation with the public, either in a General Election and/or a Referendum.

Second: I am sure that the Labour Party is absolutely right to hold its Conference and settle its policy on the basis of Party democracy, whenever Conference so decides, and to unite in supporting it.

Third: I believe we should now embark on an intense campaign for a General Election, and, in that campaign, offer a consistent and radical alternative range of policies to the public which they can choose when it takes place.

Fourth: I can see really significant long-term opportunities for ordinary people in Britain, and in the Six, if we could persuade the British public to vote for entry and then work together to change and reshape E.E.C. from the inside to convert it progressively into a democratic socialist community. This Socialist case for joining has almost gone by default. We must develop it and let it be heard. We shall surely need to look at it in the future.

The European Question is much more than a simple decision to enter or stay out, on the terms announced.

The debate on it has opened up some of the most important questions in politics. It throws new light on the nature of the Parliamentary system, on the attitudes of elected leaders to their constituents, and on the nature of democracy itself. It is my firm belief that unless on this – and most other issues – people demand more power and governments concede it we shall find that the democracy our forefathers fought for will slip through our fingers and we shall lose control over our own future.

And worse still – that as a result – we shall go under to a new authoritarian bureaucracy and our society will never be freed to generate the responsibility and leadership it now so desperately needs if it is to survive.

102

The People Must Decide*

This speech, delivered just before the House of Commons vote on the principle of British entry, sets out the background of argument that took place in the Labour Cabinet on the EEC and argues the constitutional case for public consent before the British democratic system of parliamentary government was dismantled by being subordinated to a bureaucratic supra-national system.

Mr. Anthony Wedgwood Benn (Bristol, South-East): When I set myself to prepare for this debate I hoped that I would be able to achieve four objectives: first, to be brief; second, to speak my mind; third, not to provoke; and fourth, to try to clarify the choices that the House has to make. If I may pay a tribute to a part of the Chancellor's speech, I fully agree with the words that he used at the beginning, about the "end of an era", the "parting of the ways", "a matter of judgment". However, if I may say so without disrespect, if he had been able to continue to develop his argument by recognising the truth, that we are all groping to find the right answer to difficult problems, he would have commanded more respect from the House.

But I shall not depart from my brief, which I have written myself so as to be short. I shall not be tempted by the right hon. Gentleman to provoke, and I have only one quotation to read, from which I think the House will learn but which I do not think that it will mock.

I do not share the certainties expressed in this debate by many of the principal advocates on either side. I envy the Prime Minister and the right hon. Member for Thirsk and Malton (Sir R. Turton). I envy those on either side of the House for whom this has always been absolutely clear, who have made no change of view at any stage and for whom tomorrow's debate is only a long-awaited opportunity to register a long-held view.

But I do not believe that that is the position of as many hon. Members as the debate might have suggested. I believe that the division in the country, in the House and in both parties is reflected in some sense within each of us. Indeed, even the Prime Minister, if the Gallup Polls could not reveal a single supporter for entry, might decide not to press his application. Therefore, we are talking about something which does divide us and which divides each of us.

I believe that the debate would have made more sense to the nation if more hon. Members had been prepared to confess publicly that they had argued it out in their own minds and that some doubts remained. I

*Speech in Debate on "European Communities" in House of Commons, October 27, 1971.

am very much afraid that if the people think that we have no doubts, they will think that we have not been listening to them over the last few years – because they have doubts.

I would go further and say that I think that history is unlikely to confirm any of our certainties expressed, and that what the historians will want to know is how deeply we thought about the possibilities. Moreover, a doubter listens because he wants to be convinced, while someone who is certain very often does not. It is with this approach, therefore, that I make my submission to the House.

I make no apology, in the course of having thought about this issue, for having changed the emphasis of my view at different stages. I would not regard it as being particularly honourable or necessarily desirable that in a world which is changing more rapidly than at any time in our history the one thing that remains absolutely unchanged was my view of how we should handle it. What sense does that make to an audience not only here but in Europe, which has changed its own view and its own institutions?

I was not an early European. I debated with my right hon. Friend the Member for Leeds, West (Mr. C. Pannell) when he came to my constituency 15 years ago, when I was opposed and he was in favour. He has not changed his view. I joined in the Cabinet discussions and I supported application, but I did it with doubts then, doubts of which I am not ashamed, as to whether Britain outside would be able to manage as well as inside, and whether we had the power alone to cope with the new power that had been created by modern industry. I supported the decision to apply.

But the right hon. Gentleman really must not pretend that the motives of the Labour Government in applying were comparable to his own. For example, I did not join in the Cabinet decision, neither did my right hon. Friends, in order to create a wider market to discipline the British trade union movement. When the Secretary of State for Trade and Industry spoke earlier this year about the motor tariff, he was very candid: it was to deal with wage increases in Britain. I am not criticising him. I am identifying a difference which he would want to see identified as clearly as I would. He sees in Europe a chance of market forces working unrestrained over a larger area. I do not. That was not why we applied.

The Secretary of State for Trade and Industry and the President of the Board of Trade (Mr. John Davies): Is the right hon. Gentleman implying that he has never had, and has not today, the least faith in the force of competition? That is what he appears to be saying.

Mr. Benn: I am not saying that. The right hon. Gentleman knows very well that his attitude to market forces is different from ours. I am not saying who is right, but we take a different view about the role of market forces in a society. He sees those forces having greater sway in a bigger market. We saw in the Market — and this is why my right hon. Friend the Member for Kilmarnock (Mr. Ross) said what he did say yesterday — a need for more protection for those who might be affected by the acceleration of technical change due to competition. We did not share the present Government's political motives.

It is not sensible for the House to try to isolate this central economic question from our philosophies on other economic matters, and to pretend that we can cut the question of British adherence to the Treaty of Rome from all the other aspects of policy which have guided us. That would be to mislead the public. I confess frankly that the view of entry which I took in 1967 and the application which I supported then were in the context of policies which would be followed by a Labour Government and which had very little in common — and the Secretary of State will be glad to hear me say it — with the philosophy of the right hon. Gentleman and his colleagues.

I wish to say a few words about some of my colleagues. Much play has been made about my right hon. Friends the Members for Workington (Mr. Peart), Battersea, North (Mr. Jay), Kilmarnock, Blackburn (Mrs. Castle) and others, joined later by my right hon. Friend the Member for Stepney (Mr. Shore), because it is known now, and it was known then, that they had great reservations about the application. I can say what they cannot say, because I am not seeking to claim that I had their reservations; namely, that their positions were wholly reserved within the Cabinet, and everybody knew it. An application was made, but with reserved judgment until the negotiations had been completed. [*Laughter*] Before it giggles, the House had better consider whether it wants the idea to go out to a public which is a bit more intelligent than it may think it is that Cabinets are always unanimous.

Unanimity is not the same as collective responsibility. I have no criticism of the hon. Members for Glasgow, Cathcart (Mr. Edward Taylor) and Ludlow (Mr. More), who joined the Government in the summer of 1970 knowing that the Government they entered wanted this country to enter Europe. They came out when the decision was made and it affected them most directly. It would be a very great pity — because it is a dishonest way of presenting the means by which those in politics reach their decisions — to suggest that there was unanimity in the last Government and then a total change of view. Everybody knows that in political decision-making we must reserve our position until we see how the final choice has to be made.

I must claim to reserve the same freedom to comment on the terms negotiated by another Government as I would have had in the Labour

Cabinet to comment on the terms negotiated by a Labour Government. Therefore, let us not have too much of that.

Mr. Jeremy Thorpe (Devon North): The right hon. Gentleman is a fair man. Would he logically conclude that any fellow member of the Shadow Cabinet has the right to reserve his opinion?

Mr. Benn: Yes, to reserve his opinion.

Mr. Thorpe: According to his conscience?

Mr. Benn: The right hon. Gentleman had better listen to my argument before he comments further. The greater part of my speech, if I am allowed to reach it, deals with the question of how the House should decide this matter.

I agree very much with what the Chancellor of the Exchequer said — and it enables me to shorten my argument — that the economic predictions cannot be advanced as solid ground for reaching a decision. If there is one thing which all of us should have learned over the last 25 years it is that the economic problems of Britain are not simply to do with economics. The organisational problems of the world monetary system, the political problems, the attitudes of people — all these things create the conditions in which a society grows economically.

There is a great danger of our producing for members of the public a new myth — "Vote 'yes' for more jobs in Europe" — after all the experience we have had of putting forward remedies which we promised them would produce the desired answers. No Governments since the war have succeeded in achieving growth, a balance of payments surplus, stable prices, higher productivity and full employment at the same time. If any Government had done so they would have been in power throughout the last 25 years.

The forecasts do not make sense as an answer. In my constituency I succeeded a Chancellor of the Exchequer, and I have listened to 11 others in the House. They were all good and honest men but they were all wrong in their forecasts. Therefore, I agree with the Chancellor that we should not base our case on them. But the House should at least have had a chance to know what the best Government forecasts are. The Lockheed loan of 250 million dollars was subjected to a long inquiry by a Congressional committee, and matters to which the Select Committee on Science and Technology, of which my hon. Friend the Member for Bristol, Central (Mr. Palmer) is Chairman, has devoted many sessions on issues that have received more detailed consideration than the decision which the Chancellor of the Exchequer has called "a decision which ends an era". That is our complaint — that we do not want to rely on an intervention from the right hon. and learned

Member for Hexham (Mr. Rippon) or second-hand news about what he told the Lobby.

This is not principally an economic issue; it is a political argument. The Government see it as a political argument. The people sense it as a political argument. History will confirm it to have been a political decision. Of course, it must be mainly to do with Britain's role in the world and her relationship with the United States, the Soviet Union, China and Japan. Ministers sound convincing on Europe only when they talk political language.

I wish to read a quotation, but not in order to mock or to criticise, from a speech which the Secretary of State for Trade and Industry made last year at the Agra-Europe Conference before he was a Minister. I ask the House to listen not because it represents the Government's view but because it is the best political case for entry that I have heard. No one at the end of it will be cheering or laughing. The right hon. Gentleman said:

> "what are we going to get out of it? Firstly, in a world where more and more the big battalions hold sway, we are going to move closer and closer to those who are not only our neighbours but who, for so many reasons, have interests compatible with our own. I know it is unfashionable to talk about the political objectives of the European community, but they seem to me by far the most important of all. Tensions on our continent's eastern, south-eastern and southern frontiers have not disappeared and, unhappily, are not likely to do so in the near future. The defence bulwark of the U.S.A. is to be gradually withdrawn. Western Europe grudgingly and unenthusiastically no doubt, must unite to assure the safety of its own frontiers and, no less important, its strategic negotiating strength. The first thing we buy is, to my mind, the economic unity upon which must be built the political structure capable of assuring the independence of our continent and its right to develop its own particular mixture of democracy, liberalism and the respect of the individual.
> So number one on my list is the defence of the integrity of Western Europe towards which the enlargement of the community is the fourth faltering step after NATO, the Rome Treaty and the creation of EFTA."

I read that to the House because those words explain why the Chancellor said that it is the end of an era. It has a political motive tightly linked to defence. I said that no one would cheer or laugh.

I come to the defence aspect of it. This is the best exposition of the Prime Minister's real thinking, and I suspect that of most of his Cabinet colleagues. He went through the agony of negotiation before he failed in 1963. He did not fail because of the negotiations. He knows that he failed because of the Polaris deal at Nassau. At the very moment when

107

de Gaulle wondered whether we had shifted from America to Europe, the then Prime Minister reaffirmed the special relationship, confirmed the exclusion of France from the nuclear partnership, and confirmed again the insult de Gaulle had suffered when he asked for a triumvirate to run N.A.T.O., which was denied by America and Britain.

My interpretation is that at that moment, or soon after, the right hon. Gentleman, then a Minister in an outgoing Government and now the Prime Minister, resolved that nuclear weapon technology was the golden key to lift the French veto on British entry. I can put to the Prime Minister only what I believe. It is not part of the terms, but it is an essential part of the deal. That release of that technology is now openly demanded.

I hope that the right hon. Gentleman will not forget that in the atomic world — I have had responsibility for the Atomic Energy Authority — it has always known that that is what it was about. One could not visit Harwell or other places without knowing from all the people there that it was the French exclusion from the nuclear deal that was the major barrier between Britain and France. In his speech the Foreign Secretary admitted, after an intervention from the hon. Member for Worcestershire, South (Sir G. Nabarro), that the McMahon Act was very important. I can only put it to the House, because it has not been brought into the White Paper, that a massive shift of military support linkage from the United States to France, always the sleeping partner with the Atlantic Alliance, is what lies at the heart of the Prime Minister's defence and foreign policy.

I give a parallel example. As a Minister, I negotiated the centrifuge agreement with the Germans and the Dutch. A centrifuge is not a piece of nuclear equipment; it is a little engineering component which goes round very rapidly. It is a very simple engineering component. It stemmed — and the House should know this — from the period of co-operation between Britain and the United States in this sphere. The amount of negotiation that was required to get the centrifuge agreement settled, on that simple engineering component, indicates to me the magnitude of what the Prime Minister will be undertaking if he carries through his nuclear deal.

Except in the House, I have only once debated with the right hon. Gentleman. That was on 3rd February, 1951. We were both new Members. He had been elected in February and I had been elected in November. He has probably forgotten it but I have not; I have checked. His speech was based upon the importance of the Atlantic Alliance. I found the notes of my speech. I said, "Democracy means the right to be wrong." That is still the argument I put to the House today — [*Laughter*] The question is; who has the right to be wrong? Has the Prime Minister the right to be wrong on behalf of all of us and to bring

108

about the end of an era in British history? If the Secretary of State for Trade and Industry is right, if he speaks for the Cabinet, if the renegotiation of the nuclear arrangements is undertaken, if defence and foreign policy are to be put in too for harmonisation with tariffs and taxation, we are being asked to undertake such a major political commitment that there is no parallel for it, certainly in this century.

I should have thought that it would be obvious that in such an arrangement this House would be subordinate to the bureaucrats in Brussels, or — I think that the Prime Minister sees beyond that, too — faced with subordination to Brussels, we shall demand a European suffrage and we shall have entered a fully-fledged federal European State.

In a situation where all these major decisions are taken by the Commission, the Prime Minister thinks that he can bring the second lever into play, the lever of British opinion wishing to democratise the power to which it is subject. Therefore, I claim that the Government have set out upon a course that can only be interpreted in terms of a major federal structure for Western Europe. If this is so, why is it not more apparent? I will tell the House. If it could be said that this is only a little economic arrangement one could tell the public that it is too complicated for them to understand. But it is not a little economic arrangement. By playing down the politics of it, one can be sure that the public do not understand what it is really about. By isolating the nuclear element from it and saying that it has nothing to do with the White Paper — which is true — one could complete the act of concealment.

To undertake changes of this magnitude without specific and explicit public consent is to undermine the basis of British parliamentary democracy. Either we subordinate the House of Commons to a non-accountable bureaucratic structure in Brussels, or we go on to the full federal structure.

Sir Harmar Nicholls (Peterborough): I am likely to be in the same Lobby as the right hon. Gentleman, rather surprisingly, but as he is explaining what was the concealed intention behind this Government when they were previously in office, what was the intention behind his Government when they decided to apply in 1967?

Mr. Benn: Perhaps the hon. Gentleman has not been present throughout my speech, but I said that the Conservative Party's motives for entry — I am commenting on rather than criticising what I believe to be its motives — were totally different from those that motivated my right hon. Friend the former Prime Minister and myself in presenting our application.

Let me develop my case. I am seeking not to provoke but to argue a case. I say further to the Prime Minister that this proposal will not work. It will not work because one cannot generate the will to carry through such a change without first obtaining the consent preceding the decision. If I were a long-standing European, as is the Prime Minister, I would feel that he had killed my European dream, because visions are realised only when men enter a common enterprise freely. They carry the strain. They are rewarded by their effort. One cannot march a nation into a new era and adventure on the scale — against its will. [*Interruption*] I am prepared to develop my argument as best I can. I should be grateful if the House would allow that.

A major constitutional issue lies at the heart of this question. We have talked about sovereignty, but what does it mean? Without referring to the old texts or the Treaty of Rome, it means that when people come to this Chamber we can point to the Treasury Bench and around the House and say, "This is where your laws are made and your taxes are imposed. This is where policies are explained, and you can get rid of these men yourselves." That is all there is in parliamentary democracy. Open-debate plus a secret ballot is parliamentary democracy. It has nothing to do with Mr. Speaker's wig or the mace, or all the little things the tourists come to see. It is the combination of open debate and secret ballot, that is the basis of our system. Parliamentary democracy does not mean that we control our destiny. Our future could be decided in Brussels, Peking, in the Kremlin, the Pentagon or anywhere else. What it does is to guarantee that how we respond to the circumstances of our time is decided after open debate and by secret ballot.

Sir Frederic Bennett (Torquay): The right hon. Gentleman said that one difference between the parties was motive. How would the procedures that he has outlined — the free vote and ministerial accountability — be varied if the Labour Government had stayed in office?

Mr. Benn: I have tried not to make this into an argument of the kind that we have every day. Let me develop my case. I am doing it as best I can.

The arguments about parliamentary sovereignty are not arguments about the House of Commons having any rights, because I think the House knows that we hold these rights in trust for others. I am not interested in Parliament save only as an instrument of the public. When Lord Shawcross, in one of the silliest of many silly speeches, said "We are the masters now", he broke the central principle of parliamentary democracy. This House is famous not for its wisdom or its customs or its *Hansard*, but for Erskine May. That is why people come to see this House, because in Erskine May is contained the distilled wisdom of our experience of open debate and secret ballot. We do not have a written constitution. We have got something much more formidable. We have got a constitution embedded deeply in the hearts and minds of the people who live in this country, and it is that which encourages and shapes and restrains us all.

In 1910 a small constitutional change was delayed by the Crown. In 1949 a change of control of an industry was delayed by the House of Lords. Are we to be told by the Government that a simple majority in a single day is really to put an end to this long process of development of self-government? I believe it would totally misunderstand the whole temper and nature and history of this country if a decision of this magnitude were taken in this way.

All the attention this week has been on European institutions. This debate is about a British institution and how we should decide an issue ourselves. It is, of course, in relation to the public that we have to take our decisions. It is very easy to make fun of opinion polls and referenda. The right hon. Gentleman read an extract from a pamphlet that I wrote on referenda, drawing attention to one of the difficulties of proceeding in that way. But the truth is, and every Member of the House knows, that in the 20 years since the Commission was set up there has been an enormous development of our constitution in that our electors are better informed, and they are now beginning to press us more forcibly than they have ever done before. When the demonstrators come here they do not threaten Parliament. They sustain Parliament. It is when the U.C.S. workers — [*Hon. Members:* "Oh!"] Just listen to the argument. It is when the demonstrators take a charter flight to Brussels that we shall know where power has really moved.

If the Crown is no longer a constitutional safeguard, and neither is the House of Lords, the only place which could perform this function is the House of Commons. The issue tomorrow is not keeping the flag of Europeanism flying, for no one is in any doubt where most hon. Members stand upon Europe. It rises well above party loyalty. But they should accept that the constitutional issue rises above it. The House has got the power tomorrow to reserve the position for the people. I do not believe that if my hon. Friends or hon. Members opposite who choose to vote that way did so to give the Government time to think, to reserve the position for the people, anybody would misunderstand the motives that led them to do it.

I plead with the House, before this is all brushed off as a procedural matter, to recognise that parliamentary democracy is a very fragile thing indeed. It rests upon a network of assumptions so sure and strong that power is able to pass peacefully from one group to another. When

Churchill had defeated Hitler, he was defeated by the British public. Why? Because he had been brought up to believe that in Britain power passed that way. If ever this House were to create a situation in which people thought that it no longer reflected their power ultimately to decide, I believe that parliamentary democracy, which hangs by a gossamer thread, could easily fall to the ground.

Hon. Members may think me strange to concentrate almost entirely upon this issue, but there are not many places in the world where people can turn to an assembly that shapes their lives and say, "I decide who speaks there. I can remove them and by doing so I can change the policies of my society." The party system, for all its faults — and I do not much care for people who mock it in this House and then outside at conferences, Conservative or Labour, take a different view — preserves that basic choice. All the pressures of society are trying to bring us together into the mush of men of good will and no party. The party system preserves choice.

What I warn the House of is this. If the people think that by a temporary coalition, which has never been tested at the polls, some Members of Parliament claiming a divine right that we have denied to kings, deny the people the right to decide their own future, we are in serious trouble. [*Interruption*] I believe what I am saying. We live in a world where enormous and unaccountable powers are everywhere growing, whether they be General Motors, the big companies, whether they be the mass media or the big organisations for which we work, and people see in this Chamber the one thread connecting them to a countervailing power. If we cut the thread that connects them to us I do not believe that this House could long survive.

Certainly it would not help Europe if we joined, having entered this way. The Europeans do not really need our money for their common agricultural policy. They do not even need our technology because they can buy it as anyone can, as the Japanese did, from abroad. What they really need is the thing that we must preserve, if ever we were to go in to be of value — our experience of government by consent. I say this to the Prime Minister: If you rupture the social contract in this country as a pre-condition of entry into the Community, the terms are too high for anyone, whatever his view of Europe may be.

I began by admitting to doubts, and I have described them as best I can. But I have one absolute certainty at the end, that whether the European communities are good for Britain, only Britain can decide. The Prime Minister could leave this House to sign the Treaty of Rome and no one could stop him, but he cannot take this country into Europe by signing the Treaty of Rome. A British signature on the treaty of accession, legislation forced through this place, will not be the end of the matter. It will not commit the Opposition which entirely reserves its rights. It will not commit the British people because they will have had no part in it. I say to the Prime Minister: It would precipitate a major crisis and unleash the biggest constitutional and political struggle that we have seen in this country for many years. Will that struggle be anti-European? Not at all. It will be the right of British people, if they go in, to go in freely and to carry with them the thing they value most — the right to decide their own future. I have said before in political anger, and I say it again now, quite coldly, that the Prime Minister has forgotten the people, and in the end the people will always have their way.

A Grave Breach of the Constitution*

This speech delivered at the Annual General Meeting of the Christian Socialist Movement in March 1972 was written immediately after President Pompidou had announced a referendum in France on British entry which Mr. Heath was still denying to the British people. It was the French Referendum which finally tipped the scales within the National Executive Committee and the Shadow Cabinet of the Labour Party in favour of a British referendum, confirmed at the October 1972 Labour Conference, almost exactly two years after the referendum campaign had been launched.

It would be an outrage if the French people are allowed to decide whether they want Britain in the Common Market, and the British people are denied the right to say whether they want to join.

This is the nub of the present political and constitutional crisis which Mr. Pompidou has high-lighted by his Press Conference in Paris yesterday.

What is at stake here is not a matter of Parliamentary procedure but an absolutely fundamental question of Government by consent against Government by *diktat.*

Mr. Heath is trying to usurp powers that do not and cannot belong to him, or to any Member of Parliament, in any Party, at any time.

First, he made improper use of the Royal Prerogative to sign a Constitutional Treaty that had not been approved in advance by Parliament or the electors.

*Speech at the Annual General Meeting of the Christian Socialist Movement in Kingsway Hall, London, March 17, 1972.

Second, he drafted the Bill now before the House of Commons in such a way as to prevent essential amendments to it from being debated.

Third, he is using his Parliamentary majority to cut short the Commons debate by moving closures; and is likely to use the guillotine to bring the whole debate to an end when it suits him, as he has already done with the Rents Bill.

Fourth, he plans to advise the Queen to give her Royal Assent to a Bill which is, by definition, unconstitutional because it purports to bind future Parliaments, and hence the electors who will elect them.

Fifth, he has advised the Queen to visit France in circumstances which will now be used by Pompidou to help him in his Referendum campaign; after using the Royal Prerogative at home to prevent our people from having a Referendum or Election here.

Mr. Heath cannot get away with this. It is contrary to all British traditions of democracy, fair play and common sense.

What is at stake here is not some detail of Parliamentary procedure or legal nicety. It is absolutely basic.

If the British people are herded into a federation against their will, the whole fabric of our society will be threatened.

First, we shall find ourselves governed by laws we did not make and cannot change.

Second, we shall find ourselves taxed by people we did not elect and cannot remove.

Third, we shall find ourselves locked in to economic policies that may harm us and cannot be altered because they were devised to meet the needs of others.

Fourth, we shall be governed by European bureaucrats elected by no one for whóm Ministers are only needed as a rubber stamp.

Fifth, we may find ourselves sucked into a European military machine with its own nuclear weapons shared by France, Britain and possibly Germany, over whose use the British people will have no control at all.

When the British people wake up to realise what is happening, there will be a veritable explosion of rage directed not just against Mr. Heath, but against any M.P. in any party who joins in a conspiracy to destroy 700 years of Parliamentary democratic self-government by stealth.

The strength of Parliament has always rested on the foundations of public faith in it.

Take that faith away and you destroy institutions for self-government that generations of British people have laboured long to create.

Once the people discover that Parliament has given away the people's rights, then there will be no logical argument for retaining the system.

Some voices will be raised to say that the only answer is an authoritarian Government in Britain, of extreme Right — or extreme Left — governing by decree.

And if such an extreme Government did come to power and changed the laws without Parliamentary approval, they could argue that they were only following the same constitutional practice as Mr. Heath had introduced in the Common Market Bill which does allow Government by — European — decree.

Leaders of all three parties have got to sit down quietly and think out this problem afresh.

The Conservatives have got to accept that a General Election must be held before the present Common Market Bill enters into force.

The Labour Party has got urgently to re-examine its own attitude to a referendum because in such an election the Labour Manifesto must offer the British people a distinct and separate choice on the Common Market issue to take place after a new Labour Government had tried to improve the terms to see whether these new terms were acceptable to the people.

The Liberal Party, which once stood for personal freedom, might well ask itself why its Parliamentary leaders are now keeping a Cabinet in power that is denying the people's freedom to choose their own future.

It is always difficult for political leaders to change their minds. But if circumstances change or the full implications of a course of action emerge slowly and take some time to appreciate, it is a sign of weakness, and not of strength, to stick woodenly to decisions arrived at under different circumstances and before the significance of what has happened had become apparent.

People will understand a man who says that he is ready to listen and learn. They will never trust anyone who seems to be wedded to a process of decision-making that is based on the belief that the people cannot be trusted.

The British people have faith in those of their leaders who have faith in them. They distrust leaders who distrust them. They respect those who respect them.

That is the whole essence of British democracy which has survived not because of Acts of Parliament or the details of procedure. It survived because people wanted it to survive. It rests on mutual confidence. Destroy that confidence and you destroy our whole system.

The idea of building a wider unity in Europe has inspired many men and women in Britain. It is a tragedy that now — just because of the way it is being enforced — it should have become the most divisive issue and should threaten the ideals that we hold so dear.

The case for a General Election or a Referendum has not been advanced to stop Britain entering the Common Market. It has been advanced to allow everyone to join in that decision.

It may well be that given an absolutely free and fair choice we would say 'Yes'. We certainly must also have the right to say 'No'.

The opposition to an Election or a Referendum has come from those who have so little faith in the British public that they are not prepared to put it out to the people to decide for themselves.

Democracy has always been about *how* you decide things. We have always accepted that the way you settle your differences is more important than the differences themselves. It is on that proposition that consent has been won and held for successive governments, even from amongst those who did not vote for them.

Take that away and you have nothing left.

No one wants to see British politics sink into the mush of a general consensus. Were that ever to happen, great issues would never be debated and resolved.

But it is even worse to pretend that there is a consensus based upon 'the whole-hearted consent of the British people' when that consent has neither been sought nor obtained.

It is the pretence that consent exists that is dividing old and valued political colleagues and friends one from another, and souring the minds of milllions of people in Britain who are condemned by this pretence to be mere spectators to what seem like squabbles among politicians fought out under the arc lights of the Parliamentary arena.

We must rediscover national unity based upon acceptance that issues of supreme constitutional importance cannot be settled in the lobbies in the Palace of Westminster but must be settled in the ballot box which is the ultimate safeguard of our liberty.

The course upon which the British Government is now set can only intensify bitterness, and deepen cynicism. The ultimate consequences of which no one can now foresee accurately.

Everyone, pro- or anti-Market, Labour, Conservative or Liberal, should now agree to agree on the way in which the decision should be taken

This means we must tell the British people the truth, trust the British people, and let the British people decide. There is no other way.

Why Labour Opposed Entry*

This exchange of letters with Dr. Mansholt, then President of the European Commission, came at a time when many European Social Democrats were still unaware of the majority view of the Labour Party because most of their personal contacts were, understandably, with the pro-European minority within the Party. Mansholt's understanding of the working of British parliamentary democracy is shown to be most superficial.

House of Commons
London, SW1

March 28, 1972

Dear Dr. Mansholt:

Your press conference in Brussels on Monday was widely covered in the British press, including your comments on the policy of the British Labour Party towards entry into the Communities.

You are reported as saying that you are "ashamed to see my Socialist friends adopt such a negative attitude"; that "there is no reason why the Socialists in Britain could not accept the terms"; and, later of our "stupidity".

You are entitled to your own opinion. But you also have a duty both to understand and to explain the reasons why the Labour Party has taken the view it has taken.

The entire British Labour movement, by clear majorities, at the Trades Union Congress, the annual conference, amongst Labour M.Ps, on the National Executive Committee and in the Shadow Cabinet agreed to oppose entry on two grounds.

First that the present terms were unfair and unfavourable; and second that on a matter of such historic importance the people should be consulted.

The peoples of Denmark, Norway, Ireland and France are to have a vote. The British people are to have the decision forced upon them. We are therefore demanding a general election, or failing that some other method of consultation.

The British Labour party has always been internationalist, but its policy is democratically decided; and in this case it is also championing the rights of the British people, as a whole, to have their say.

If Britain is dragged in without its consent we would lose before we entered our traditions of democracy which the communities so notably lack in their present structures.

Instead of calling us stupid you should be supporting our demands,

117

with your authority, and insisting as President of the Commission, that the British Government allows us all to choose our own future.

Yours fraternally
Anthony Wedgwood Benn

Dr. S. Mansholt
President of the European Commission
Brussels

Commission Des   ] Brussels, 12th April 1972
Communautes Europeennes
Le President

Mr. Anthony Wedgwood Benn M.P.
House of Commons
London, SW1

Dear Mr. Wedgwood Benn,

Your letter of March 28th surprised me.

When I see that all socialist parties in continental Europe are in favour of European cooperation in general and of the European Communities in particular, I cannot be but "ashamed to see my socialist friends adopt such a negative attitude". What you do, in effect, is to desert from the socialist family. "Right or wrong my country" was for a long time a conservative slogan in your country, you seem to have taken over that slogan.

It has been, and still is, a good socialist tradition to abide by democratic parliamentary decisions. The democratic parliamentary decision to enter into the Community has been taken by your House of Commons.

The debate in your country, after that vote, should be over now. Instead the Labour Party should prepare itself for the new situation and work closely together with the other socialist parties in order to make out of our Europe the socialist Europe we want it to be.

Yours fraternally,
S. L. Mansholt

From Anthony Wedgwood Benn MP
April 28 1972

Dear President Mansholt

Your surprise at receiving my letter was nothing to the surprise I got at receiving yours today.

You attribute to the Labour Party the doctrine of 'my country right or wrong'. But that is not the basis upon which we have taken our stand on entry into the community.

Democracy means that the people are given the chance to decide what is right or wrong for their country. The British people have been given no such chance – unlike the French, the Danes, the Norwegians and the Irish. We insist they should be given that right through the ballot box.

You speak of democratic Parliamentary decisions as binding on Socialists. But since when have Socialist MPs ever been bound by decisions taken by a Conservative majority against their own agreed policy? If we did that we should all pack up shop and accept Society as successive Conservative governments have shaped it.

If the Parliamentary leadership of the Labour Party had ignored our policy decisions taken by a majority at every level to give the British people a voice in this historic decision, we should have destroyed the British Labour movement before we entered; and we would have had little of value to offer to the Socialist parties in the Community.

I wish you would come to Britain yourself to meet and talk with those who represent the majority view that we have expressed. Come to our Conference at Blackpool this autumn. I believe you would find out for yourself that the banner we have hoisted is not labelled 'nationalism' but 'democracy'. You would be very welcome.

Yours fraternally
Anthony Wedgwood Benn

Dr. S. Mansholt
President of the European Commission
Brussels

We Must Have that Referendum*

By April 1972, the Shadow Cabinet had decided to support a referendum on the Common Market. It was decided to support a Conservative amendment calling for a referendum instead of tabling our own and I was invited to speak on it.

I ask the indulgence of the Committee to intervene briefly to convey officially the support of the Opposition for the Amendment moved by the hon. Member for Banbury (Mr. Marten). I am very conscious of the fact, and the House of Commons knows it from

*Contribution to the House of Commons debate on the "European Communities Bill", April 18, 1972.

following the newspapers, that the majority on the Labour side in favour of that Amendment is narrow. Both in the Executive and in the Shadow Cabinet, and even in the Parliamentary Labour Party, there was a substantial body of people who thought that Amendment to be wrong, but in conveying our view and recommendation to the Committee that it should support the Amendment I want to give some reasons why that should be done. I have to be careful and moderate in my recommendations since my right hon. Friend the Leader of the Opposition has described it as a repugnant procedure. I disagree with him, but he said it and I shall therefore have to moderate my own view.

Where I share the view of the opponents of a referendum, including many of my hon. Friends on the back benches, is that it is a pity that a major constitutional change − and to have a referendum even on this is a major constitutional change − should have come up so late in the debate and should occupy so little time in our discussions on the Bill. The truth is that the question of how we decide the European matter has emerged late in the debate, not from lack of trying by some of us to get it discussed earlier. I believe, and hon. Members know it to be my view, that how we decide whether we enter the Common Market is at least as important as what that decision itself is.

Turning to a practical argument that has not found much space in the debates we have had so far today, the House of Commons is divided on Europe. Both parties are divided on Europe. Indeed I would go further and say that the House is fragmented on the European question, for I agree with the hon. and gallant Member for Lewes (Sir T. Beamish) that there are many different views.

To go further, I think there are many hon. Members who lack the certainty that is given to some and who find that their attitudes and anxieties extend even into their own judgment. But instead of laughing at each other, as has happened today, instead of exchanging quotations and mocking each other as we approach this issue. I think the Committee would do well to approach the matter with a greater respect for the difficulty of reaching a wise decision. It cannot have given much pleasure to my right hon. Friend the Member for Birmingham, Stechford (Mr. Roy Jenkins) or our right hon. Friends who resigned with him to have parted company with their colleagues on a matter of this kind. It cannot really give much pleasure to hon. Gentlemen opposite, including the hon. Member for Banbury, who has tabled Amendment No. 205, who like most Members of this House have tried to give devoted service to their party to find themselves in a position in which they might prefer to see the other side in power to avoid the consequences they fear would be so serious for the country. When Members of Parliament on both sides who have a long record of service to their parties find themselves in the position in which we find

120

ourselves put, this is not a moment to mock, to laugh, to trade quotations that may somehow help our short-term interests.

Mr. Thorpe: If the right hon. Gentleman is right, and I think he is, in his thesis that the House of Commons is fragmented and if he feels compassion for those in all parts of the House who find themselves in disagreement, does it not make it sheer hypocrisy for him to have supported throughout the whipping system being applied to the vote in October and still more in February?

Mr. Benn: My concern throughout has been a free vote of the British people. The right hon. Gentleman cannot get away with that. He knows very well that the effect of the vote of 18th October and the effect of the votes tonight will be to deny to the British public the right he claims as a Member of Parliament.

Mr. Thorpe: Let us hear about this place first.

Mr. Benn: That is no recommendation for the parliamentary system. I will deal with the right hon. Gentleman's points as they come. The British parliamentary system cannot survive if we are to have distinguished parliamentarians saying "Let us think about this place first", because if that is what Parliament is about there is no reason why anybody outside should support it.

Mr. Thorpe: Freedom starts here.

Mr. Benn: Now we have it. Freedom began before the House of Commons was set up. Freedom was forced on the House by people outside it. Freedom is defended by the ballot box and not by the Division Lobby. If the Liberal Party now says that freedom rests in Parliament instead of seeing itself as the guardian of freedom outside Parliament, no wonder it is a tiny minority. I began with a pledge to be conciliatory and it is not my wish that I should provoke the one party in the House that has consistently supported the view of entry from the beginning.

There are factors in this debate which the House of Commons must take seriously. I believe the first such factor to be that neither side will accept the verdict of the House of Commons on the European question. Those who favour entry will never give up their advocacy of entry. We have seen that from those who have separated themselves from my colleagues and myself on this question. Similarly, they must learn that those who will not support entry without consent will never support entry without consent. Even if that entry is forced through the House of Commons, forced to Royal Assent, and the celebrations in Brussels take place in January, that will not be accepted.

Mr. Robert Maclennan (Caithness and Sutherland) *rose –*

Mr. Benn: Let me finish this point. This is the difficulty which we face. We could cope with our own disagreement if it were this place first. We could cope with our disagreement in the ordinary parliamentary way. What we cannot do is to cope ourselves, in the ordinary parliamentary way, with deep differences reflecting deep interests that have been wholly shut out from the decision we are asked to take.

Mr. Maclennan: My right hon. Friend has rested his argument on the inflexibility of those who are committed in favour of the Common Market and those who are against it, but some of us remember very clearly – indeed, his own example speaks loud in this matter – how flexible some politicians are able to be.

Mr. Benn: I take my hon. Friend's point. I am not one of these – and I have made this clear every time I have spoken in the House – who have been committed at all costs to our joining the Common Market or to our staying out. I have been consistent in saying for many years that this issue must be decided by the people, and I will accept the popular verdict, whichever way it goes. But if flexibility in response to a developing situation is an offence, there is not one man, including my hon. Friend, who will be able to claim that he came down the motorway of life without turning the steering wheel to left or to right to take account of changing circumstances.

The vote on 28th October was a majority that was not normally reached. It was reached before the treaty was published and before the Bill was published. It was reached by a coalition of people voting together who had never sought together the mandate which they claimed they had in the Lobby that day. It is a constitutional change. It is an irreversible decision. I heard the hon. and gallant Member for Lewes say on television that it was not irreversible, but that cannot easily be said by leaders on the Front Bench. If our Continental partners-to-be thought that we were lighthearted about our attitude to entry, they would not have us in. So the case must be presented as being a solemn, irreversible decision.

There is a growing cynicism with politics. This argument is advanced by both sides in this controversy. We differ about what causes the cynicism. Some say that it is caused by politicians who change their minds. Others say that it is caused by Members of Parliament with a contempt for their electors, supporters and people generally.

When members of the public see Parliament trying to solve this problem in this way, they see one of two things. They may see the House of Commons united under the Whips, knowing that they are men of conscience voting against their conscience. I get no satisfaction from seeing the House trying to settle this matter in a way in which Members are unable to follow their consciences. Indeed, I have a deep sense of repugnance against it.

Mr. Rippon: A free vote.

Mr. Benn: Yes — and a free vote by the British public. The right hon. and learned Gentleman missed the earlier part of the debate when we dealt with this matter. I am putting forward my view. I should like to see the British public, on a free vote, decide the matter on the basis of a recommendation which came from a free vote of the House. What I will not accept is the House, on a free vote, using that vote to deny the electors the right to say whether they wish Britain to join. That is the alternative which the right hon. and learned Gentleman proposes, and it is not acceptable.

Mr. Selwyn Gummer: The right hon. Gentleman says that we have already dealt with this matter. He has been asked a specific question, namely given that we have a party system and a whipping system, why did the right hon. Gentleman deny Members of Parliament the right to make their own decision on the merits of the matter?

Mr. Benn: That is a very fair point to make if we couple it with a decision that the result of a Commons vote would be our advice to the people when they voted themselves. The point of substance is that either members of the public see men of conscience voting against their consciences, which shakes their confidence in Parliament, or they see both parties divided, which also shakes their confidence in Parliament, because both parties being divided and carrying through a major constitutional changes without a mandate is destructive of the basis upon which our system works.

[Sir Robert Grant-Ferris *in the Chair*]

Sir Alfred — [*Interruption*] I beg your pardon, Sir Robert. The chairmanship of the Committee changes as rapidly as the views, so I am told, of some of our colleagues.

There are various choices open to the House of Commons. We can go on with the Bill as we have been doing and continue to exclude members of the public from the decision. They do not reply to postal votes sent out by Members. They know that nobody will take the slightest notice of them. If we exclude members of the public, they will have only one thing to be interested in — the personal squabbles, as they see it, of Members of Parliament; and do not be surprised when confidence in Parliament diminishes if people are confined to understanding those aspects of the parliamentary scene which they are allowed to understand, namely, the arguments we have between ourselves.

One day the people will wake up to find that the powers they lent to their Members are no longer available to take back to themselves. The House may think that not many people are interested in this matter, but when the electors discover that the laws which have been made and are enforced in the courts cannot be changed by any man they elect — Labour, Liberal, Conservative or Communist — the explosion of rage should not take us by surprise. Do we imagine that Scotland and Wales will be unaffected when this happens? There are already stresses and strains among people in Scotland and Wales about their being governed by an English majority from London. Why should they accept being governed from Brussels and represented by Englishmen from London? The demand either to secede altogether or to join independently will develop if we are carried in without consent.

Mr. Nicholas Edwards (Pembroke): Some Members on both sides of the House will resent the right hon. Gentleman's suggestion that Scotland and Wales are represented by English Members from London. Some of us like to think that Welsh constituencies, and no doubt Scottish constituencies, are represented by Welshmen and Scotsmen, from those constituencies.

Mr. Benn: The hon. Gentleman has misunderstood me. I said that Welsh and Scottish interests will be represented in Brussels by a predominantly English Parliament. The feeling of remoteness among Scottish and Welsh people will become greater. If I put the point wrongly, I apologise.

Another respect in which public anger will be caused is this. If there is further development of the Community, if we have an economic and monetary union, if we have a defence community and political reunification, and if every time the French proceed by referenda we are hogtied by Clause 2, the public will not understand it. People will not accept that the Government, without consent, have put a statutory straitjacket on parliamentary debate in advancing the Community, whereas France is allowed to proceed by popular vote.

Although referenda in France have been the agents of presidents, they have also destroyed presidents. President de Gaulle disappeared, hoist on his own petard. There are safeguards in a referendum for the French which are utterly denied us — not just now, but in any development of the Community.

I do not want to sound alarmist, but we should be very foolish if we supposed that there were not people in this country who cared as much about being subordinated to Brussels without consent as so-called loyalist Protestants in Northern Ireland care about being subordinated to Dublin without consent. They may be a small minority, as minorities are everywhere when violence errupts, but if the feeling that the independent right of the electors, through the ballot box, to decide constitutional questions is as deeply entrenched as the feeling of Ulster loyalists, as I believe it is, there could well be trouble following a decision to enter. No doubt the Government, with their police and perhaps a little advice from the French police in Calais, could put it down. It is better to say it now than wait until it happens and then wonder why it has happened. [Hon. Members: "Stir it up"] I am not stirring it up.

I say this to the Government. The capacity to put down that sort of thing, if it arises, depends upon one's being able to say to the man whom one is putting down "Change your Members of Parliament, change the law, and you can have your way by peaceful means". However, if some power, some law — the power to tax, for example — is put outside the control of the British electorate, one destroys at any rate a part of the moral authority that allows one to deal with those who struggle against what has been done.

The Government cannot, on the one hand, stand on the issue of law and order and, on the other hand, themselves deliberately fracture the delicate social fabric of the social contract upon which our system of government has been founded.

How does the House of Commons settle the issue? A General Election is the traditional way, if it is to be that way. I personally would accept unhesitatingly, as I think that the whole House of Commons would, a Conservative re-election at any election that occurred now on this basis, as settling the European question. Of course it would settle it, because the country knows the Bill, it knows the terms and it knows the treaty. If the Government were to be re-elected, we would accept that.

However, the Government would not be re-elected. An hon. Member can get a round of cheers by mocking his constituents in the Chamber. Today I have heard many hon. Members laughing at the ignorance of their constituents. Hon. Members have asked "Who knows what a referendum is?" By God, the miners won the right to strike and their battle in the recent dispute on a referendum. The British people know the meaning of the right to choose through the ballot box. Hon. Members can mock their electors with impunity from the safety of the Chamber, but when the battle is taken to a General Election the Government would be utterly defeated if they were to deny the British public the right to decide the matter. I warn hon. Members not to be surprised if the British public laughs at the British Parliament if hon. Members are so quick to laugh at the British public when debating its rights.

125

If there is an election, I believe that the Labour Party will come out for a referendum in its manifesto. I will say why – because it is the only way to put this issue to the public. If we were to say "Vote Labour, and we will never enter Europe", we should be just as guilty as the right hon. and learned Gentleman. We should be denying those in Britain who want to join Europe the right to do so. If we were to say that we would renegotiate and go in without consent, we should be guilty of the same offence, because we would be saying "You must take our word instead of that of the present Prime Minister".

I therefore believe that a referendum must and will be offered in a General Election. After all, if the Labour Party is to offer a referendum in its manifesto, why wait? We can do it tonight. We have a parliamentary majority tonight if the Opposition support their colleagues for a referendum tonight. If the Government will not accept a referendum, we get an election, which is what all my hon. Friends want. Therefore, the issue of a General Election and that of a referendum are inextricably bound up together.

I will now deal shortly with the arguments which have been advanced against a referendum. The first was that it would split political parties. Does anybody seriously think that the division in our parties is not well enough understood for a short referendum campaign to worsen it? Indeed, it would settle it, because both factions in both parties would accept the public's verdict.

Second, would it defeat entry? The hon. and gallant Member for Lewes said that it might given the wrong result, and then he corrected himself. There are those who oppose a referendum because they think that the British public would not accept entry. There are those who say that it would somehow magically reproduce Nazi Germany, Gaullist France or the stodgy Swiss. But a referendum is only a ballot box. It reflects the people and the values that go to the ballot box. A Danish referendum gives a Danish result. A Nazi referendum gives a Nazi result. A Swiss referendum gives a Swiss result.

Are we so far from our own electorate that we are frightened that they might vote in the ballot box in such a way as suddenly to transform Britain from a parliamentary democracy into a tyranny at the mercy of the Executive or the electorate, albeit any more Conservative in a referendum than they are in far too many General Elections? Are we to be told that we are to be frightened of our own electorate?

I think that the real reasons why this is rejected are worth studying. If the Committee will bear with me for a minute or two I will try to analyse the real reasons against the referendum. First, it is contrary to our traditions and the whole basis of representative parliamentary democracy. Second, it establishes a precedent which, if followed, would lead to serious consequences. Third, the public are not really equipped to reach decisions of this kind. Fourth, Britain is different from other countries. Fifth, the advocates are insincere, they have changed their minds and are motivated by expediency or, as *The Times* parliamentary correspondent put it today with marvellous economy of words, are "humbugs". Those are the reasons which have been argued against the referendum.

Mr. Rippon: Does the right hon. Gentleman agree that every one of those arguments except the last has been reiterated over and over and over again by the leader of his own party?

Mr. Benn: Let the right hon. and learned Gentleman wait, if he has the time, to hear what Lord Salisbury said about Disraeli in 1867, which is the most marvellous quotation of them all.

If the arguments that I have summarised are valid, the case against the referendum is overwhelming. I cannot hope in one speech to deal with all of these arguments. What I can do is to show the Committee the historical origins of these arguments.

Sir Robert Peel, in opposing the Reform Bill, said this in 1831:

"I am convinced that it is not founded on the acknowledged principles of the constitution – because it does not give security to the prerogative of the Crown – because it does not guarantee the legitimate rights, influences and privileges of both Houses of Parliament."

Peel said this first when he opposed the Reform Bill. This argument about its being contrary to our parliamentary traditions has been used in opposition to any extension of the people's rights which has been proposed over the past 140 years.

The second argument is that it establishes a precedent. I invite hon. Members to listen to this quotation from Asquith on votes for women in 1910:

"In the long run, if you grant the franchise to women, you will have to grant it on the widest possible basis, and with all the consequences to which I have referred . . . " – [*Official Report*, 12th July, 1910; Vol. 19, c. 250.]

Asquith was against votes for women because it would open the way to votes for everyone. That is exactly the argument that we have had in the course of this debate.

Lord Cranborne, later Lord Salisbury, attacked Disraeli's Reform Bill in 1867 on the same grounds.

The third argument is that the public are not equipped to reach decisions. Bagehot is the man to listen to here. He said this in 1872:

"In plain English, what I fear is that both our political authorities will bid for the support of the working man; that both of them will promise to do as he likes if he will only tell them what it is, that, as he now holds the casting vote in our affairs, both parties will beg and pray him to give that vote to them. I can conceive of nothing more corrupting or worse for a set of poor ignorant people than that two combinations of well-taught and rich men should constantly offer to defer to their decision, and compete for the office of executing it. *Vox populi* will be *Vox diaboli* if it is worked in that manner."

That is the case against the referendum. If it is looked at in one way, of course it is the case against the referendum. If it is looked at in another way, this having happened, it is our traditional parliamentary way of life that we are being asked to defend.

Britain is different. Asquith explained why votes for women in Australia were all right because Australia had such a sparse population, but Britain was different.

The fifth argument is that the advocates are not sincere. One cannot do better than David Wood's attack on humbug. The arguments against the referendum are the very same arguments as have been used against every extension of the people's rights for 140 years. It follows the same pattern. First, the argument is ignored. It is described as a fringe issue. It is then described as trendy. Then it is mocked. Then it is laughed at. Then hon. Members who do not support the referendum laugh at their own constituents and laugh at those who advocate the referendum. Then they warn against the referendum and against its dangers. Then they denounce it. Then they capitulate. Then they forget and hope that everyone else forgets too. It is always the same process – ignore, mock, laugh, warn, denounce, capitulate, then forget and then hope that everybody else forgets that one has gone through the process.

That was how the British Empire became decolonised and there were just as many humbugs, according to *The Times*, voting for freedom in the colonies as there will be voting for the referendum tonight because there were many people who wished that the public, the people, would go away. But when they did not go away, they found it more advisable to accommodate themselves to what the public wanted. The arguments are always the same. They are always wrong and when they are brought up again they are always supported by certain minorities.

They are supported by the rich because, of course, the rich are afraid that the public, if they had a vote, might be interested in the redistribution of wealth. They are opposed by racial minorities because all racial minorities are a bit nervous and that is why we hear about immigrants. They are opposed by a particular section of the Left who are afraid that if they had to convince the public that Socialism was right they would never succeed. Therefore they would rather sneak into

Parliament to do it before the public discover.

We heard that argument a little tonight, that one would never convince the public on nationalisation. Why not? It is a very powerful case. I am not interested in the sort of democratic Socialism that is so little democratic that one does not try to convert the public but slips in at the back door and does it when they do not notice.

Mr. Harold Lever rose —

Mr. Benn: I will give way to my right hon. Friend because I like him.

Mr. Lever: There is a mutual response although we are both able to dissimulate our affection. My right hon. Friend calls voting nationalisation through the House and the abolition of hanging sneaking it through the House. Does that mean that he has now reached the position in his thinking that he will regard any such future actions by any Government as sneaking things through the House?

Mr. Benn: The right hon. Gentleman, who is a dear friend — and I seriously mean that — is a member of a European minority too and is reflecting some anxiety about minorities. As to the argument about hanging, may I put it to him like this. If the abolition of capital punishment is the case for parliamentary democracy it emerged on the scene 900 years too late and no one would have dreamed of advocating parliamentary democracy on the grounds that it abolished capital punishment, because the House of Commons was very slow to abolish capital punishment.

I would not like to base my case for parliamentary democracy on the ground that we succeed in defying public opinion over a prolonged period for such successes would be temporary and have no merit. In the end parliamentary democracy must mean that the people have their way. We can — for a time — dampen their passions, dilute their aspirations and defy their wishes, but in the end a democracy can only mean that the people have their way. The parliamentary tradition which I uphold is not in rigid rules. It is not frozen at particular times and is not tied to any one balance of power struck between Government and governed. It has always evolved by enlarging the public role.

Tonight will not settle this matter. Even if the Amendment fails by the vote of the Government and by some abstentions from my hon. Friends, the clamour of those outside the House of Commons will continue to grow until it is heard on this and, if I might add, on other issues in which they believe that Parliament pays too little attention to their needs.

I would venture to prophesy that hon. Members who vote against or abstain will later live to hide today's *Hansard* from their grandchildren, particularly its Division List, because they will want to avoid the embarrassment of explaining why they voted as they did. I believe they will be ashamed at their blindness in failing to see that what they opposed in the name of parliamentary democracy was the floodtide of popular consent without which parliamentary democracy cannot survive. Trust between Parliament and the people must be a mutual trust. If we do not trust them, then not for long will they trust us.

Boycott European Institutions*

This speech, advocating a boycott by Labour MP's of the European Parliament, was delivered at the Tribune *meeting held during the TUC Conference in September 1972, a few weeks before the Labour Conference at which the Boilermakers' resolution calling for a boycott of European institutions was carried.*

In the event the Shadow Cabinet and the Parliamentary Labour Party upheld this view when Parliament met after Conference and no Labour MPs have attended the EEC Assembly since.

This decision was important because it was the only decision the Labour Party could take for itself and make effective by itself. This boycott has done more than any other single thing to convince the EEC that Labour is in earnest about renegotiation, both before, and even more since, the February 1974 General Election.

The Parliamentary Labour Party should completely boycott all European Community institutions and procedures if Britain is taken into the Common Market on January 1, 1973 without popular consent, first expressed through a General Election or Referendum.

Labour MPs should not serve in the European Parliament, and possibly not even on the committee to be set up at Westminster with little scope to do more than study the flow of Community laws and regulations, which are to be enforceable in Britain, even though they have been made by non-elected officials in the Commission.

A clear statement of intention to recommend this to the PLP should be given when the Labour Conference discusses the Common Market at Blackpool, and then put to the PLP for decision when Parliament meets.

*Speech at the Tribune Meeting on the eve of the TUC, Hotel Metropole, Brighton, September 3, 1972.

The case for non-co-operation is immensely powerful.

1. *The European Communities Bill is wholly unconstitutional.* No single Parliament has the moral or constitutional authority to place the British people — and future Parliaments elected by them — under an outside authority, by sub-contracting power for making the law and raising taxes to such a body.

2. *This legislation does not become constitutional simply because it has come into force.*

It becomes unconstitutional on January 1.

The battle to give the British people a say in their own future begins in earnest next year.

3. *The Government wants to commit the Opposition to support its policy on the EEC.* The Prime Minister hopes that if Labour MPs can be drawn into day-to-day Community work some of his responsibility for what happens can be shuffled off on to the Opposition.

But we cannot possibly abandon our campaign against the unacceptable terms of entry, against the undemocratic legislation and against the constitutional malpractice for which the Prime Minister is responsible, just at the moment when our warnings will be seen to have been right.

4. *Non-co-operation is essential if we are to keep faith with millions of our fellow countrymen.* They believe us when we say that every voter in Britain has a right to decide the question of British entry in a General Election or a Referendum as plainly set out in 'Labour's Programme for Britain' to be discussed at Conference.

The Labour Opposition must remain absolutely free to fight for the interests of the British people, against higher food prices, VAT and European taxes levied on us to pay for the expenses of the Commission and against any policies, like the CAP or Regional Policy, it is pursuing, that run counter to our interests, and for policies that create jobs.

5. *Non-co-operation is essential if any future renegotiation is to have any chance of success.* At present leading members of the Community do not appear to take Labour's determination to renegotiate seriously, and to let the people decide, and some have said so.

They must be taught from the outset that we are in deadly earnest.

They must be brought to understand that unless they are ready to meet Labour's terms and able to win British public opinion over, in a Referendum or Election, Britain would not remain with the Communities.

6. *Non-co-operation, announced now, will also alert the Community to the dangers for them which would follow from dragging a resentful Britain in against its will.*

If the present EEC Governments accept Heath's plan to treat the British public with contempt, they will run the risk of doing unnecessary damage to the existing Community in the future, when Labour gives the British people their say.

It is, therefore, in the interests of the present Community members themselves to insist that between now and January 1 there should be a General Election or Referendum in Britain to test Mr. Heath's claim to speak for Britain. Eire has already consulted its people. Norway and Denmark will be consulting theirs.

Only the British people are to be ignored. It will not do.

7. *A boycott of the European Communities by the Parliamentary Labour Party involves no breach of the law.*

The Government itself flatly refused to allow any amendments to the European Communities Bill even to make statutory provision for permanent all-Party delegations to the European Parliament.

If Labour MPs do not co-operate we shall therefore not be in breach of the Act. Indeed we shall be upholding the Rule of the Law.

8. *Non-co-operation is essential if we are to preserve public faith in Parliamentary government.*

This faith has suffered some setbacks in the last few years. If the powers which the electors lend to each successive Parliament are taken away, without their consent, so that future Parliaments cannot reverse the policies of their predecessors, public confidence in Parliament as a means of democratic self-government may be seriously undermined, opening the way for those who would like to see some form of managerial despotism or others who are peddling revolutionary solutions.

For these reasons a clear recommendation by the Parliamentary leadership not to co-operate endorsed by the Parliamentary Labour Party must be taken before the end of this Session.

Only in this way can we preserve the rights of the British people to be exercised when they elect a Government that is pledged to consult them, and to abide by their decision.

Only the British people can take Britain into the Common Market.

Mr. Heath may have the power to push through a Bill under the guillotine.

He may have public funds to pay for a fanfare of trumpets on January 1.

But he has not got that full-hearted consent of the people which he solemnly promised he would obtain, and which helped him win his election victory.

Now he is in power he is behaving as if he owned us.

He does not.

The British people cannot be disposed of as if we were his personal possession.

The national campaign to teach him that simple democratic lesson is only just beginning.

Meanwhile we must not weaken ourselves by helping Mr. Heath to carry through an unconstitutional Act, passed by methods that symbolize his obvious contempt for the people he was elected to serve.

We shall fight hard for our people and we shall win back for them the power to decide whether they want their future to be inside an enlarged European Community or not.

Re-negotiation*

This speech delivered at the Foreign Press Association lunch just before the 1973 Labour Party Conference spelled out the effects of Labour's policy of promising a ballot box decision on the Common Market on the forthcoming General Election by showing why Conservatives and Liberals might have to vote Labour if they wished to win the right to vote on European membership. The Community is now aware that the British people will have the last word and this above everything else is what makes our renegotiation real.

... The only way in which a British voter can safeguard his rights of self-determination on the Common Market question will be by voting Labour. A Labour Government will seek to renegotiate the terms on a basis that will entirely safeguard our national interest. In any case we are bound to amend the European Communities Act in such a way as to return all the sovereign powers passed to Brussels, back to the British people to be exercised by Parliament.

It is too early to say how these renegotiations will proceed and what the time-scale will be. But if, as I hope and believe, they begin with a total freezing of all payments due under the terms of our membership, and a suspension of arrangements like those involved in the Common Agricultural Policy, the pressure for a speedy conclusion will come from the other members of the Community, who would not be able to accept long drawn out and protracted talks because of their effect upon the Community itself.

Nor is it possible to forecast whether the demands that a Labour Government will make will be acceptable to other nations in the

*Extract from a speech at a lunch given by the Foreign Press Association in London September 17, 1973.

Community. As for their acceptability in Britain, the Cabinet will review the position when the renegotiations are over and then make a recommendation to the public who will have the responsibility for deciding the matter through the ballot box.

At this stage, everyone in Britain, whatever their party allegiance, will be able to join in the decision. The knowledge that only a Labour Government will give them this opportunity will certainly have an effect on the outcome of the election itself. It is quite clear that many Conservative and Liberal voters who are hostile to Labour's domestic programme will still feel it to be their public duty to bring about or accept the election of a Labour Government solely and simply to win for themselves the right of self-determination on this question, which is central to the future of our country.

I very much hope that our friends in Europe, and elsewhere, will now begin to take Labour policy on Europe seriously and not dismiss it as a minority view, or a pledge to be set aside, once we are in office.

One of the difficulties we have experienced in getting our policy taken seriously up to now is that so many of the people who have been most closely involved in developing and maintaining our links with our friends in the EEC helped by the mass media have themselves tended to minimise the real nature of British opposition to enforced entry. They have tried to suggest that the tumult will soon die away and everybody will accept the inevitable, with as much grace as they can muster. This is not the case. It is important that what we say on this matter should be studied carefully — all the more so since the prospects of a Labour Government being elected are very real. . .

IV

The Mass Media

Broadcasting and Democracy*

This speech outlining the role of Broadcasting in a modern democracy set off a storm of protest and led to many critical leading articles repudiating these views.

Although it explicitly excluded "direct or indirect Government control of the mass media to which I would be wholly opposed" it was reported as posing a threat of censorship. The key sentence in it **"Broadcasting is really too important to be left to the broadcasters** *and somehow we must find some new way of using radio and television to allow us to talk to each other" was never quoted in full, always stopping after the first eleven words to reinforce the false impression of favouring Government control.*

But once the dust had settled, the issues – especially of the need for access to the media – began to be discussed more soberly. The 'Free Communications Group' carried the debate further. In 1972 the Party established a study group which published its report "The People and its Media" in the summer of 1974.

The decision of the Labour Party to make communications one of the central issues in its debate on policy in the '70's is one of the most significant things to have come out of the Blackpool Conference.

The mass media, and especially broadcasting, now play a large part in shaping our attitudes, our outlook, our values and indeed the whole nature of our society. The wider this debate ranges, the better. It should cover the structure, finance, technology and, above all, the role and function of the mass media in a modern society.

Those engaged in active politics who speak or write about these matters are suspect on two grounds.

First, because the complete independence of the mass media from Government control is an essential ingredient of our special brand of personal freedom. Even too great a political interest is automatically taken to imply a deep plot to impose some form of censorship.

Secondly, because of the notorious love-hate relationship between

*Speech to a meeting of Hanham Labour Party, Bristol, October 18, 1968.

135

politicians and the broadcasters which is so permanent and intense that a politician's criticisms are almost automatically dismissed as being motivated by party feeling.

These suspicions provide a valuable subconscious protection against the dangers of political interference. But they cannot be regarded as any sort of a justification for a bar on political comment on these problems. Political interest is inescapable even if only because the structure of mass communications shapes our constitutional forms and indeed shapes the whole nature of political controversy and may even decide the issues which are to be the subject of that controversy.

The views I want to express are my own personal views, in no sense committing the Labour Party and still less the Government. They are put forward more to open up discussion than to resolve it; to ask questions rather than to answer them. And to focus the argument more clearly I want to talk about the role of the B.B.C. as the prime national instrument in broadcasting.

It may help to dispel suspicion if I make it clear at the outset what I am *not* talking about.

I am *not* proposing direct or indirect Government control of the mass media to which I would be wholly opposed.

Nor am I making, for the purpose of this argument, any complaint of political bias. Arguments about political balance are quite separate and ought to be conducted quite separately from any debate on the future of mass communications.

The political parties are always complaining about party balance and if they allow their discontent about that to cloud everything they say about the B.B.C., they cannot expect to get a hearing on the much more fundamental problems which need to be debated.

We have to start by writing an operational requirement. The first essential in such a requirement is that broadcasting should be used, to the full, to help individual men and women to live useful and full lives. That is to say that in its broadest sense, communications should serve the people and not become their master.

But if it is to do this, it has to make available the sort of information and programmes which are really relevant to human needs. These needs include the need to be entertained, informed and educated. The original B.B.C. charter recognised this.

Now a new dimension has to be added to this basic requirement. This is the need for helping us to adjust to the enormous changes which are occurring in society, and which are far greater for this generation than for any generation that has ever gone before it.

We must also concern ourselves with the means by which all this is to be achieved. The objectives set out above are unexceptionable. But of course they could also be used to justify a paternalistic control.

We therefore have to add a new criterion relating to the method. If the broadcasting organisations are to perform their task they must allow us to meet our objectives by talking to each other. Availability of access to the mass media becomes an integral part of our operational requirement.

Let us try to apply these tests to the B.B.C. alone, so as to exclude extraneous arguments about advertising, commercial ownership and other factors which, though highly relevant, may confuse the main argument.

The B.B.C. is a completely independent public corporation. It is financed entirely by a license fee which it was intended should liberate it from the influence of Government interference or commercial pressures. It thus constitutes a perfect − if untypical − case study for judging the performance of mass communications.

Looking back over the history of the B.B.C., it is impossible to overestimate the constructive contribution that it has made. It brought broadcasting to the nation under the initial impetus of dedicated leadership adhering to standards of truthfulness and balance which earned for it a deserved world-wide reputation.

During those years, the general level of information, education and culture have risen sharply. It has also given pleasure to millions of people by bringing them entertainment, sporting events, drama and music. Criticisms must be set in the balance against the formidable achievements and a record of service to the public which is widely recognised and appreciated.

What then are the criticisms that can be made?

The B.B.C. handling of news earned it early recognition. With a conscious and sustained effort to be objective it brought the news to people quickly and reliably and set a standard by which the other mass media were judged.

However in recent years this objectivity has been replaced by a growing tendency to personalise news presentation. The news reader has almost become a commentator; the gap between news and comment has greatly narrowed. This tendency to personalisation, carrying with it editorial powers, exercised by individual commentators, has even more serious implications for other types of programmes.

For many years the B.B.C. steered clear of comment altogether. For a time it avoided all controversy, whether religious or political.

This early caution was too restrictive and so, later on, programmes of carefully balanced controversy were introduced. Until recent years the B.B.C. itself stayed aloof from these, presenting them rather than participating directly by interventions of their own.

Now the position has completely changed. The B.B.C. retains, either on the staff or on contract, a whole host of commentators who, being

137

quite free to comment, carry with them some inevitable suggestion of B.B.C. authority. True, the B.B.C., through its Board of Governors, has no collective view on public matters and very rarely issues a statement of any kind. But listeners and viewers have come to expect from certain well-known broadcasters a particular line of thought which is peculiar to them, but which, through the power of the medium, inevitably shapes public thinking.

Nobody wants to go back to the earlier tradition. Quite the reverse. What is wrong is that availability of access is still too restricted in that it is almost limited to a few hundred broadcasters, chosen by the B.B.C.

When you add to this the fact that all programmes on current affairs — their subjects and treatment — are also chosen by a few hundred executive producers, the influence of B.B.C. editorial power becomes even stronger.

First in respect of the choice of subjects. Britain has thousands of problems which would merit the attention of the broadcasting authorities. Certain ones are regularly picked out for treatment. They include the most important, but do not by any means cover all those that are important. The choice is supposedly influenced by the interests of the mass audience and it is here that the influence of the programme ratings begins to be felt. It would be surprising if the sort of subjects that are guaranteed to get a large audience in the popular newspapers were not equally effective on the radio or T.V. This is exactly what is happening.

Second in respect of the presentation of the subject. Here, too, the influence of the ratings is very strong and so is the pressure of time. Important subjects are skimped, important discussions are telescoped and conflicts are artificially sharpened. The result is inevitably to make for triviality and superficiality, over-simplifying what is immensely complicated and sensationalising almost everything that is touched on.

Thirdly by choice of people. Any B.B.C. producer soon learns that a certain sort of person will give him just what he wants, in the time allowed, in colourful language and with an agreeable manner, and these people are used again and again. They may well not be the best qualified people in their field. They are not chosen because they are. They are chosen because they fit neatly into an editorial slot.

If these criticisms are put to the B.B.C., you will get a variety of answers.

While professing a general sympathy with the desire to deal with matters more deeply, they point out that the public won't have any patience with longer expositions which they find boring. Just as an editor of a popular daily will modestly describe himself as a servant of his readers, so will a B.B.C. producer, when hard-pressed by the same criticism.

In support of this argument the B.B.C. points out that if the Corporation were to do this, and its audience ratings were to fall, relative to I.T.V., then there would be a mounting volume of public criticism against the licence fee and the B.B.C.'s whole future would be in peril. But this does not dispose of the argument. If the B.B.C., which does not depend on advertising, follows a programme policy that is indistinguishable from I.T.V. which does, then people might well ask what is the case for having a licence fee and a public service corporation anyway? There is a real dilemma here, and it arises from the fundamental weakness in the method by which competitive broadcasting was introduced in 1955.

The B.B.C. ultimately rests its case upon its own profound belief in its editorial duty. What began as a Reithian concept that was openly paternalistic has broadened into a view that runs something like this: The B.B.C. has a positive duty, acting for the public, to probe and challenge and question all the centres of power that are growing up in the modern society – political, industrial and social. Seen like this the idea of balance has now become for them a balance between the B.B.C., and the people they are investigating, so that half of every argument belongs, as of right, to the B.B.C., as it performs its painful, relentless but necessary duty to the British public.

Under this banner, it has appointed itself investigator-in-chief into the alleged inefficiencies of British management, the alleged obstructionism of British trade unions and, of course, the wilful way of foreigners. When British interests are threatened, the Government no longer sends a gun-boat. The B.B.C. sends the 'Panorama' team with instructions to bring back the head of the offender, to be shown on the box.

All this amounts to an enormous accumulation of power. With the exception of Government itself there is scarcely any other body in Britain enjoying as much power as the B.B.C. And since the Government, quite properly, keeps at arm's length from the B.B.C., and makes no effort whatsoever to make it account for what it does, it stands in a position of almost unique and unchallenged influence.

Of course the Board of Governors are appointed to supervise the Corporation in the public interest. They are men and women of distinction and a fine awareness of human values. But unlike the Governors of the I.T.A., they actually employ the people whom it is their duty to supervise, and they would not be human if they did not have a protective interest in their own employees which expresses itself in an understandable preference for issuing their directives in private, thus depriving the public of any knowledge of the operation of such public accountability as does exist.

Virtually the entire output of the B.B.C. is produced under editorial conditions. The subjects, handling and people are chosen by the staff to fit in programme slots which have been pre-determined quarter by quarter. Occasionally the framework is adapted, as for example at Party Conferences or major sporting events. But even there the presentation is by and through the B.B.C.

It is as if the only printed material available for us were newspapers.

There is no publishing done by the B.B.C., on radio or television. Nobody (except in Party political or election broadcasts) is ever allowed to develop an argument in his own way, and at sufficient length, to confront the public with what would be the broadcasting equivalent of a book.

We have lived with this publishing gap since the B.B.C. was established, and we may be so used to it that many of us do not realise what we are missing. What we are missing, is the opportunity to hear directly from those who have something to say to us all, what it is they want to say to us.

Perhaps the most immediate example of this at this moment comes from the expected demonstrations by students and others in London and other major cities. We all know that if these demonstrations follow the pattern of some earlier ones they will get extensive television coverage on the day. If there are tussles, we shall see them, in vivid pictures in the news bulletins and trigger off a whole series of discussions among the usual panel of pundits who will talk predictably about their significance and the problems of law and order.

But the one thing we shan't get, either before, during or after, is any opportunity to hear, first-hand, at length, and in peace, the views of those who are organising these demonstrations.

If they were invited to speak, what they might say would be very unacceptable to millions of people and probably the overwhelming majority. In part they are protesting against the very denial to them and others of any real access for their views on the mass media. All they can be certain of is that their demonstrations will be fully covered on the mass media and undoubtedly that knowledge itself stimulates the demonstrations. If law and order were ever to break down, in part or in whole, in Britain, the policy of restricted access and unrestricted coverage would have to bear a very considerable part of the responsibility.

But, of course, it is not only the demonstrators who ought to be heard. According to the motor manufacturers, this country has lost £48 million of exports this year due to industrial disputes. There have been countless snippets about this on news bulletins and comments in current affairs programmes. But to the best of my knowledge, neither the motor manufacturers nor the trade unions have been offered even an hour apiece to tell the public how they see it, or even to address their own managements or members.

Almost all we see of trade union or business leaders are hurried little street interviews when they are pinned against a wall by a battery of accusing microphones, wielded by interrogators who have just come from covering an air crash and are on their way to the hospital where some quins have been born. Is it any wonder that so few of us really understand the complexity of some current problems in industrial relations which are really going to condition our prospects of economic success or failure?

It is here that the B.B.C.'s greatest weakness in the handling of public affairs becomes most apparent. It is not a question of balance between Labour and Conservative that matters. It is the B.B.C.'s failure to provide the means by which the true complexity of affairs can be explained, without which the gap between political leaders and people will inevitably tend to widen and widen. If politics are dealt with superficially and politicians are presented in a context designed to extract the maximum entertainment value for them, it is not surprising that the public should learn from the B.B.C. handling a contempt for all those in public life.

I am certainly not arguing that it is the duty of the B.B.C. to put on politicians in a way that makes them appear to be attractive or to create a favourable impression. Indeed, it may very well be that if the full depth of thinking that lies behind certain political arguments was fully deployed on the air, it would stimulate far more fundamental criticisms. What is wrong now is that most politicians are being criticised for the wrong reason.

But it would be a great mistake to think that the need for a publishing function is confined to public affairs and politics. There are thousands of organisations – from the British Medical Association through to the engineering institutions, or the consumer or women's organisations – who have a great deal to say and are now denied access. If broadcasting is not reorganised to enable us to hear, in our own time, what those who are working on contemporary problems want to tell us, then the task of adapting ourselves will become almost impossible.

All this involves a complete re-definition of the meaning of 'topicality'. The common definition of topicality is that which is happening today. But as the time scale of development lengthens, the meaning of topicality must change too. What is actually topical today is what is being decided today, even though the consequences of that decision may not be apparent for five or ten years.

For example, the run-down of the coal industry is regarded as a very topical subject. But properly defined it was actually topical in the early '50s, when all the technical work on nuclear power was going on, culminating in the announcement of the first nuclear power programme over ten years ago. No doubt this featured in some science programme then, presented in simple language. But the implications of that research and those decisions were never explored at length, nor published. And because they weren't, the miners were not prepared for what was going to happen to them. And the Government in the late '50s and early '60s was never pressed, by a public interest stimulated by the B.B.C., into thinking out the implications of what it had decided.

The same sort of thing is happening today all along the line. For example, the container revolution is now under way, and the authorities concerned are trying to cope with the implications of that. The public have never yet been confronted with what it will mean and even the vague anxieties of the dockers only find expression through the T.V. news coverage of their march to the House of Commons against immigrants.

It is the same with metrication. The big decisions are being made now. But they are too dull to merit serious consideration on the topical B.B.C. We shall have to wait until 1975 when, maybe, a few thousand workers find themselves redundant because the firms in which they work forgot to metricate. Then, no doubt, the B.B.C. will put on sensational programmes on what went wrong. Now is the time to discuss it.

If the telephone service is not as good as it might be, you should ask why, year by year in the pre-war and post-war years, there was not a serious annual discussion on the telecommunications investment programme.

These are just a handful of examples that might be given of the failure of the B.B.C. to provide the facilities by means of which we could talk through our problems and our future and use the mass media to help us to make sense of it all.

Parliament imperfectly performed this function in the centuries that preceded the adoption of the universal franchise. Through talk, we tamed kings, restrained tyrants, averted revolution and ultimately reflected public needs in such a way as to help to shape public policy. In this sense, the B.B.C. has assumed some of the role of Parliament. It is the current talking shop, the national town meeting of the air, the village council. But access to it is strictly limited. Admission is by ticket only. It is just not enough.

In a way it is unfair to blame the B.B.C. for all this. Every criticism I have made could be made with far greater force against all the other mass media. The B.B.C. are undoubtedly doing their best, and they regard the liberalisation of comment since the days of Auntie B.B.C. image as having been a conscious effort to meet some of the objectives which I have described.

But it is not enough. We have got to find a better way and give access to far more people than now are allowed to broadcast.

The trouble is that we have extended the overwhelming technical case for having a monolithic broadcasting organisation into a case for unifying programme output control under a single Board of Governors.

Broadcasting is really too important to be left to the broadcasters, and somehow we must find some new way of using radio and television to allow us to talk to each other.

We've got to fight all over again, the same battles that were fought centuries ago to get rid of the licence to print and the same battles to establish representative broadcasting in place of the benevolent paternalism by the constitutional monarchs who reside in the palatial Broadcasting House.

It is now a prime national task to find some ways of doing that. It must be based on, and built around, the firm framework of public service control and operation, and not dismembered and handed over to the commercial forces which already control every other one of the mass media except the B.B.C. For in the B.B.C. we have an instrument of responsible communication which is quite capable of being re-fashioned to meet our needs in the '70s and '80s as it did so brilliantly in the '20s, '30s and '40s.

Direct Access for Unions*

This speech, given at the 1971 Glasgow May Day demonstrations, criticised the media for their handling of the Trades Unions and called for the unions to be allowed to produce their own programmes. Harlech TV took up this suggestion and the Transport and General Workers' Union in Bristol was given all the necessary facilities to produce a programme projecting its work which it called "My Brother's Keeper"; it was shown on HTV but never networked.

The unions and especially shop stewards still remain largely without access to the public on the issues which concern their members.

... The trade union movement stands today, as it has done since its earliest years, in the front line of defence of the ordinary family and its living standards. That is why the Government has chosen to launch a sustained attack on them through their Industrial Relations Bill.

This campaign against the trade unions has been enthusiastically taken up by many newspapers and commentators on radio and TV. It is

*Extract from a speech given at a May Day Demonstration of the Glasgow City Labour Party in Queen's Park, Glasgow, May 2, 1971.

an astonishing thing that working men and women do not yet have the means to speak to their fellows through the mass media, and have to sit back day after day and read or listen and watch — on BBC and ITV — while a one-sided picture of the nation's industrial problems is presented to them.

The time has come when the trade union movement should demand the right to regular programmes of its own on the BBC and ITV to allow it to speak directly to its members without having everything they say edited away by self-appointed pundits and producers. Surely the trade union movement, with nearly ten million members, should be entitled, as an absolute minimum, to say a quarter of an hour out of the 200 hours of BBC output each week, and also time on other major networks so that it could present, in depth and free from bullying interrogators, the needs and problems of those who earn their living in industry. If that meant giving the same time to the CBI as well, at least we should be hearing from managers who are also experiencing the complex problems of human relations in industry.

What is intolerable is not so much the bias against trade unionists in the mass media — although there is bias — but the lack of experience of those who filter the news through in such a way as to give a largely false impression of what is going on. We shall never be able to solve these problems unless everyone is able to learn about them at first hand from those who are actually doing the job. The editor, the producer, the cameraman, the interviewer are all one stage removed, and lectures from so called experts, written in the comfort of their air-conditioned offices, are wide of the mark.

Soon after the trade union movement began to grow in the nineteenth century, its leaders realised that they could only make real progress if they had access to Parliament as well. Today, some of the power of Parliament has passed to the mass media, which can shape the thinking of the nation by the way it presents the news, selects the issues and describes the choices. Most of these people are accountable to no-one, elected by no-one, and enjoy security of tenure while they continue to please their employers by proving their capacity to hold the attention of mass audiences.

But if, in order to get big ratings or big circulation, the news has to be presented superficially and the issues have to be sharpened up to attract attention, we shall find ourselves paying too high a price in terms of lack of understanding; and if people don't understand the problems, our prospects of finding a remedy for them will be greatly diminished.

The right of direct access by ordinary people to the community as a whole is going to be a key one from now on. Of course the trade unions would need technical advice on how to present their material. But even here the so-called expertise is much over-estimated in order to preserve the position of those who have a monopoly today.

Let us suppose for a moment that the trade union movement had had half an hour a week to talk to the nation over the last twelve months. They would certainly have dealt with some industrial disputes. But they would also have dealt with industrial accidents which lose us two-and-a-half times as many working days as are lost by strikes. And they would have taken up the problems of rising unemployment, which by the end of the year could lose us as many days of lost production every fortnight as are lost by industrial disputes every year.

I hope the trade union movement will now formulate a clear demand to the BBC and the commercial television companies for a programme of their own to allow them to set the record straight. If they did so, it would represent a substantial advance in democratic development that would immensely enrich our society. Indeed I think it would pave the way for a new and better communication system which would give other people the opportunity to state their case and would underpin Parliament with a broader base of public understanding. We should not then again have to put up with the sort of treatment that so many shop stewards and others have experienced in some of their recent claims for better living conditions on behalf of their members . . .

A Voice for the People*

This paper prepared for the Fourth Manchester University symposium on Broadcasting policy in February 1972 was printed in full in The *Guardian.*

It sets out the case for reshaping broadcasting in Britain to allow it to be used more fully by the people and reproduces ten criteria for a truly democratic system.

It is impossible to separate broadcasting policy and the influences which shape it from the other information-disseminating systems in society, and the restraints under which they operate.

The whole political process in a democracy rests on the maintenance of a delicate fabric of communication within society which reveals the common interest that exists, identifies conflict where it arises, and painfully builds the consent which leads people to accept the policies that emerge as these conflicts are resolved by upholding the ground rules of the system.

*Given as a paper for the Fourth Manchester University Symposium on Broadcasting Policy and reproduced in *The Guardian* of February 9, 1972.

Similarly the whole educational system is an information-disseminating system passing wisdom from generation to generation, sustaining and reflecting the inheritance we have acquired from the past and bringing human genius to bear on the problems of society in such a way as to allow mankind to adapt itself more easily to the changes that are occurring, and to anticipate future events as they loom up on the horizon. Legislation governing the educational system and its accepted value structure have shaped its pattern.

The media are engaged in the same process and are so much more effective in disseminating information simultaneously to large groups of people that they not only supplement the political and educational systems but in some respects supplant them, because of their enormous power. But they do so without the restraints that have been built into the political and educational systems over the centuries. The tension that is building up between the media, politics, and education arises in part because we have not yet developed a framework of public responsibility expressed through external influences within which the media can operate so as to maximise their value and minimise the dangers that must necessarily follow from the irresponsible use of so much power.

Examples of this tension can be found in every country in the world. A series of arguments in Britain — too well known to need repeating — between political leaders and the broadcasters culminated in the recent clash between Westminster and Stormont Ministers and the BBC over the Ulster programme which highlighted the problem in a most vivid way. The sustained attack by Vice-President Agnew on the American television networks has headlined the same problem in the US. The role of the mass media in accelerating the liberalisation in Czechoslovakia during the Dubcek period, thus contributing to the.Soviet decision to intervene militarily, offers an interesting example from the Communist world.

Similarly the anxieties being expressed world-wide about the effect of violence and sex on television as a corrupting force undermining the traditional role of the educational system in preserving cohesive social values within society, indicates a growing suspicion that the influence of television may be greater than the influence of schools in shaping the whole character of our people.

These questions are far more important than the subject most usually raised by politicians and broadcasters in public debate — whether or not the mass media are fair to the political parties and individual parliamentary leaders. Since everyone suspects that any politician talking about the media is likely to be motivated by discontent at the way politicians are treated, I should like to make it clear that this is not the basis of my comment, and I am not advancing any argument for controlling the mass media by Government in the interests of political leaders.

The nub of the political system in Britain is and always has been its twin capacity, first to secure free debate, secondly to give an expanding electorate progressive power to select its participants in that debate through the extension of the franchise.

Long before Parliament – the talking shop – was in any sense democratic, it had a creative and positive role in probing the exercise of power by kings and landowners and it opened up policy for public examination and acted as a safety valve for public discontent. Later as the vote was extended to more and more citizens the representative character of MPs was enlarged and the right of selection of those MPs by the public was the basis of this process of the democratisation of power.

Thus the exercise of power in the political system is governed by some very important constitutional statutes such as the Parliament and Representation of the People Acts operating as an external restraint, and the common law developments described in Erskine May which provides the ground rules of the system. In the House of Commons itself the choice of speakers to be called is regarded as so sensitive a matter as to require the discretion to be exercised by the Speaker, a man who separates himself from all party loyalties as a price he must pay for winning the trust of the House.

By contrast the mass media operate under very different restraints that have grown up only in the past 50 years and which provide for broad political balance but very little else. The choice of people to broadcast, and be given access to the public greater even than an MP can hope to aspire to, is regarded as the proper function of the producer of the programme who is himself appointed by the BBC or ITV company on the basis of his abilities as revealed to his employers.

Nor is there adequate provision for the judgment exercised by the broadcasters to be called to democratic account. In the case of independent television there is the ITA, a licensing body with some power over the companies including the right to disallow programmes and ultimately to grant or withhold the licence to continue broadcasting. In the case of the BBC the Board of Governors themselves influenced by outside comment sit in judgment on their own employees, and whatever complaints procedure they may institute, they are still judging in their own case.

Moreover the Governors of the BBC and the ITA are both appointed by the Government of the day, and just because of the potential power this gives to the Government it normally bends over backwards to avoid exercising its power and leaving itself open to a charge of censorship.

As compared with the parliamentary system of communications the system as operated by the mass media is therefore seriously defective and inadequate in that it is basically undemocratic and there is no accountability of power.

This poses a major challenge to those who are thinking about the future of British broadcasting. Nobody wants Governmental political control but the present combination of corporate or commercial control theoretically answerable to politically appointed boards of governors is not in any sense a democratic enough procedure to control the power the broadcasters have.

What is required therefore is some way of developing a new framework to democratise this power without falling into the trap of state control or confusing commercial competition and free enterprise control with the free expression of different views on the air.

Undoubtedly as technical developments proceed and the number of channels increases either by air transmissions or by the development of multi-channel coaxial cables the problem will get easier rather than more difficult. But even here there will be problems of accountability to be faced which may need to be worked out well in advance.

One method of democratisation worth further exploration would involve an external attempt to democratise the internal structure of the broadcasting organisations so that the actual production units had a greater say over their own output but were collectively held fully accountable to those outside for the use that they made of that freedom. I am not referring to the producers alone but to the whole team including directors, studio managers, script writers, cameramen, sound recordists, technicians, secretaries and other workers.

If these discrete units could be identified and democratised so that they discussed their own policy and output, the men in charge within them would be accountable to their own subordinates and colleagues and external complaints about the programmes they put out would then also have to be discussed within the same democratic framework. This is the way of industrial democracy or workers' self-management and although it must sound strange or foreign, or unrealistic or alarming to those brought up in the hierarchical traditions of British organisational practice, it has great potential and is well worth serious consideration.

Those complaining of unfairness would thus be directing their complaints, initially, to the whole team that made the programme and the whole team would have to agree on its response and in the debate that ensued there would be pressure from inside to change policy where this seemed necessary. Moreover everyone involved would be forced to accept his responsibility for the output of the unit of which he was a member.

At the moment those working in broadcasting can very often slough off their responsibility by pointing out quite accurately that the responsibility for the conception and execution of the programmes upon which they are engaged has nothing whatsoever to do with them. There is, in short, no code of conduct accepted by broadcasters as a whole.

The second road to democratisation involves a fresh look at the whole question of access to the media which has been debated with growing intensity over the past few years.

It is, on the face of it, quite absurd that only the BBC and the ITV companies should have any say on who should appear on the air and what subjects should be discussed. It is as if the ownership of a printing press was the only means by which anyone could get anything published unless he could persuade somebody else with a printing press to accord him this right.

The publishing function has been very largely neglected until recently and almost the whole output on all channels has been devised and presented under editorial direction. This has had serious political consequences. Since those with something constructive to say, together with others expressing discontents in society have been denied the right to "publish" their views, some important grievances have festered until they reach explosion point. And when the explosion comes the mass media have been only too ready to give extensive coverage to the demonstrations and violence that resulted and to pontificate endlessly *after the event* on the reasons why things had gone wrong.

What they should have been doing was to provide ample time for these views to be expressed beforehand so as to provide society with the feedback essential to correct its errors before they do too much damage, and the chance to understand future choices by having the alternatives presented to them.

The arguments used against giving access have been various and it is worth examining some of them to test their validity.

First, it has been argued that there is no time available for this purpose and that if an attempt was made to provide it the public at large would be bored and would switch off.

But are we to accept the ratings as the final determinant of what should and should not be broadcast? The BBC, though financed by the licence and not by advertisements, is subject, through competition to exactly the same pressures as commercial companies and therefore demonstrates in its output no greater evidence of public responsibility.

Some cultural minorities are well catered for. What is evidently not accepted is that the minority who are really interested in a penetrating study of social problems — industrial relations, race relations or Ulster — are equally entitled to have access to the information they need to help them form a judgment.

Secondly, it is also argued that the problem of selection of groups and individuals to whom access should be given poses impossible difficulties for those who would be called upon to make a choice between them.

There are difficulties but they are not insuperable, and many of the groups to whom access should be given are self-selecting because they represent important interests in the State that are capable of throwing up their own representatives through their own internal selection processes.

For example, the televising of Parliament would involve giving Parliament direct access to the people by allowing the cameras to observe what happens there. The fault here lies with Parliament and not the broadcasting authorities and it no doubt soon will be resolved.

Similarly the trade union movement with its enormous national membership should certainly be entitled to its own regular programmes showing its policies to the public.

Industry too could legitimately lay claim to its right to direct access. The discontent so forcibly expressed by so many trade unionists at the way in which industrial issues are handled by the media is exactly matched by the discontent felt by industrialists, many of whom greatly dislike television coverage of their problems.

The professions too could properly claim to talk directly about the subjects in which they are most qualified to speak, and so could different regional authorities which represent important areas of the country who feel that they have been improperly treated by the community as a whole.

Then there are the thousands of pressure groups representing racial minorities, special interests, and a host of other concerns that at present depend solely on the possibility that they may be invited to contribute a speaker to a discussion that has been set up by a producer to fill a slot in his schedule.

It is said that these subjects are already dealt with in regular programmes or schools programmes or special features. These should obviously continue but there is all the difference in the world between a programme devised by a producer, and a programme presenting the considered view of a group that has something to say and is entitled to be heard.

Thirdly, it is argued that the intervention of a professional communicator is necessary because ordinary people are so inarticulate and cannot be relied upon to express themselves clearly. But most people are very articulate when they are talking about what they know best.

The argument for wider access has already gained substantial ground in recent years and there are now some examples which can be cited to illustrate how it would work.

Quite apart from the Dutch system which has aroused some interest in Britain as part of the argument over the fourth channel, there are some domestic examples worth noting.

The recent Ulster programme itself offered a very interesting case history and was one of the most important developments in the use of television in public affairs that we have seen in this country.

It was undertaken in a spirit of high responsibility and the audience were treated throughout as completely adult. It was open ended and escaped from the artificial pressures imposed by programme schedules. The questioning was done by men who were respected in their own right instead of by professional interviewers and there was no attempt to bully or hector those who took part. As a result of this the temperature remained low, and in the absence of any sense of confrontation those who spoke did so moderately and intimately rather than rhetorically. There was no production gimmick, no music over captions, no studio audience to interrupt, and very few reaction shots. It was international — bringing together people from Britain and the Republic as well as Ulster, and those who were chosen were chosen because they were representative and not just because they could be relied upon to argue well in a debate situation.

Perhaps the most important statement made on the programme came from Lord Devlin in summing up when he said: "On questions of principle every citizen has a duty to form his own view." This constitutional doctrine must necessarily carry with it the right of every citizen to have access to all the necessary information that will allow him to form his own views. Whether by design or not the Devlin doctrine of the responsibility of a citizen conferred upon the media a duty that parliamentarians have hitherto claimed to be their special preserve. Indeed, the transcript of the BBC Ulster programme constitutes a State Paper of considerable importance and the programme itself was certainly more influential than the debates that have occurred in the Parliaments at Westminster, Stormont, or Dublin, all of which have necessarily been limited by their composition and the exclusion of the general public from the audience. The BBC programme reached millions of people.

Another recent example of the innovation in television coverage was the Harlech TV programme "My Brother's Keeper", transmitted last month, which was actually made by the Transport and General Workers' Union in Bristol with the help of highly qualified staff provided by Harlech and in which the union presented itself without the intervention of any professional communicator as an intermediary.

Similarly some BBC local radio stations are beginning to work with local pressure groups to allow them to get their case across.

The Open University is perhaps the biggest single example of the

151

transfer of substantial periods of broadcasting time to an outside body which uses the network purely as a publishing agent.

In conclusion I submit the following criteria by which we might judge the media, and determine the framework within which broadcasting should be contained, with a view to developing the necessary external and internal influences that ought to be brought to bear:

1. Is the content free from Government control?
2. Do they provide regular access to allow individuals and groups to express specialist and minority views?
3. Do they sustain and reflect the rich and diverse inheritance that each community they serve draws from its past?
4. Is their coverage international in the sense that uncensored material from other countries is regularly made available to their audiences?
5. Do they include serious and sustained education as part of their output?
6. Do they inform their communities about the future in time to allow public opinion to understand and influence their decisions before they are reached?
7. Is the majority of their revenue drawn from the service they provide, or does it come from advertising?
8. Do they operate any system of workers' self-management or industrial democracy?
9. Do those who work in them maintain any code of professional conduct?
10. Is there any independent body to whom they are accountable and which can investigate complaints made against them?

An ideal system would yield a positive answer to each of these questions.

V

Civil Liberties

The Case of Dr. Joseph Cort*

In 1954 Dr. Joseph Cort, an American working in Birmingham, was ordered to report for military duty in the United States. His health record was so poor that it was clear that it was a political move, prompted by his left-wing activities as a student.

He appealed to the Home Office for permission to remain in Britain. This was refused and he was forced to leave the country.

This speech, delivered in the House of Commons, described these events and the issues of Civil Liberties involved.

The subject which I want to raise this afternoon is the decision of the Home Secretary not to renew the residence permit of Dr. Joseph Cort, the American doctor, who has been living here for three years. The burden of my argument is that the Home Secretary reached a wrong decision and reached it in a wrong way.

At the outset, I should like to declare my own interest in this matter, which is simply that Dr. Cort chose to write to me in April about this difficulty. Even after that I did not meet him for some months. I have only known him personally for some six weeks and I have tried, as a Member of this House, to help him. I am always very moved on these occasions when the House of Commons — although perhaps not very full of Members at the moment — turns its mind from great affairs like the one which we have been debating, the question of Malaya, to the personal difficulties of an individual, because this House would not deserve its reputation if it were not able to move from big things to what, to some people, might seem to be small ones.

I should like to say one other thing before I get into my argument. That is, that although, as I have said, I believe that the Home Secretary was totally wrong in the decision he reached, I have nothing but gratitude to him personally and to the Joint Under-Secretary who is to reply to this debate today, for the personal courtesy which they have shown me throughout, and in going out of their way to offer me every

*Extract from a speech in the House of Commons on July 30, 1954.

facility to make the best case I could. I am grateful to them for that.

I will not detain the House with the facts of this case, which are well-known, but I should like briefly to trace the story of Dr. Cort's application and what has happened. Dr. Cort is an American. So far as one can make out from the best technical advice one gets, he is a very brilliant doctor. There is plenty of evidence to suggest that, and one does not have to look far to find it, because in 1948 he got a year's Fellowship at Cambridge to study there and subsequently a second Fellowship, and up to recently he has held a Lectureship at Birmingham University. In between his two visits to Cambridge, he went back to Yale to finish his medical training, and while he was there he joined the Communist Party.

I do not think that that needs additional comment from me, but I ask the House not to be too heavy-handed about someone who once, as an undergraduate, became a Communist. There are some Members of this House who have been members of the Communist Party in their time. I think that all that one can say about that is, that when we look at the story of Dr. Cort we find that all his difficulties, in my view, date from the period when he was a member of the Communist Party.

When Dr. Cort came to this country in 1951, he left the Communist Party. He went to Cambridge, and he has been working here ever since. I am sure that the Under-Secretary will correct me if I am wrong when I say that there is no suggestion that while Dr. Cort has been here he was engaged in any political activity, or that there is any other objection to him. I deduce this from the fact that no hint or suggestion has been made by anyone that that is not so, and I cannot believe that if that was the real reason behind the Home Secretary's decision he would not have conveyed it discreetly to some hon. Members on this side of the House who have taken the case up.

When Dr. Cort came to this country he started at Cambridge, and within three or four months he received a letter from the American Embassy telling him to hand in his passport and return to the United States. Dr. Cort wrote and asked, why? No reason was given him and he declined to fall in with those instructions. Shortly after that, a Congressional inquiry was made into Communism in American universities and Dr. Cort was frequently named, and his friends were closely questioned. As a result of that many of his friends lost their jobs and have been dispersed. Dr. Cort felt, and still feels, that were he to return to the United States he would suffer victimisation.

It was only after the United States Embassy had told him to return, without giving a reason, and only after the Congressional hearing that he received his call-up papers. I will come back to the simple question of whether this man is a "draft dodger," to use an American expression, but I think that it is worth noting that his call-up papers came long after other attempts had been made to get him back to the United States in December of last year.

As Dr. Cort failed to respond to the call-up papers he was summoned by the police in Birmingham to make a statement. As a result of that, the Home Office, hearing that he might lose his citizenship, decided that they could not renew his permit to remain in this country. I should like to make one point which is important if the House is to reach a fair decision about the motives of Dr. Cort. This is in connection with the publicity attached to this case.

I can say – and I believe that there is plenty of evidence to support it – that the last thing that Dr. Cort ever wanted was publicity for his case when he was making his application to be allowed to remain in this country. I have a letter from him which was addressed to Professor A. V. Hill, of London University, an ex-Member of this House and a member of the party opposite, in which he said that he wished to be allowed to remain here quietly to carry on his work without publicity to himself or the university of which he was a member – Birmingham University. The University wrote to the Home Secretary or to the Joint Under-Secretary asking whether they would not allow Dr. Cort to remain.

I think it is important, if the House is to get a proper account of this story, to explain that in the early stages there was not a request for political asylum. In the early stages – and this is really the crux of the whole question – Dr. Cort was asking to be allowed to remain here because he wanted to continue his work. At any rate, that is the outline of the story, and I do not believe that anyone would say that these facts were not correct.

Before I get on to the issues which this case raises, I should like to deal with some points which arise out of the Home Office's handling of the case. I do not want to make too much of them, but I think that they are important and I would be grateful if the Under-Secretary would deal with them. In the first place, I was very concerned – and I think that many hon. Members were – at the fact that an alien resident in this country should be interrogated by the British police on behalf of a foreign government, without the Home Office and the Aliens Department knowing anything about it until afterwards.

This seems to me to be a very important principle. The Home Secretary does not deny that the Birmingham police interviewed Dr. Cort and that he himself only learned of it when the report was sent in from Birmingham. I think that the House would be rightly angry if aliens, although enjoying only the temporary protection of this country, were able to be got at by a foreign Government through the agency of our own police, particularly so as no one has suggested that Dr. Cort had been guilty of any offence which comes within the

155

provisions of the extradition treaty. There is no suggestion of that. Although I can understand that if extradition proceedings are commenced the British police may feel that they ought to find out what they can for the sake of the foreign Government concerned, in this case that did not arise.

The second point, and it ties up closely with the question of interrogation by the Birmingham police, is that of the Home Secretary's answer to the House when he was asked to give a general statement on the decision. The Home Secretary, in a written answer to the House, used these words about that interview. He said that he had been asked

" . . . to explain why he had done so and what were his intentions with reference to his duties under the United States Selective Service Act, he had refused to make a statement." − [*Official Report,* 24th, June, 1954; Vol. 529, c.49.]

I suggest that that was a misleading statement by the Home Secretary.

I have in my hand the statement made by Dr. Cort. Admittedly, it was made at the second interview by the police, but it was delayed only because he felt that he ought to take legal advice before making a statement under those circumstances. I believe that the Home Secretary's error was a very unfortunate thing, and it has not helped us to reach a proper decision about the matter.

In the statement Dr. Cort said:

"I should like to make it clear that I am ready at any time to give the Home Office any information which it may desire for its own use and will co-operate to the best of my ability in any request of the British authorities."

I am not saying that it was a particularly good statement, but I think that he did the right thing. When reaching this very important decision about his future, the Home Office made no attempt to interrogate him or to give him an opportunity to make a statement about his position, thereby depriving him of the only hearing open to an alien since no judicial proceedings could have arisen at any stage in the case. I regard that as an unfortunate example of the handling of the case by the Department.

Finally, and much more serious, there is the letter which I received from the Under-Secretary about the general handling of aliens' matters. Writing on 28th May, the Under-Secretary said:

"Except in the case of refugees whose homes are behind the Iron Curtain, the Home Secretary is not prepared to allow foreigners to settle here."

That was a reference to those who had lost, or were about to lose, their own nationality. Although the Home Secretary said later that that was simply a statement of general view and was what usually happened, it seemed to those of us who read that letter that there was a clear division in the minds of the Home Office between refugees from Iron Curtain countries and those from other parts of the world. I cannot refrain from mentioning this handling of the case, although it does not bear on the immediate issue.

The first question that we must dispose of is the simple question of whether Dr. Cort is really somebody who has sought to live here only to avoid his military service obligations. Had I thought that was the case, I should never have taken the matter up; nor do I believe that my right hon. Friend the Member for South Shields (Mr. Ede), who, in his time, has occupied the Home Secretary's position, would have taken up the case had he been of that opinion.

Dr. Cort registered in 1946 with his age group as an ordinary non-medical person, for he was not then a doctor. He had bad eyesight and a dangerous condition which made it also almost impossible for him to have certain injections, and also the remnants of infantile paralysis. In 1948, he had to register again, and by that time he had contracted tuberculosis. He made no attempt to evade either of those medical examinations, and the result was perfectly clear.

In 1951, before he came to Britain, Dr. Cort registered with the American authorities. I have seen his registration chit, which makes it clear that before he left he wanted to get all that side of his affairs cleared up. He subsequently provided the American authorities with his address in England to which call-up notices should be sent if that were necessary. That was not the action of a man who was going abroad to evade military service. I do not believe that the Home Secretary can himself believe that Dr. Cort was simply a "draft dodger."

The real question is this. Dr. Cort happens to be a good doctor. He happens also — I know him slightly now — to be a very pleasant person. He wants to remain here; he is happy in this country. He is being sent away because the Home Secretary has used his undoubted discretion on the grounds that he is likely to lose his native citizenship. There is nothing against Dr. Cort. He has the support of the highest university authorities and of many others.

We then have to consider why he should be turned away. Last November, when the House was debating the question of aliens, as we do almost every year, the Under-Secretary of State, replying to the debate, laid down what is, I understand, Home Office practice in matters of this kind. The hon. Gentleman dealt with various sorts of visitors to Britain, described the position of a man who comes temporarily but later wishes to reside here permanently, and said:

"They come in for 12 months in the first instance, but if their work and behaviour is satisfactory they get a renewal as a matter of course. In the ordinary way, after four years' approved employment here the conditions are removed and they are able to stay under exactly the same conditions as any ordinary resident." – [*Official Report,* 26th November, 1953; Vol. 521, c. 562.]

There are many hon. Members on this side of the House who are doubtful – quite frankly, I am – about this absolute discretion that is given to the Home Secretary, but we are satisfied year after year, when we raise this point, by the very reasonable statements, of the kind which I have read, in which the responsible Minister tells us how he exercises that discretion. It is because I believe that it should be exercised in that way that I think the present decision has been a wrong one.

The real issue between the Minister and myself is that Dr. Cort has asked for certain political factors to be taken into consideration. I deliberately do not use the phrase "political asylum" because that was not the phrase that was used in the first instance when application was made for Dr. Cort to remain. But Dr. Cort says – I think, rightly – that political factors, if there are any, should be taken into consideration.

What are those political factors? The first is the general state of American public opinion. I say this more than deliberately, because I do not want to refer specifically to the American Government in this case. Any hon. Member who, as I do, had an affection and regard for the United States, has watched with concern the development of intolerance in certain places over there in recent years. Most of us believe that in the end the good sense of the American people will put a stop to it. In fact, this very day, perhaps even at this very hour, Senator Flanders, in Washington, is moving a motion of censure on Senator McCarthy for behaviour that is as reprehensible to me as, no doubt, it is to the Under-Secretary of State.

We do not believe that that state of affairs will become permanent, but it is a real fact. There is plenty of evidence that a man who has been a Communist and who has not purged himself in the way that some professional ex-Communists have done is suffering. People lose jobs at universities. Dr. Cort had four jobs in the offing from universities, but they were all withdrawn when his name was mentioned. He has many friends who have lost their jobs. In general, he may feel that the atmosphere at home was by no means congenial to him – in fact, it is the very reverse; and this ought to be taken into account by the Home Secretary when exercising his undoubted discretion.

I am putting the case moderately, because the last thing I want to do is to make it an occasion for an attack on the United States of America. But we would be deceiving ourselves if we did not recognise that this is a real factor and should be taken into consideration . . .

. . . I come to my last word and I ask the pardon of the House for detaining it so long. I come to the outcome of this event because it is on the consequences that the Home Secretary will ultimately be judged. The month's extension given to Dr. Cort has come to an end. I have received a letter from him, and I propose to read an extract from it to the House. Dr. Cort says:

> "Dear Mr. Benn,
> This is to tell you that Ruth and I are going to Czechoslovakia. We are very grateful to the Czech Government for granting us asylum and making it possible for us to carry on our medical work. We wish to say that we leave with feelings of warm gratitude to the British people who have treated us so hospitably and supported us so strongly in our efforts to remain in England."

When I read that letter from someone I had come to know slightly during the last few months it emphasised the utter absurdity of the Home Secretary's decision, because to my mind here is a man whose only offence was that he was a Communist as an undergraduate. Yet the apparatus of two modern States is turned on him to hound him out and hound him behind the Iron Curtain.

Both these people wanted to work here and both wanted to settle here. They wanted to become naturalised. Because of the nature of their work they were never able to raise a family. They wanted to raise one, and they wanted to go back to their own country which they love, as any ordinary human being would love the land of his birth, and visit their own people when this tide of prejudice had abated.

I greatly regret this decision that they have taken to go to Czechoslovakia. But I cannot find it in my heart to criticise them for going there, because it is one place which is open to them – for all I know the only place – where they can carry on their work and where they can do the job which they are fitted to do. The irony of it is that Dr. Cort's father is a Russian by birth and that he left the Soviet Union as a result of the Revolution. He went to America for freedom, and his child is now being pushed back again by the hamhandedness, lack of imagination and meanness of the people of the Western world. . .

159

Security Vetting*

This speech was delivered in Parliament in 1956 during the cold war at a time when the government was introducing new vetting procedures for civil servants.

Eighteen years later the issue is still a live one, and we know a great deal more about the activities of the security services themselves, in Britain and many other countries, which now seem to constitute a potential internal threat to political freedom as serious as some of the external dangers against which they are intended to guard us.

The right to think for oneself and speak one's mind is the only real safeguard against dictatorship.

. . . There is a very great difference between regarding a man as unreliable because of what he thinks and regarding him as unreliable because of what he has done. My view is that, far from increasing the security of the State, if we had a lot of police inquiries, a lot of dossiers and files designed to show what men in the Civil Service have thought in the past or think now, we would be likely to encourage such great caution on the part of those civil servants that their capacity for free thought and independent inquiry would be seriously harmed and, as a result, the State would lose some of the benefit of their services. To take an exaggerated example, far from dismissing any member of the Foreign Office who had read Karl Marx, my inclination would be to dismiss anyone who had not read Karl Marx.

. . . Then we come up against the question of character defect and the man living with somebody who is supposed to be a Communist sympathiser. [*Interruption.*] My hon. Friend forgets that if a civil servant whose wife was a Communist sympathiser left his wife he might be in trouble on the ground of character defect. I think the answer to the extremists on security is ridicule. I hope that the sense of humour which is supposed to be one of our British characteristics will always prevent us from becoming too absurd in our inquiries into the views of civil servants.

. . . We come to the third part of the problem. The safeguarding of the free society was the first, and the second was the dangers to which we are exposed. Now we come to the methods to be employed by the Government in searching out security risks. It has already been pointed out, and I think it is worth re-emphasising, that the loyalty boards are not designed in order to catch spies, but it is purely preventive work —

"Prevent us, O Lord, in all our doings" in its true sense is what the security board is designed to do. Therefore, we are only undertaking all these inquiries to expose certain people who might be dangerous to us.

*Extracts from a speech in the House of Commons on March 21, 1956.

What happens, so far as one can make out from hon. Members who have spoken, and we all have experience of this, is that the police make inquiries to find out all about a man, all that is good, bad and indifferent. That all goes down higgledy-piggledy into the record, depending on the judgment of the man who compiles the record. It is made available to the board which decided whether the man is suitable to be employed further or not. Then we come to the stage when the man is informed of the decision, and he has an opportunity of appealing to "the three wise men." Here I think there are very grave defects in the machinery provided by the White Paper.

It is argued that one cannot have an accused person interrogating witnesses because they might be doing secret work for the security forces. That might be true if a Communist is confronted with non-Communist police spies. At such a hearing the value of the police agents would at once disappear. But if they cannot be cross-examined by the accused himself, is that any bar to their being cross-examined by someone acting for the accused? We come back to the question of the right of advocacy on behalf of someone who is brought before the board.

Secondly, it is said that we cannot have a public trial and, in most cases, men are not charged but are brought up on suspicion. Is there any reason why a private trial should not be made more effective and more in accord with judicial procedures which we have in this country? I put these points most sincerely to the Government because I believe that, when the immediate pressures of the Communist world relax, sooner or later all these practices will have to be replaced by our traditional practices.

I finish with a quotation from a man who was jointly responsible for security measures in the United States with President Truman, Dean Acheson, a very distinguished American and, I believe, a very great American Secretary of State. He referred to the three Presidential executive orders made in the years 1947, 1950 and 1953 which were adopted to deal with exactly this problem, and he devotes a great chapter to the problem in which he finishes with these words:

> "I was an officer of that Administration and share wifh it the responsibility for what I am now convinced was a grave mistake and a failure to foresee consequences which were inevitable. That responsibility cannot be escaped or obscured."

With such an authority to support me, I ask the Government to look again at the White Paper before it becomes the established practice of this country.

161

Computers and Freedom*

This lecture was given in November 1970 at a workshop on "The Data Bank Society", organised by the National Council for Civil Liberties. It warns against the dangers of computers as agents of repression and argues that we must re-assert our control over this new power. By the time this lecture was given I had had nearly six years of experience as a Minister who had had responsibility for computers within Government.

This is one of the most important conferences I have ever attended, and I congratulate the NCCL on having established it. Three years ago I attended a conference in Edinburgh on data processing and there was a Soviet professor who began his speech by saying that in the last twenty-five years there had been three great scientific developments: one was nuclear energy, which at Hiroshima and Nagasaki shocked the world; the second was the discovery of man's capacity to travel in space, which thrilled the world; the third was the discovery and invention of the computer, which went more or less unnoticed, and which was the most important of the three. I entirely share this view because, when one looks at the future of our society, it is communications technology that provides the central nervous system of all organizations – governmental, military and industrial. Information is the new man-made raw material, upon which all societies in future will live. The creation, the evaluation, the packaging, the transmission and the using of knowledge, is going to be the basis for man's life from now on.

What we are discussing at this Workshop is man's place in this system, and it is not a technical problem we are discussing but a political one. This does not require technical knowledge in order to understand what is happening and what the problem is.

. . . We are not talking about a Luddite answer, but about the regulations and control by law of this enormous power. Is data collected openly? Is it collected secretly? Is it collected directly or indirectly? We must regulate and control those who are authorized to collect it, to store it, to use it, to transmit it. We must decide to whom they may transmit it and for what purpose, where it is kept, and by whom, for how long it is kept – for ever? And if it's for ever, why? Who will supervise its disposition? Is it accurate? Who checks it? Is it double-checked? How do you protect Sir Alec Douglas-Home from having his name submitted to the Yippies as a would-be member, so that all the computers recording this begin to identify him as an undesirable and dangerous figure? Who is responsible at every stage for the information? If we are

*Extracts from a lecture at the workshop organized by the National Council for Civil Liberties, November 18, 1970.

talking about the end of privacy, let us end the privacy of those who record the facts about us, and let those who are the librarians of this system have to put their imprint on each bit of information they store, so that later, if it turns out to be inaccurate, we know who put the inaccurate information in the machine. The doctrine of personal responsibility has to be re-injected into these systems. What rights has the citizen got? Has he the right to know that information about him is being collected, to decline to have it collected, to be told why it's collected, who is collecting it and how long it is to be collected? Is he entitled to receive a print-out, to have it destroyed under certain conditions? To whom does he appeal? Against what? What powers should the appeal tribunal have? What damages might be paid to a man for inaccurate information wrongly used? And where does the government and the supervision of government activity come into the picture of defence and protection which we are now considering?

Some alarmist things have been said, but if it's any comfort to anyone here, I found as a Minister with industrial responsibility that huge blocks of information collected by government were quite properly refused to me. Even quite surprisingly innocent things, such as figures for the imports by a particular firm of a particular product which we might have wanted to know about, to see if it was worth supporting a similar product at home. This was declined on the grounds that the Customs and Excise were in a position of trust with importers. So one must not be too alarmist, though the potentiality of abuse exists.

Two final points. The first question I would ask you is whether privacy is actually what we are talking about. I think anonymity of modern urban life is one of the most soul-destroying things that has ever happened to society. When you have created the totally anonymous society, then you pay for psychiatrists to listen to you, personnel officers to consider human factors, members of parliament and welfare officers, to whom you can write to break through the curtain of anonymity. Do not base this campaign on privacy on the sacred right and duty of everybody to live wholly separate from his fellow men.

Second, make it clear – and this is the political significance of what we are doing – that as a community we recognize the great potential and value of the system that is now at our disposal, and that we do not intend to surrender our power by default to those who have the information that, if abused, could take away our civil rights. And do not be pessimistic about the capacity of winning this battle. I know that many people in this area get very depressed because no one seems to be interested in it, and yet all the great changes in our society – the development of the trade unions, the welfare state, the health service,

SPEECHES BY TONY BENN

proper education, and now the war against pollution — have bubbled up from below when sufficient people were concerned about the problem to demand an answer to it. I have absolutely no doubt that when the history of this particular issue comes to be written, this seminar will be seen as a significant stepping-off ground to the point where we really can see that the public as a whole know the significance of what is happening.

Law and Order*

This paper was prepared for a Shadow Cabinet discussion on law and order. It begins with an analysis of how the Government might be planning their electoral strategy; goes on to consider three principles upon which our democratic tradition rests; and ends with some proposals on our relations with the Unions and the problem of the mass media. In fact it was never submitted.

Since 1970 the trade unions have been in the front line. They have had to bear the brunt of government policy, whether it was in killing off "lame ducks", reversing regional policies with its consequences in redundancy and higher unemployment. The Industrial Relations Act was aimed directly at them, and they are now being drawn into what looks more and more like a political trap set by Mr. Heath.

The Chequers talks were much more than a new initiative on inflation. By deliberately raising public expectations, and appearing to be so reasonable, the Cabinet was making a crude bid for public support, and simultaneously preparing the ground for a further assault on the unions.

It is widely believed that if a voluntary policy for controlling wages is not acceptable the Government will quickly move to a statutory policy. Then if industrial disputes take place, they will switch at once to a "Who governs Britain?" campaign directed against the trade union movement holding them responsible for unemployment, inflation and for undermining law and order.

The mass media are daily high-lighting violence of all kinds as if to provide the perfect setting to give such a campaign the best chance of success. By reporting every mugging and student unrest as well as the real horrors in Northern Ireland, they are building for the moment when picketing, or even an angry strike meeting could be shown as part of a pattern of anarchy. From then it is easy to demand strong

*Paper prepared for the Shadow Cabinet, October 31, 1972.

164

counter-measures of a kind that "only Mr. Heath can provide."

It is easy to see why the Government are adopting this policy. They have nothing else they can try. Almost every policy on which they were elected has had to be abandoned, with the exception of their policy on the Common Market which has not won majority support. With prices rocketing, their 1970 election appeal to the housewives cannot be repeated. They have got to try something new. The theme of anarchy, deliberately raising public anxiety and putting the blame on the trade unions is undoubtedly their best bet as they see it.

It is, therefore, a political campaign directed against them that the trade union movement now has to face, and we are deeply involved. If we are to respond effectively we shall have to re-examine some of the fundamentals of our political faith.

Democracy and socialism in Britain are built upon three principles, which we have struggled to establish over the years, and which form the basis of consent upon which our system of government rests.

The first is the supremacy of conscience over the law. The second is the accountability of power to the people. The third is the sovereignty of the people over Parliament.

These three principles are now under direct attack. The Tory campaign on Law and Order is designed to get us to accept the idea that all laws made by the State must be blindly obeyed.

The Industrial Relations Act has been drafted and interpreted in such a way as to try to overturn the accountability of trade union leaders to their own members, by substituting a statutory duty of trade unionists to obey their elected leaders as if they were just employees in a labour contracting company.

Finally, the way the Common Market question has been handled has been quite unconstitutional — because it has ridden rough shod over the sovereignty of the people by trying to usurp that power by a temporary House of Commons majority.

We are, therefore, confronted in Britain with the need to look again at the fundamentals of our system of politics and government; and in doing so we are greatly helped if we can trace their origins back, in order to understand how deep the roots are.

The supremacy of conscience over the law is the oldest principle of all. It derives from the idea of the brotherhood of man which itself comes from the monotheistic teaching that there is only one God. Whether one believes in this theological superstructure or not, there is no doubt that the brotherhood of man does derive from the fatherhood of God and that is the greatest contribution of Judaism.

The Ten Commandments brought down from Mount Sinai by Moses spelled out the law derived from that moral principle of responsibility. Later Prophets added other essential elements to it.

165

The Prophet Amos, Chapter 5, Verses 21-24 introduced the idea of righteousness:

> I hate, I despise your feast days, and I will take no delight in your solemn assemblies.
> Though ye offer me burnt offerings and your meat offerings, I will not accept them: neither will I regard the peace offerings of your fat beasts.
> Take thou away from me the noise of thy songs; for I will not hear the melody of thy viols.
> But let judgment run down as waters, and righteousness as a mighty stream.

As a criticism of a materialistic society, it is pretty strong stuff; and the idea that righteousness has a force of its own, independent of what the law may require, is one important ingredient in the idea of conscience.

The Prophet Micah, Chapter 6, Verses 6-8 repeats the same contempt for materialism, and spells out the need of justice, mercy and humility:

> Will the Lord be pleased with thousands of rams, or with ten thousands of rivers of oil? Shall I give my firstborn for my transgression, the fruit of my body for the sin of my soul?
> 8 He hath shewed thee, O man, what is good; and what doth the Lord require of thee, but to do justly, and to love mercy, and to walk humbly with thy God?

Here again is a moral challenge that stands over and above whatever the law may require.

So too does the concept of love which was carried over from Judaism to play a leading role in Christian teaching.

The idea of conscience being above, and beyond, the law, can be traced straight through to the Christians who insisted upon it in more modern times.

Those who did so include a long line of Christian dissenters who were arguing their right to freedom of thought against a disciplined interpretation of Christian belief that got embodied in civil statutes, and was enforced through the courts.

For example, in 1592 an Act was passed "for the punishment of persons obstinately refusing to come to Church". This Act was directed against the Congregationalists. Henry Barrow and John Greenwood were hanged at Tyburn for disobeying the law. Kellett's Short History of Religions explained the Congregationalists' view on page 504:

> They asserted, for instance, that the only head of the Church is Jesus Christ — thus implicitly denying the supremacy of the Crown. The only statute-book, they said, was the Word of God, whereas the

Articles of Religion, and the Common Prayer, are Acts of Parliament. They maintained that the Church must be wholly separate from the world, whereas the Elizabethan doctrine was that Church and State were one. Each congregation of godly believers, said they, was independent of every other, and had the power of choosing its own ministers, whereas the established system first put the whole Church under the Crown, and then organised it into provinces, dioceses, archdeaconries, and parishes, all under the same discipline, and set up officers whom it was totally out of the power of the laity either to elect or to dismiss.

It was this belief that the Pilgrim Fathers carried with them to America and which opened a gateway to religious liberty through which many others have since passed. It was based on the idea of the "Priesthood of all Believers" — under which every person interpreted the moral law, for himself.

There were other martyrs too who laid claim to the same right. When David Lewis, the Catholic Bishop of Llandaff was hanged at Usk in Monmouthshire on August 27, 1679, he used these words on the scaffold:

Please now observe, I was condemned for reading mass, hearing confessions, administering the sacraments, anointing the sick, christening, marrying, preaching! As for reading the mass, it was the old, and still is, the accustomed and laudable liturgy of the Holy Church; and all the other acts, which are acts of religion tending to the worship of God; and for this dying, I die for religion. Moreover, know that when last May I was in London under examination concerning the plot, a prime examinant told me that to save my life and increase my fortunes I must make some discovery of the plot, or conform. Discover a plot I could not, for I knew of none; conform I would not, because it was against my conscience! Then by consequence, I must die, and so now, dying, I die for conscience and religion; and dying upon such good scores, as far as human frailty permits, I die with alacrity, interior and exterior! From the abundance of the heart, let not only mouths, but faces also speak.

Later still this "gateway of conscience" was used to emancipate the Jews in Britain and even atheists like Charles Bradlaugh.

In more recent times this country, along with its wartime allies, entrenched that principle of placing conscience above the law in the Nuremburg judgment against the Nazi war criminals. On September 30, 1946, the International Military Tribunal in its summing up said: "The German people, therefore, with all their resources, were to be organised as a great political military army schooled to obey — without question — any policy decreed by the State."

We laid down at Nuremburg the principle that even if you were a soldier, under military discipline, you had a moral duty to your fellow

men which you were obliged to follow even if you were ordered to kill
an innocent civilian, or a Jew, or in some other way to commit a crime
against humanity. This is a very important principle, and it must
occupy a central position in our system of values. Nor is it so very
revolutionary as it is sometimes made to appear. Lord Wedgwood, a
former Liberal who later joined the Labour Party, wrote in his book
"Testament to Democracy" published in 1942, a passage which makes
it very plain and connects it directly with the traditions I have
described:

The British Attitude Towards Law

Professor Dicey discussed the influence of law upon public
opinion. Which creates which, may be debated for ever; but that
conscience created the public opinion of the lawmakers of Victorian
Britain is certain. They put individual conscience above law, and I
am well content to think that the British are now the champion
breakers both of law and of public opinion. The Lord Chief Justice
adjures me: "How dare you say that I put my law above my
conscience!" The High Church Whig, Lord Hugh Cecil, speaking in
the Commons, defines the boundaries for Christians: "Acts of
Parliament do not make things right or wrong." The suffragettes,
like Mr. Gandhi, gloried in gaol; while to have defied the police is
almost a *sine qua non* for a labour leader. In Parliament, because we
see how laws are made and how soon most of them die, we treat
them with perhaps excessive levity. In America I believe they regard
every new law as the Act of the People and therefore the Act of
God! Here, the ordinary citizen's reaction to a new law is
indignation against the impertinent interference of Government and
the pusillanimity of Parliament in allowing it.

In short, it is Parliament as the sounding-board, not Parliament as
a law factory, that makes public opinion – shapes opinion, not only
for the schools and for the Press, but for the Church and for the
philosopher. All the tossing elements go into a thinking-vat, are there
blunged and blended; and in that mixture ferments the political
education; from it pours forth the understood responsibility of
self-control and liberty. For this blending and fermenting the British
Parliament stands unrivalled.

That concept of law-breaking in pursuit of conscience rests on our
belief that our prime duty is to each other. If this leads individuals into
conflict with the law, these individuals must be ready to take the
consequences non-violently. In our democracy no man should tell
another man to break the law, nor should any man break the law to
bypass Parliament. But a person who is punished for breaking an unjust
law may, if he is sincere and his cause wins public sympathy, create a
public demand to have that unjust law changed through Parliament.
Moreover this belief in the supremacy of moral responsibility has a

positive and negative quality. It does not just permit the law to be broken. It calls upon us to go *beyond* the law in the pursuit of our responsibility. It is a challenge not an excuse. And the directness of the challenge can be measured by the response, for example, to my own recent speech saying that workers in mass media "have a responsibility to see that what is written about us is true." The virulence of the counter-attack proved the strength of the challenge.

We know, as a fact, that you cannot run any society, least of all a complicated modern society, let alone change it, without responsibility. We concentrate much too much on the laws we will pass to solve this or that problem. We ignore education and teaching about the need for that responsibility.

British Socialism itself grew out of the idea of responsibility. Robert Owen, for example, tried to find industrial institutions that would reflect it. So did the Israeli Kibbutz movement.

We owe a lot to the critical analysis that Karl Marx and the Fabians and others brought to bear on the problems of socialism, but these are additional to the moral precept which must underpin it.

So much for the idea of conscience and its relationship to law and the way in which it gave birth to socialist ideas.

What about the accountability of power – the birth of democracy from underneath? Here too there is a very easy bridge between the ancient and modern parts of our heritage.

Morgan Phillips pointed out that the Labour Party owes more to Methodism than to Marx. The trade unions were born out of the chapel. Journalists still call their branches 'chapels'. Early trade unionists learned their democracy from the dissenting chapels. When the Congregational Federation was refounded recently, in the Memorial Hall (where the Labour Party itself was formed), its Constitution re-stated the principles of its founders. Indeed, the method of representation, including voting arrangements, with the provision for a "paper" – or "card" vote was the very model from which the Labour Party Constitution was itself drawn up:

A. Constitution (5C, 14 A) Recommended that:

The Assembly adopts the following Constitution:

Foundation Principle: In solemn renewal of the declaration made in the Congregational Library, London, on 13 May 1831 and affirmed by the Conference in Lyndhurst Road Congregational Church, London, on 13 May 1972 and by the Assembly in Westminster Chapel on 14 October 1972 the Federation of continuing Congregational Churches is *founded on a full recognition of their own distinctive principle, namely, the scriptural right of every separate Church to maintain perfect independence in the government and administration of its own particular affairs; and therefore that the Federation shall not in any case assume legislative authority, or become a court of appeal.*

B. Voting Arrangements (5 B, 13 F) Recommended that:

The Assembly accepts the following voting procedures: Voting shall normally be by show of hands of the Representative Members and the Personal members present. If, however, a paper vote is required, the voting paper or papers deposited on behalf of each Church shall in total indicate the number of members currently on the roll. A representative of several churches may deposit a separate voting paper on behalf of each of them.

Any alteration to the Constitution shall require a majority of three-quarters of those present and voting by show of hands or, in the case of a paper vote, three-quarters of the total number of Church members represented in it.

Trade Union democracy and Party democracy came out of the people organised in their dissenting chapels, and they are still in conflict with the idea of authoritarian democracy which sees the role of people as little more than participating members of a system that consults them but that does not allow them to decide anything for themselves.

It is this principle that is being challenged by the Industrial Relations Act in respect of trade unions, and that is used by those who have absorbed the ideas of Edmund Burke, to fend off the pressure for more democratic control by the people. This second principle of British democracy, accountable to its members, within the Party, was established mainly as a result of trade union pressure to make Parliament democratic. Free trade unionism rests on that principle and so does a free parliament.

The third principle is based on the belief that our National Sovereignty belongs to the people. We only lend that sovereignty to our representatives to use for five years at a time. The powers of Parliament are held in trust, temporarily, and must be returned intact when the next general election comes. Any Government, or MP, pretending to give away these sovereign powers without the explicit consent of the people is acting unconstitutionally. Laws that pretend to take away these powers permanently have no moral authority.

So it is not hard to trace back the origins of our democratic socialism to Judaism and Christianity. But it is very relevant to do so, since each of these principles that I have described are under direct attack.

The new hue and cry about law and order, which is being made an excuse for a return to authoritarianism, cannot be resisted unless Law and Order are seen in the context of Justice and Responsibility.

Trade Union and Party democracy cannot be defended adequately unless their origins are understood.

The case for national sovereignty, as the property of the people, can only be understood as a very ancient right for which many have fought and died.

This is our common inheritance, whether we realize it or not. These are the roots of British democratic socialism. We should acknowledge it more openly so that people are reminded of the long history that lies behind our political and democratic traditions. In the end it is these values that make us what we are, and will shape our future, and protect us from totalitarianism of the extreme right or the extreme left.

It is against this background that the tri-partite talks between Labour's National Executive, the Shadow Cabinet and the TUC General Council have now to see their tasks. This important Liaison Committee began its work earlier this year. Its first report went both to the Brighton Congress of the TUC and to the Blackpool Party Conference. Starting with agreement on the total, immediate and unconditional repeal of the Industrial Relations Act by the next Labour Government, it outlined the agreed legislation that would replace it and strengthen free trade unionism. It promised further talks on economic policy. These have now begun.

But it is now quite clear that more will be required. For if the Unions, and the Party, are to face an election campaign on the issue which the Cabinet would like to make central, unity between the whole Labour movement has got to be complete.

We have got to think in terms of a Joint Programme covering a complete range of policies, discussed and agreed between us, and on which we can fight together for public support to form the basis upon which the next Labour government will work.

Much of the ground work has already been done. We have removed the main obstacles that divided us during the last government. "Labour's Programme for Britain" supplemented by Conference decisions, taken with the TUC Economic Review in conjunction with the resolution passed at Brighton, contain a mass of policy common to us both. Some of these need to be further defined. There are gaps to be filled and details to be worked out, but this will not prove difficult.

The Liaison Committee already reports both to the National Executive and to the TUC General Council. If these two major bodies can agree on the need for a joint programme, and say so plainly, work can begin on it, in earnest and at once.

There is no reason why such a Joint Programme should not be laid before both the 1973 TUC Congress, and the Party Conference. Indeed, if necessary, the TUC might wish to summon a Special Congress, and the Labour Party a Special Conference, to discuss a draft programme even earlier than that.

The advantages of a Joint Programme are easy to see. It would represent the re-creation of the Grand Coalition of Labour which was in the minds of the founders of the Labour Party when the trade unions first set it up. It would mobilise trade unionists alongside constituency parties for the Election Campaign whenever it comes. It would make all the organisation problems easier by bringing together constituency parties and trade union branches in factories and offices at the local level where they have so much to offer each other.

But it is not enough just to agree a Joint Programme, contained in a Labour Election Manifesto, and endorsed by the trade union movement. This programme must be got across to the British people as a whole against the massive advertising campaign financed by their rich business and industrial allies which has already begun.

"Working together" would be a first rate slogan for us — if the Tories and their business friends had not already appropriated it. A Joint Programme does mean "working together" to replace Heath and his policies with a Government committed to policies devised in the interests of working people.

The acceptance of a Joint Programme will not prevent the TUC from continuing to perform its other role as spokesman for its affiliated unions in dealing with the Government. It will not prevent the Labour Party from discharging its Parliamentary responsibilities in opposition or in government. But the very fact that we have a Joint Programme will excite imagination of many of those who have been disappointed in the past, and who wonder how it can be different in the future.

It can be different, and it will work, if we commit ourselves together, consciously, not just to an election strategy but to the long-term aim of completing the task which we were set up to discharge — by joint action, jointly agreed.

This leaves one outstanding problem to be discussed. The bias against working people, arising out of the control and working of the mass media is not a new one, but it is important. It has been neglected as a policy issue because of the difficulty in finding the right answer, and indeed, of identifying the exact problem.

It is important to state the problem correctly. The main point is not the treatment accorded to Labour leaders — or even the Party as such. These people are able to look after themselves and if they give the impression that their only interest in the media derives from personal resentment at what is said about them, no one will really listen to their comments about the much wider problem of seeing that mass media treat the community as a whole decently and fairly, and use their enormous power with that objective. In any case, over-kill in press attacks on Labour leaders is usually counter-productive.

The greatest complaint against the media is that its power is used to dominate the community, that it excludes ordinary people and that it is not accountable in any way, save by the crude test of market success.

The main victims are the trade unions whose motives are regularly distorted, whose members are insulted or ignored, and who are presented in a way that denies them the opportunity to describe their work and interests properly.

The NEC has now agreed to set up a working party to look at our policy for the mass media. This policy is bound to include a fuller consideration of the role of advertising; a look at the future pattern of broadcasting; and may give consideration to various ideas ranging from a subsidy to newsprint or the stimulation of more outlets that would allow a wider range of views to get across. This work will take some time and we must not expect it to help us in the short run.

Government censorship direct or indirect would be totally wrong and unacceptable. This has to be stated time and time again since the mass media would like to dismiss any serious discussion by raising the bogey of government control – thus preventing any debate from taking place.

Similarly the idea that industrial action, exercised by workers within the industry, could or should be an acceptable substitute for Government censorship is equally wrong. The unaccountable power now exercised by the proprietors, editors or broadcasting chiefs would be equally unacceptable if it were arbitrarily exercised by anyone in the production chain who took exception to anything that was being printed or transmitted, and stopped it.

The immediate situation may best be tackled by carrying forward the debate triggered off by the crude intervention into politics by some newspapers and television companies. The problem has also got to be seen from the point of view of those who work in the mass media – journalists, broadcasters and others who are themselves victims of the present authoritarian trends.

The trade unions too will need to be encouraged to take a more active interest in the disadvantages that flow from the distorted presentation of their work – especially if this distortion is a part of a careful pre-election build up to an "Anarchy" scare poll.

The long debate about access to the mass media is now leading to results. Some BBC local radio stations are actually giving time to local community groups and allowing them to present their case directly.

The trade union movement might well think it worthwhile directly approaching the Board of Governors of the BBC and the Chairman of the programme companies to make two specific requests:

First that a Code of Conduct be agreed under which industrial disputes would be handled on the basis of equality of treatment from both sides in news and feature coverage; *Second*, that the TUC

173

should be allocated a certain number of hours every year – like the political parties – which they could use to present their policies and explain the position of member unions. Were such a scheme to be agreed there would be no reason why the CBI should not be given equal time on the same basis.

The problem of accountability may also need to be looked at in a new way. Always excluding Government control, the Press Council and new Complaints Committee set up by the BBC are too remote, slow and clumsy to be effective.

Hitherto trade unions in the mass media have concentrated rather too narrowly on their traditional tasks of negotiating about wages, salaries and conditions. The attempt by the Free Communications Group to cater for a wider interest has not been successful partly because it did not connect up with the trade unions involved.

However, recently moves to bring about a Federation of Broadcasting Unions may offer the first real opportunity of consolidating the interests of the unions, and extending them into the wider area of responsibility for output.

A similar Federation of Press Unions, if it could be set up, might assume a similar role. Ultimately a Federation of Mass Media Unions would provide the best forum of all.

For if accountability could be achieved *inside* the newspapers or broadcasting units, a completely new situation might be created.

The points for discussion at meetings of this kind might include the following:

1 The publication of directives

The provision that all policy directives from proprietors, editors and broadcasting chiefs must be in written form and must themselves be published or broadcast so that everyone knows what is going on. This would follow the pattern laid down for directives given to nationalised industries by Ministers. Though it would not actually eliminate private and indirect pressure, it would act as a sort of check and would throw some light on the inner workings of the media which are now shrouded in complete secrecy.

2 The development of Codes of Conduct

The drafting of a Code of Conduct to be signed by all those who work in the media, laying down the personal responsibility that each one of them has – whatever they do – for seeing that the output is true and fair and the comment free from internal or external pressure. This might also protect journalists and others, who fear for their jobs if they write or broadcast material that is unacceptable to their superiors on policy grounds.

3 The establishment of internal councils

The establishment within *each* newspaper or broadcasting unit of a council or committee elected by the whole labour force which would have the responsibility for receiving complaints directed to it, either by outsiders who felt aggrieved or by those working for the Paper or Broadcasting unit who were dismissed or victimised for what they had written or said. This Council would discuss these complaints with the Editor or management but would have no power, other than the power of making a report which would then be published. Criticism on grounds of balance from the inside would be much more formidable as an influence than criticism from the outside. Complaints would be discussed and a body of agreed policy would slowly build up, which would influence future treatment of news and features. No-one would want to encumber the daily process of producing news for programmes (with its very tight time-scale of operation) by having a committee breathing down the neck of the man responsible. But accountability *afterwards* is perfectly practicable and would influence future action.

VI

Bristol

Against Hereditary Peerage

In 1960 my father, William Wedgwood Benn, long time a Labour MP and made a peer in 1942 on his retirement from the Commons, died.

His peerage, conferred before life peers were introduced, had been an hereditary one, and with the death of my elder brother, Michael, a war-time RAF pilot in 1944, I was left his heir. At the moment of his death I was disqualified from the Commons after ten years' service there and a by-election was declared to fill the vacancy.

My local Party re-adopted me and the electors returned me with an increased majority on May 4, 1961.

This speech, prepared for delivery at the Bar of the House of Commons on May 8, 1961 was never spoken since the House would not hear me. It summarised the simple democratic issues involved in the peerage battle. In the event after the House had rejected my request to be heard my defeated opponent petitioned the Election Court which declared my election invalid and seated him as MP for Bristol South East. But the power of the electors who had voted me back despite my 'disqualification' was so great that it stirred public opinion until the law had to be changed, as it was in 1963.

After nearly three years I was re-elected to represent the people who had stuck by me so resolutely and the victory was theirs.

I am here to claim my seat as Member of Parliament for the Constituency of Bristol South East.

My sole authority for doing so is that the electors of that constituency have decisively chosen me to represent them here. This is certified in the statutory declaration of election made on Friday last by the Sheriff of Bristol acting as Returning Officer in pursuance of a decision of this House that an election should be held for that purpose.

I assert no personal rights in this matter – but solely the rights of my constituents to choose any member not debarred by Act of Parliament.

We who are members of this House of Commons do not sit here at the whim of the Crown, or by courtesy of the Lords. We do not come here at the discretion of Mr. Speaker or even by consent of the House – and least of all by virtue of any personal merit. We sit here because we have been elected by our constituents and for no other reason whatsoever. We cannot stay here if they reverse their decision in another election. And so gravely do we regard the duties imposed on us that an M.P. cannot even resign his seat – but has instead to go through the legal fiction of applying for the Chiltern Hundreds in order to disqualify himself.

This entrenched constitutional principle of elected service bears testimony to the sovereignty of the people of Britain in the Government of their affairs. And is their main safeguard against any attacks upon that sovereignty.

It should therefore be clearly understood that the issue today is a simple one: Are the people of Bristol South East to have the right to choose their own Member or is this right to be usurped by the Government of the day, using its Parliamentary majority under the discipline of the whips? No other issue arises.

I have done everything in my power to avoid the election which has just been forced upon them.

In 1955 – 5 years before my father died – the Lord Mayor, Aldermen and Burgesses of the City of Bristol petitioned both Houses of Parliament to permit me to remain their representative. Parliament took no action.

Last November, on the death of my father, I petitioned this House in the same sense. It was referred to the Committee of Privileges. In its report the Committee saw fit to make no reference whatsoever to the rights of my constituents and contented itself instead with a microscopic study of medieval customs.

In April, 10,000 of my constituents petitioned this House. The House brushed it aside as of no account and proceeded to disqualify me by resolution.

There was therefore no other course open to me than to take this issue back to those who had elected me and to ask for their judgment upon it. They have sent me here four times and it was for them to dismiss me.

During the election campaign all these matters were fully presented. The issues were clearly understood. The verdict was unmistakable.

I come now not as a supplicant for special favours but as the servant of those whose will must be sovereign. What happens to me matters not at all. But their right of free choice is of tremendous constitutional importance and it is my clear duty to defend it – whatever the consequences for me may be.

My opponent has declared his intention to petition the Election Court to claim the seat. If he succeeds and is seated here (backed by the party whips) it will make a mockery of Parliamentary democracy and all it stands for.

For my part I would rather be disqualified for life than sit and vote here in flat contradiction to the expressed wishes of those whom one is intended to represent.

What then should the House do today? It should surely first seek a way of giving effect to the will of the people of Bristol. This presents no great problem. There is no statutory barrier to administering the oath. Decisions as to membership of this House are entirely for the House to make. Once more such decisions are privileged — and cannot be questioned in any place outside this House.

The House has therefore full power to act in this case. There is no binding law. The only obstacles to action are customs and practices which stemmed from circumstances that have long since changed. It is true that to set them aside would be to create a precedent. But the history of Parliament is the history of precedents, wisely created to meet new conditions.

Finally I ask the House to approve this matter in the spirit of our constitutional development. The manifest absurdity of heredity disqualification is widely recognized and overwhelmingly rejected. To enforce it today against the wishes of my electors will inevitably bring British Parliamentary government into disrepute.

The great glory of this House is its record of defence of freedom against all who have sought to undermine it. In the world of today political freedom is still so rare a thing that it ought not to be lightly set aside but rather should be especially cherished.

I ask therefore that I should now be permitted to proceed to the table to take the oath in the prescribed manner and to assume the Parliamentary responsibilities freshly re-imposed upon me by the people of Bristol, whose servant I am.

The New Bristol Group*

The New Bristol Group was founded in June 1962 with the following aims.
1. To bring together those people in Bristol who care sufficiently about the City to work to secure its future growth and welfare.
2. To begin an active study of the problems now facing or likely to face the citizens of Bristol and to work out constructive proposals designed to meet them.
3. To stimulate a wider public discussion of these issues in the City so

*Preface from "Output 1" published by New Bristol Group, June 1963.

as to mobilise the skill and energy of thoughtful people in the task of carrying through the necessary reforms.

The response was astonishing. Well over a hundred people became Associates. They included councillors, magistrates, engineers, doctors, trade unionists, students, teachers, designers, university professors, and a farmer – many of whom have never been involved in this work before.

Specialist groups were set up to study various problems. Voluntary organizations in the city were asked to fill in questionnaires to help us do our work. In the hours of discussion that have taken place over the last year we have tried to bridge the dangerous gap between experts in various fields and those in local and national government who are grappling with the practical problems that arise.

The broadsheets which are published in this booklet are the result of that one year's work. They cover a wide variety of subjects each of them of tremendous importance to the people who live in Bristol.

I want to stress one thing. The New Bristol Group is not a party political organization that makes policy and campaigns for its acceptance. That is for others to do – or for ourselves in our individual capacities. We have no collective view. The Group is simply concerned to study the problems and to offer its recommendations as being worthy of public consideration.

This then is an experiment in responsible citizenship and an attempt to harness the knowledge to be found in the city, to the task of making Bristol as great in the future as it has been in the past.

This is only the beginning. We plan to go on and tackle more problems and publish more broadsheets. If you would like to join with us in this endeavour we should be pleased to welcome you into the New Bristol Group.

The New Bristol Group in Action*

The New Bristol Group was founded as an experiment. Those of us who sponsored it were convinced that the problems facing a modern community could only be tackled effectively by breaking down the barriers that separate us into little water-tight compartments according to our occupations or specialized knowledge and experience.

We therefore invited teachers, doctors, students, aldermen, professors, trade union officials, local government officers and many

*Preface from "Output 2" published by the New Bristol Group, September 1964.

others to join us in studying the city: its difficulties and its opportunities. It has been intensely exhilarating working together, and the result is to be found in *Output* 1962/63 and now this new edition *Output* 1963/64. The twenty-four broadsheets already published cover a very wide range of subjects that are of immediate concern to the citizens of Bristol. Requests for our broadsheets and for details of our work have come from many other parts of the country and a number of similar groups, based on our experience, are being set up elsewhere.

The New Bristol Group has no officers, no organization, no party affiliations and it has never voted on anything. Its broadsheets are simply published as being "worthy of public consideration". The task of getting our ideas taken up is not our concern, except as individuals. Some of our past proposals, for example on the future of secondary education, have now been accepted. Others, like the proposed new Citizenship Council, are being resisted. The important thing is that they should all be discussed. Informed controversy is an essential part of community renewal.

Among the subjects we intend to tackle next are broadcasting, the Press, political organizations, the care of the elderly, regional government, the hospitals and the future of Bristol's direct-grant schools. We always welcome new members and we need a little more financial support to help pay for a wider circulation of the broadsheets.

After two years the New Bristol Group is firmly established. There is a lot of work still to do.

The New Bristol Group Concludes its Work*

The New Bristol Group was set up in the summer of 1962, and in the four years since then it has produced over 30 broadsheets covering a wide range of subjects which have been of interest and concern to Bristolians in this period. Now we come to the end of the work of the Group. Admittedly, the nature of its task has been modified in the course of four years. It has not attempted to make the detailed survey of Bristol life envisaged in the first broadsheet (*Output 1*) and its approach has been somewhat less systematic in consequence. Nevertheless, we venture to think that there are not many matters which have been regarded as important in Bristol during this period which have not had an airing in one or more of these broadsheets.

*Preface from "Output 3" published by the New Bristol Group, 1966.

Whether or not our work has made a significant impact on policymaking in Bristol, it is not for us to judge. We have good reason to suppose, however, that the views which we have expressed on Secondary Education, the Fluoridation of Water Supplies, Health Centres, the Integration of Coloured Immigrants, and a variety of other topics, have been taken seriously by those in positions of public responsibility.

The production of *Output 3* has been long delayed by changes in personnel and by the elevation of some of our leading members to offices of national responsibility. As a result, some of the broadsheets which appear in this collection have dated a little, in the sense that some of their recommendations have already been fulfilled. We have thought it best however to let them stand as they were written, rather than try to adjust them in detail. This collection of broadsheets is characteristic of the wide range of interests of the Group, and it is hoped that Bristolians will find the inset on "Facts and Figures" particularly valuable.

In bringing the work of the New Bristol Group to an end, we are not implying that there is nothing more to be done in the way of suggesting constructive reforms in civic life. This was a continuing task which will never be complete. What we are saying is that this particular radical initiative has run its course, and that it is time to hand over the work to other groups, coming to it, perhaps, with fresh ideas. We earnestly hope that such groups will arise, and many of our members will doubtless wish to be associated with them.

The Index of Community Action*

The Index of Community Action, launched just after the 1970 Election, was a pilot scheme designed to reconnect Parliamentary politics to the grass roots organisations which speak for the people as they organise themselves. It listed all the local trade unions as well as other community groups and became a reference book for those who wanted to make the democratic system work for them.

The idea of offering consultative status to such groups to help the Labour Party to renew and extend its role as spokesman for the people has since been accepted by the National Executive Committee.

The Bristol *Index of Community Action* published today contains the most comprehensive list of community and voluntary organisations ever compiled for any city in Britain.

Work on the *Index* began early in 1971 at the suggestion of Mr. Anthony Wedgwood Benn MP for Bristol South East and was undertaken by a group of volunteers led by Oonagh McDonald, a philosophy lecturer at Bristol University who has since been adopted as prospective Parliamentary Labour candidate for South Gloucestershire.

The *Index* describes all those organisations which could be traced as working within the Greater Bristol area that were not either governmental, local authority or commerical in character.

Entries, based on a questionnaire drawn up with the help and advice of IBM contain the name of the organisation, the address of its secretary, its membership qualifications, its objectives and brief details of its activities and meetings where this is known.

All this information has been fed into the computer at the Bristol Polytechnic, who are the publishers of the *Index*. The Polytechnic have agreed to make it available for those who wish to use it.

Miss McDonald, commenting on the work involved in preparing the Index and on its possible use said:

"The work involved a team of volunteers using all the available sources — newspapers, advertisements, personal contacts and so on, for the names and addresses of the various organisations in Bristol. We then sent out questionnaires and based the information in the *Index* on the information we received. We were impressed by the sheer number and variety of the voluntary organisations in Bristol and the work this' represents. It is extremely difficult to trace in this way all the voluntary organisations in Bristol, and we are aware that we have not been able to contact all the organisations which exist. We are confident that the publication will attract entries from many more organisations once they realise the value of the *Index*.

*Press Release, November 9, 1973.

183

The *Index* is primarily a means of communication. It will provide an immediate contact with a suitable society or group for newcomers to Bristol, those with new-found interests or needs, those requiring companionship and many others. It will enable social workers and counsellors of all kinds to provide additional support and friendship for those whom they are trying to help. These are the social uses of the *Index*. It will provide a means of consultation for those who are responsible for planning the community at the level of local and national government and the community. It will enable societies such as churches and pressure groups which informally represent the community and the planners and the politicians to speak to each other. Finally it will be used as a means of communication between voluntary organisations and the public and between voluntary organisations themselves."

Mr. Wedgwood Benn MP, at whose suggestion the *Index* was compiled, said:

"I have already used the *Index* to contact organisations able to help personal cases that come to me as an MP; to consult others on policy proposals and to receive from these groups their own views on matters that are of concern to them. It is exactly organisations of this kind with which the Labour Party wishes to establish informal 'Consultative Status' so that, without in any way compromising their complete independence, their policy proposals can be considered when our programme is being drawn up locally or nationally."

Mr. Benn added: "Community politics is not something that can be appropriated by a single political party, claiming to speak for all these groups. They must speak for themselves and all political parties must be ready to listen to what they have to say."

Statistical note for editors:

The *Index* has a total number of 1007 entries. Of these there are: for example:

Organisations dealing with:

Blind	6	Ex-Servicemen	14	Old People	25
Children	28	International	36	Political	22
Community Assns	30	understanding		Sailing	25
Conservation	34	Motoring	18	Social clubs	19
Drama	45	Music	36	Women	30

VII

Women and Youth Today

Listening to the New Generation*

This article, published in the Melody Maker *in October 1970, was written in response to an article by Mick Farren, a leader of the Yippie movement, about "Rock as a political force". It contained a reference to the only real revolutionary principle that 'the man next to you really is your brother' and in responding I tried to unearth this principle and separate it from much of the rest of his argument with its false emphasis on drugs.*

Mick Farren's article "Rock — energy for revolution" was certainly one of the most interesting statements from his generation addressed to my own, that I have yet to read.

There can be few parents who will not have felt, from the other side of the age barrier, the alienation that he describes and attributes to the fact that "Rock is not something you understand, it is something that you feel in your body and you know."

Every new generation has always thought its parents were old-fashioned and out of touch and limited in their vision and hidebound in their ideas. But the gap today seems wider, and is wider, for two new and important reasons. First, the rate of change is now so rapid that the old now, for the first time in history, find it harder to understand the world than their own children do.

And secondly because the new generation are not only rejecting the ideas and values of the past (or seem to be doing so) but some are discovering a new physical awareness that Eldridge Cleaver described as "a generation of whites getting back into their bodies."

When Mick Farren calls for "a real alternative to the life-long, mind-twisting routine of office or factory" he is saying something very important that makes sense to a lot of older people as well. Indeed what he says is directly mirrored in some of the writings of the best management philosophers too.

Robert Townsend, the American management consultant in his

*Article in *Melody Maker,* October 24, 1970. Reprinted by kind permission of *Melody Maker.*

book *Up the Organisation* wrote: "We've become a nation of
boys. Monster corporations like General Motors and monster
cies like the Defence Department have grown like cancer until they
take up nearly all of the living working space ... Two solutions
confront each of us:

"Solution One is a cop-out: you can decide that what is must be
inevitable, grab your share of the cash and fringes; and comfort yourself
with the distractions you call leisure.

"Solution Two is non-violent guerilla warfare: start dismantling our
organizations where we're serving them, leaving only the parts where
they're serving us. It will take millions of such subversives to make
much difference."

To work to dismantle bureaucracy thus provides a common interest
between the generations which has not been fully developed and has
great potential.

However, when Mick Farren says "our parents are making only
meagre attempts to cure the sickness in their society" he opens up a
wider range of issues which need to be explored. The argument here is
not as simple as an argument between those who want to put society
right – the young – and those who don't care – the old.

Society has always been criticised by the young and they have
always clamoured for radical change. But up until a generation ago the
main remedy appeared to lie in the mobilization of state power to deal
with current social ills. The problem of ill health prompted Nye Bevan
to work for a National Health Service administered by the State. The
curse of unemployment suggested the need for public ownership and
better central economic planning. The direct threat of fascism called
forth a vast national and international military effort. Thus the older
generation still tend to think of *national* action to deal with *national*
problems.

When the young say that this argument does not go far enough and
that national action may lead to greater bureaucracy and create new
problems as it solves old ones I think they are partly right. But faced
with the enormous accumulation of power in the world in which we
live I cannot visualise remedies that don't include the mobilisation of
national and international power to make strategic choices and force
private centres of power to be accountable.

Where the young are wholly right is in arguing that these policies will
not in themselves secure an enlargement of human development unless
we revolutionize our relationships with each other.

Here we come near to the central moral argument. Probably the
majority of older people do half-believe that we live in a society where
moral standards are deteriorating and where society is going "to pot",
literally and figuratively.

My own experience of the new generation does not in any way confirm this general middle-aged pessimism. Indeed I would support Mick Farren's counter attack on the values of an older generation that seems to accept violence as an instrument of policy, guide its life by personal financial gain and tolerate a society where the profit and loss account is dominant.

The drug issue is in my opinion much the biggest barrier to an understanding. However illogical the opposition to drugs may seem to be from a society that consumes millions of tons of tobacco and hundreds of thousands of gallons of alcohol, the fact is that most parents are genuinely afraid of them and, many, like myself, do not believe that real human relationships can be achieved if they depend upon drugs to get them started and sustain them; and we cannot accept the idea of a wealthy society seeking synthetic pleasure in the midst of a world that faces the problems of starvation.

Contrast this with what Mick Farren says at the end of his article "there is now a choice that none of us can ignore. If we carry on as we are now we are a frightened overcrowded species on a dying planet. If we work on the principle (and this is really the only revolutionary principle) that the man next to you really is your brother, and that you need each other in order to survive, then may be, even at this late stage, we may still have a chance to become a free and dignified people."

If this is the message of the young to the old it is a message of supreme importance. It not only enshrines all that is best, in the greatest teaching from history but it could well be written into the preamble of the United Nations charter and inscribed in stone lettering in the Houses of Parliament and incorporated into the memorandum of association of every industrial enterprise.

It is the doctrine of human responsibility, clearly stated and if it were really that that took a quarter of a million people to the open air pop festivals in Woodstock or on the Isle of Wight then it would certainly be one of the most important social movements of our time.

187

Woman's Place*

This speech delivered at the Yorkshire Labour Women's Rally in June 1971 was an attempt to analyse the relationship between the new movement for women's rights and the historic struggle of the trade union movement which has so often ignored women in its own work.

The objective of the speech was to see these two movements as twin aspects of the same struggle and to warn against the danger of allowing them to conflict with each other, thus weakening both.

I want to speak today about the role of women in society. It is a very risky thing for a man to presume to talk to women, about women, and so I hope you'll be patient with me as I develop my argument and take it in the spirit in which it is intended. I am really trying to think aloud.

Incredible as it now seems, women were altogether denied even the vote until 53 years ago and only won the franchise at 21 ten years after that. If we are considering what is still called 'the women's question' we have got to see it against a background of centuries when women were specifically and categorically discriminated against by men, as indeed they still are. In feudal times they were just chattels, as they still are in some parts of the world. But even after some of them escaped from male domination they were denied political representation. Today, even in Britain, they still suffer from laws passed by Parliament before women had to vote, which are enforced by the courts in such a way as to keep them as second-class citizens. But the problem goes far deeper than that. Public attitudes adopted by many men, and accepted by many women, are now a hundred years out of date.

It is appropriate that the new women's movement which has become active in recent years in America and Europe should have demanded liberation, for that is what the battle is about. In part inspired by the colonial liberation movements, and in part by the powerful pressure groups for racial equality established by those who had suffered discrimination, the new women's movement draws much of its energy from a history of clear injustice, which has not yet ended. And it is growing much more rapidly than many people realise. It is no good ignoring it in the hope that it will go away – because it won't. Moreover it has tremendous and untapped political potential.

Many people mock the women's movement today by picking on some of its tactics just as the feminist movement was mocked at the time the suffragettes began their campaigns. But every struggle for rights by an oppressed group is exposed to ridicule by those who are

*Speech given at the Yorkshire Labour Women's Rally at the Clifton Hall, Rotherham, on June 5, 1971.

frightened of the power it generates. Those who are privileged know that if a progressive movement succeeds in its objectives the privileges which they have enjoyed will be threatened. No wonder some men are uneasy at the knowledge that some women are now openly objecting to their arrogance in determining how much freedom women should have.

It is also true that the leaders of a new movement for social change are always liable to be accused of being unrepresentative. How easy to dismiss them as a lunatic fringe commanding no real support amongst their own constituency of women. But just the same was said of the trade union and socialist pioneers or the Chartists in the 19th century, who were written off as wild men and agitators in a deliberate effort to separate them from a supposedly sensible body of people who, the public was told, were quite content with their lot.

I have mentioned this because if we are to see this new movement in its proper historical perspective we must see it as part of a much wider movement for human rights and human equality which is being fought for against all sorts of privileges all over the world. It is, in fact, a natural part of our fight for a socialist society. Our campaign for women's rights must include women's right to be fully equal with men as workers and individuals.

One of the most interesting things about the new women's movement is the extent to which it has struck a responsive chord in women of all ages and cuts across class barriers. It is perhaps not surprising that many young women should be profoundly discontented when they come across examples of the discrimination in education and jobs and opportunity that are still tolerated in modern society. But is equally true that many older women whose first political experience was the fight for the vote should now, sometimes as pensioners, be waking up to the fact that the winning of the vote did not achieve what they expected it would. It was only the first step, giving women the outward form of political freedom with some marginal liberalisation, but leaving the inner substance of human equality beyond their grasp. They find they are excited by the new wave of feeling among their children and grandchildren. They want to see them succeed where they failed. Even though the extreme expressions of views we hear do not command majority support, that movement has already helped to awaken a political feeling among women.

The generalised discontent among women has now assumed the proportions of a real national — indeed international — movement. Whether we support it or not — and I am arguing strongly that we should do — it is a political force to be reckoned with.

The movement towards greater women's rights has remained for too long on the edge of our policy-making. We have not been concerned as we ought to have been with it. We must now integrate it more clearly into our own political philosophy as a movement based upon human equality, and human development.

The polls tell us that a majority of British women vote Conservative. It may be that while so many women are working at home we have failed to relate our pressure for social change to their concerns as women and have allowed their discontents to be exploited by our opponents.

Certainly the Tory Party has consistently tried to win their support. In the post-war period there was the Housewives' League created by Lord Woolton.

It is worth remembering how the 1970 Conservative campaign was mounted. There were the usual posters and leaflets about rises in the cost of living. But then towards the end a new note was introduced. The Conservatives deliberately played on the fact that many women were no longer prepared to vote as their husbands wished. They therefore encouraged them into deliberately voting against the men by playing on trade union wage claims and male selfishness – so it was argued – in keeping the increases to themselves and leaving their wives with the same housekeeping money to cope with rising prices. The assumption that women were *only* interested in their homes and money was a limited one – but this appeal had some effect. The attempt to divide women from an equal concern with men on those issues which the Trade Unions and Labour Party were fighting for, was successful.

The campaign to put the blame for rising prices on to the trade unions is still directed mainly at women, and every strike reported in the press or on the radio and TV will, it is hoped, consolidate political support among women against the Labour movement as a whole and the Labour Party in particular. We would be very foolish to ignore this campaign. It is part of the long-term systematic strategy of the Conservatives based on continuing market research surveys done among women to exploit some discontents that most women feel, diverting them from the issues that have to be settled if real equality is to be achieved.

Thus, not for the first time, the Tory Party hopes to divide two great political movements – the movement for better pay and working conditions which the Trade Unions are leading; and the movement for women's rights – by trying to get them to cancel each other out. And every time there is discrimination against women by men at work, which there is; or men treat women inconsiderately, this tension helps the Right. Even the opposition by some men to family allowances with the 'claw back' was turned to the political advantage of the Tories.

Against this, superficial Labour propaganda 'aimed at the women's vote' is relatively ineffective. A leaflet on the prices of school meals, or housing, important as these issues are, merely scratches at the surface of the problem of bringing these two movements together so that they can reinforce each other in support of the ordinary family which is held back — men, women and children together — by the privileges we still tolerate in our society. The Trade Union movement could and should do more to help women in their struggle. Whatever its official policy may be, there is still serious discrimination in practice.

If we are serious in our desire to create this unity we have got to see it against a background of industrial change which sets the framework for all political analysis.

Modern technology has done a lot more than re-equip our factories with new machines and spread car ownership. It has begun a revolution of home life, as well as life at work. Domestic appliances have lifted some of the back-breaking drudgery of keeping a home from those women who can afford to buy them, though millions cannot. For some it has opened up a leisure unknown before these appliances were invented, and could be afforded, when they worked from their childhood into the last days of their retirement, cooking and cleaning and mending and serving their menfolk, without pay.

And with leisure has come a whole new source of information and ideas through the popular press, radio and television. Instead of being locked away in an isolated village kitchen with nothing but gossip to feed them with information, more women today have an opportunity to be better informed. All sorts of new ideas are coming into every household, and there is a massive and entirely justified discontent among women as well as men — all part of the revolution of rising expectations.

Some of these ideas go right to the heart of family life. All of a sudden, instead of an apparently inescapable life of childbearing, more women have now discovered that you can theoretically plan your family, and instead of inevitably occupying all the years of life until you are prematurely aged by having and raising children, free time may be waiting for you round the corner in your early thirties when your youngest child is off at school, or earlier if you have no children.

So many a married woman who is still young and full of energy and ideas will find that she has perhaps 30 years of her life up to 65 (and a longer and less exhausting period than her grandmother had after that) in which she can make choices about what she does. In other cases, where husbands are unemployed, disabled or lower-paid workers, many wives have to go out to work to supplement the family income — whether they want to or not. But for women with children, and a home to maintain, who work, the physical strain and effort of this double shift is considerable. They have t fight two battles.

We call leisure 'freedom'. But when you come to look at this freedom it can only be enjoyed if you have been educated to use it and have a sufficient income to allow you freedom from anxiety. Many a woman of 35 only then discovers, too late to put it right, that *all* she was encouraged to learn at school was cooking, dress-making and typing which is now graced under the description of 'domestic science' and 'Business Studies'. She finds she was only equipped for a life that she may not have to lead – or want to lead. There is also the problem of an 'identity crisis' for some mothers when they discover their children no longer depend on them and they have no education to help them cope.

No wonder there is so much combustible material about. No wonder the Conservatives would like to see it directed against the Trade Unions in case it became dangerously threatening to the fabric of a male-dominated, consumer-orientated capitalist society, and our unfair educational system which is the cause of much of the trouble.

The phenomenon of the women's movement cannot possibly be understood without some attempt to integrate important changes in social attitudes into our political thinking. An extraordinary gap still exists between the accepted national view – about the way that people are supposed to behave and the way in which society has actually been moving.

Parliament, and those who sit in it, are still 'officially' wedded to a view of human relations – which supposes that men will be educated to work, and women will be trained to marry them, and they will then all pair off and produce families and live happily ever after. But rightly or wrongly – and I am not passing any moral judgments at all – that is not what actually happens in many cases.

Take a simple example. Though most women marry; and nowadays marry younger, some women don't marry; they want to be educated for a job and to get a job appropriate to their qualifications. And many find it hard because some people treat them as if they were kicking over the traces instead of settling down with a 'nice man', washing his shirts and raising his children and having his slippers ready when he comes back at night.

Some do get married, but things don't work out and they part, and they marry again; and perhaps have children or perhaps not.

Some women have children without marrying, and some want to marry and not have children, and some don't like men at all.

All this is demonstrable, a statistical fact, and the implications are enormous. It means that a lot of women want to do things, or are doing things, that in a way aren't accepted by society and they find themselves discriminated against because of it. The traditional role of the family as a united partnership for life, which it is for the majority, is not threatened by accepting other life-styles for the minority, though some try to argue that it is.

Remember one thing. This freedom has been accepted for centuries, but for men only. Men have always been generous to themselves, in approving their own life styles. But the old double standards are no longer acceptable. Now new options are beginning to open up for women. This is the stuff of which revolutions are made, because it involves a change of values which threatens the existing pattern of male domination.

But all freedom requires choice. What do people want to do with their freedom? Once anyone gets over the shock of being able to do what they like, they will settle down to work out their own life style that conforms to their basic nature and reflects their values. The right to make our own choices is fundamental. It would certainly be wrong to suppose that the women's movement is against moral standards. It is, if anything, rather puritanical. For many men this is the most surprising thing about it.

Parliament has recognised these changes over the years by passing a number of laws that give people greater freedom to handle these matters for themselves instead of laying down the law from the top. In doing so, Parliament has certainly not approved the behaviour that is now legal under them. We have made it easier for people to make choices for themselves in matters that affect their own lives. It certainly doesn't stop us, as individuals, from arguing against the abuse of the freedom people have won. Not at all. But the fact that the Churches have now distinguished between *sin* and *crime* liberated Parliament from trying to legislate on personal moral questions. Some of those who oppose this policy are really trying to close Pandora's box and get women back 'where they belong' as the nice reliable uncomplaining unpaid work force for men.

It is very difficult to run a modern community successfully and it is particularly difficult to see things changing so rapidly without getting frightened. Yet you and I know that we are aiming for unity in diversity; for letting people lead their own lives so long as they do not make life hell for everyone else.

And if women are to be allowed to lead fuller lives there will have to be a lot of changes made, and most of them will require a complete re-education of men.

To start with we have got to change the whole educational system and completely abandon the conditioning of girls in our schools designed to brainwash them into accepting a subordinate role in life. We have got to break the monopoly of good jobs enjoyed by men. We have also got to open up job opportunities and provide far more day nurseries and other facilities women need to free them for work. We must make provision for women of any age who want to upgrade their level of skill or re-enter the working population if they can't have children or have had their children or for any other reason they want or need to work. Here the second chance of adult education, or the Open University, could be so important for women.

We have got to sweep away all the discrimination against women that clutters up our statute book and tax laws, and that disfigure our working practices in industry, especially the continued denial of equal pay. We must make it clear that a person is a person, whether male or female, black or white, rich or poor. That's what Socialism is all about. And in doing so we are no more attacking femininity than we would be attacking masculinity if men were the victims of discrimination. The issue is one of freedom, and where femininity is used as an excuse to deny that freedom it must be exposed as an unfair practice.

But it would be wrong to suggest that the only thing we need is changes in the law. The Labour Party which itself has a long way to go has sometimes been too ready to believe that if you passed a bill you solved the problem. We will have to change the law and we will have to make resources available to advance women's rights. But above all we will have to change attitudes. And there are real conflicts of interest at the heart of this issue that have to be faced and resolved.

In the end the whole character of any society is dictated by its values. You can have any number of laws, but if they don't reflect the spirit of the people they are just dead letters. It is how people regard their fellow creatures and how much responsibility they feel for them that makes a healthy society, or a happy family, or a happy person.

Looked at like this the women's movement which is campaigning on such a programme can be clearly seen as a powerful ally in the struggle for human rights which, if it wins, will help to liberate men too.

We are all fighting the same battle. The things that women are fighting against – bad housing, inadequate social services, bad education, discrimination, lack of opportunity and outdated ideas – are the very same enemies that men are fighting. A victory for the one is a victory for us all. And if the women's movement looks as if it is middle class, it is because sensitivity to some advanced forms of discrimination only become apparent when basic problems of poverty have been solved.

If we could only ally ourselves to many of the new movements, what a terrific source of ideas and strength we could tap for democratic socialism in Britain.

And what better time to start than now, when so many women are utterly disillusioned with the total failure and cynicism of the Government they helped to elect last year, and when the Labour Party is now busy reconstructing itself for the task of winning power again and helping to make fundamental changes in our society that will benefit women and men alike.

We ought to make this next year 'Women's Year' in the Labour and

Trade Union Movement, allying ourselves deliberately and specifically with women in this country in their struggle for equality. And it would be a good start to give women their proper role in the Labour and Trade Union Movement where they still do not enjoy full equality. We should work more consciously with it for the fuller development of women's rights and reflect its aspirations and fight its battles and underline its political significance for those women who may not be fully aware of the fundamental changes they will need if they are to achieve real equality.

Above all, let us listen to what the Women's Movement is saying to us, because their message is a very important one.

VIII

The Honours System

This memorandum – never published before – was submitted to the Home Policy Committee of the National Executive Committee of the Labour Party in January 1964.

The Honours System remains an obvious candidate for action by a Labour Government, costing no money, involving no expenditure of Parliamentary time, but indicating unmistakably that we mean to change the outward appearances of a class-dominated society.

What's wrong with the Honours System

The present system is unsatisfactory for the following reasons.

1. *Hereditary honours* are wrong in themselves since they confer status and privilege on those who succeed to them without any regard to their merit. Where this also carries a seat in Parliament it represents a political threat to the supremacy of the Commons and hence to the programme of a Labour Government. This is not dealt with in this paper.

2. *Honours carrying a personal title.* Even though these are not hereditary they undoubtedly buttress the class structure in Britain dividing people into social categories built on the idea of superior and inferior human beings. Every society includes people who think they are better than others. What characterises Britain is that those who are supposed to be inferior have been persuaded that they actually are and accept their predetermined lot. There is no more depressing social phenomenon than this.

3. *Non-titular awards for public service.* Any society must have a system for rewarding service but what is peculiar about the British system is that awards are given on the basis of the status of the person who has performed the service rather than the quality or character of the service for which he or she is being rewarded. Thus a senior civil servant will move progressively up from say an O.B.E. to a G.B.E. as

*Extracts from a paper on "Honours and Awards" submitted to Labour Party Home Policy Sub-Committee, January, 1964.

he rises in the office while a Sub-Postmistress who bravely grapples with a murderous criminal and thus protects a bag of registered mail will get a B.E.M.

4. *Decorations for gallantry.* This same criticism also applies to most decorations. Commissioned officers get the D.S.O., D.S.C., M.C. or D.F.C., while non-commissioned officers and other ranks do not receive this order or these crosses but only plain medals – the C.G.M., D.C.M., D.S.M., M.M. or D.F.M., which rate below officers' decorations regardless of the degree of courage shown. Only the V.C., and G.C., are awarded to all ranks. There is no justification whatsoever for maintaining any distinction in honouring gallantry according to a man's rank rather than the guts he has shown.

General Objections to the Honours System

In addition to these detailed criticisms there are other major defects in the Honours System.

(a) The machinery for recommending and dispensing Honours is almost exclusively in the hands of the Establishment and the personal patronage of the Prime Minister is not infrequently abused as with Macmillan's extravagant parting gifts of a peerage and several knighthoods to his personal staff and Home's improper elevation of Wakefield to make room for Hogg.

(b) The numbers of awards given is hopelessly out of balance between civil service and military men as compared with everyone in other occupations. The low status accorded by our society to science, technology, industry and .production, not to mention the arts, is underlined and re-inforced by their skimpy ration of awards.

(c) The fiction of the Crown as the sole source of Honour is now completely out of date as is the College of Heralds with its unchanged feudal commercialism under which almost anyone can buy a coat of arms for a fee. As the distinguished constitutional lawyer, Blackstone, wrote two hundred years ago:

> "The marshalling of coat armour has fallen into the hands of certain officers called Heralds, who have allowed for lucre such falsity and confusion to creep into their records that even their common seal can no longer be received as evidence in any Court of Justice."

The plethora of Orders cooked up during the Victorian and Edwardian eras are just phoney imitations of medieval customs that have no place in a modern democratic society.

Towards a new Honours System

It would in fact be very simple to change the Honours System since no legislation whatsoever is required and the whole thing comes within the prerogative exercised on the advice of the Prime Minister or within the powers that can be exercised by resolution of either House of Parliament.

A solution along the following lines could therefore be carried through with the minimum of fuss and practically without expenditure of Parliamentary time.

1. *No more hereditary titles.* The creation of hereditary titles can be stopped by the simple process of the Prime Minister not recommending that anyone be given such a title. In addition he could advise the Crown positively not to make any more. If necessary, this advice could be buttressed by tabling an address to the Crown in the House of Commons. This was done in the Canadian Parliament by a Private Member in 1918 praying the Crown not to confer any titles, whether hereditary or not, on Canadians. The address was passed, conveyed to the King and acted upon. The practice has continued to the present day with the exception of the years 1934 and 1935 when the Bennett Government in Canada did recommend Canadians for titles. A similar address tabled in the House of Commons could be disposed of in half a day or a day.

2. *Promotion to the Lords without ennoblement.* The establishment of life peerages is a slight improvement on the old system under which Labour Prime Ministers had to create hereditary peerages. But it would be much better to find another way of putting people in the House of Lords that did not involve making them peers at all. This could be done by reviving and extending the practice of sending out Writs of Attendance to commoners and amending the Standing Orders of the Lords to permit those who receive them to participate in debates there.

Conclusion

For some people the Honours System may seem to be of small importance compared to the major economic and political changes which a Labour Government has to carry through. But politics is about social attitudes just as much as it is about exports and the balance of payments. If the Party really wants to build a New Britain it has got to show that it is interested in more than inheriting power in order to run an old Britain for its own advantage. Nothing would create more disillusionment than the feeling that a change of Government only meant that it was our turn to dish out honours to our people and exercise the powers of patronage for our own purposes.

IX

Open Government

Developing a Participating Democracy*

This speech was delivered just after the Paris uprising in May, 1968. It was an attempt to consider the political consequences of technological change and identify ways and means of extending democratic control by redistributing political power downwards and outwards.

Controversy centred around the proposal that referenda should be seriously re-considered as an instrument of democratic development.

Among other points made was the need for open government, greater access to the mass media, which has since moved into the centre of political debate, and a new look at the role of Community Action.

The speech also called for greater devolution. Finally, it urged a re-examination of the role of the Labour Party in advancing these policies and the need for greater party democracy.

For a whole generation Britain has been obsessed by its economic problems. This is inevitable. Until we get a balance of payments surplus, and growth with full employment and stable prices this must be our first concern.

But today I want to talk particularly about our political system and how it should develop. This is partly because life is not only about economics and partly because we will never ever get our economic system right, unless the political processes of decision-making are right too.

Just as technology is revolutionising industry, so it is outdating our political institutions as well. Our educational system, our system of local government, the civil service and the legal system are all now under critical examination because technology has made them obsolescent.

But what about Parliament itself? Can we assume that it will go on, in exactly the same form as we now have it, for ever and ever? I very much doubt it.

*Speech to the Annual Conference of the Welsh Council of Labour given at the Winter Gardens Pavilion, Llandudno, May 25, 1968.

Much of the present wave of anxiety, disenchantment and discontent is actually directed at the present Parliamentary structure. Many people do not think that it is responding quickly enough to the mounting pressure of events or the individual or collective aspirations of the community.

It would be foolish to assume that people will be satisfied, for much longer, with a system which confines their national political role to the marking of a ballot paper with a single cross once every five years.

People want a much greater say. That certainly explains some of the student protests against the authoritarian hierarchies in some of our universities and their sense of isolation from the problems of real life.

Much of the industrial unrest — especially in unofficial strikes — stems from worker resentment and their sense of exclusion from the decision-making process, whether by their employers or, sometimes, by their union leaders.

Frustration too provides much of the driving force for nationalism in Wales and Scotland among those who want to participate more fully in policy-making.

Even the Black Power movement is an indication that coloured immigrants are not prepared to rely entirely on white liberals to champion their cause and are determined to assume a more direct responsibility for securing their rights.

All these tendencies are indicative of a general — and inevitable — trend away from authoritarianism and towards personal responsibility. Even relatively benign and temporary authoritarianism that rests upon elected power is being challenged.

We are moving rapidly towards a situation where the pressure for the redistribution of political power will have to be faced as a major political issue. The implications of this for our system of Parliamentary democracy, and for the Labour Party which works within it, are far-reaching.

The redistribution of political power does not mean that it will all be decentralised. Indeed, in some military, industrial and technical areas, centralisation is inevitable. The existence of international organisations, large international corporations, and the acceptance of international standards of measurement and performance all remind us of our interdependence. To dream of living in splendid isolation grouped together according to historical culture is to follow a completely romantic illusion.

The redistribution of power by decentralising it is of great importance. But it is much more complicated than an exercise in geographical fragmentation. It means finding the right level for each decision and seeing that it can be taken at that level. It also means transferring much more power right back to the individual

Our Parliamentary system has changed radically over the centuries. At first it was little more than a means by which feudal landowners tamed the power of kings. In the nineteenth century the landowners and industrialists were forced to share their power by the emergence of the middle and working classes. But these people were not content to be represented by anyone other than themselves. That is how the Labour Party came to be formed.

Looking ahead we must expect equally radical changes to be made in our system of government to meet the requirements of a new generation. I am not dealing here with the demand for the ownership or control of growing sections of the economy. I am thinking of the demand for more political responsibility and power for the individual than the present system of Parliamentary democracy provides.

I am thinking of a participating democracy under which more and more people will have an opportunity to make their influence felt on decisions that affect them. If that is our objective, as I believe it must be, what special characteristics would a popular democracy have that is now lacking in the Parliamentary democracy? It seems to me that there are six areas in which change will have to be made.

The first requirement for a participating democracy involves giving people the right to know more about government and what it is doing.

Nothing buttresses the established order so effectively as secrecy. The searchlight of publicity shone on the decision-making processes of government would be the best thing that could possibly happen. For centuries this was the only power the House of Commons had. The new Ombudsman, the probing of the specialist committees and the partial lifting of the old fifty-year clamp on public records are all moves in the right direction. Opening the Commons Chamber to the television cameras would help too.

But I would be surprised if the process stopped there. In Sweden departmental and even Cabinet papers are, unless they involve national security, named individuals or commerical secrets, available for public inspection. In this country there is already considerable pressure to reveal exactly how the intricate structure of inter-departmental and Cabinet committees actually works.

The more light we throw on the workings of government the less we shall have of the obsession with personalities. While the public and the press are denied the right to know what is being discussed and how decisions are being arrived at we are bound to have columns and columns of personal tittle-tattle masquerading as serious political comment.

The second requirement for a participating democracy is that government should be allowed to know a great deal more than it does know about the community it was elected to serve.

This requirement is essential if we want to see decisions made on the basis of accurate fact. You cannot manage an advanced society, which is a vast complex inter-connecting system unless the facts are available. That is one reason why we are now strengthening the statistical services and encouraging the publication of much more data of all kinds. No economic policy can work unless its effects can be forecast accurately, or its consequences be simultaneously monitored to provide for rapid feed-back.

In the 'seventies computers will be widely used for managing the economy by means of a sophisticated process-control system not dissimilar from that now used in large automated plants. The value judgements will all be human and political but we shall have a reasonable chance of doing what we want to do and achieving what we set out to achieve. All this depends on having information available to programme the system.

If we had this information available to guide us in social policy the present arguments about selectivity would fade away. The day will come, not long hence, when taxation and social security systems will be capable of complete integration. Then we shall be able to decide politically what to do about means and needs on a personal basis, entirely free from anomalies. Each individual will then be in a position to settle his cash account with the community in an orderly way paying tax or receiving benefit according to his circumstances.

The possibilities that are opening up are not without serious dangers. Processed information about individuals could be the basis for a police state and a mass of new safeguards would be required. But on the positive side this information could and should compel government to take account of every single individual in the development of its policy. Just to exist will be to participate. We are a long way from that now.

The third requirement in a participating democracy will certainly involve the direct sharing of decision-making with the electorate as a whole.

The five-yearly cross on the ballot paper is just not going to be enough. Inevitably we shall have to look again at the objections to the holding of referenda and see if they are still valid. Public opinion polls — now studied under a microscope by every serious politician — are no substitute. The samples interviewed are only a tiny percentage of the population and even those who are questioned share no responsibility for the answers they give.

If some real issues — perhaps for a start of the kind that are now decided by private Members' Bills — were actually put out for a decision in principle by referendum the situation would be transformed. This would involve real responsibility. We might not all like the result. But at any rate by sharing responsibility an interest in public policy would be stirred in every household.

Here too technology may ultimately help us. Electronic referenda will be feasible within a generation and with it could come a considerable up-rating of the responsibility and understanding of ordinary people.

The fourth pre-requisite for a participating democracy involves a radical re-examination of the way in which our mass communications are handled.

Considering the power the mass media now exercise it is surprising how little thought has been given to the inter-relationship between them and democracy.

A Prime Minister can address the whole nation, if necessary at an hour's notice. A press tycoon can print his own article on the front pages of his own newspapers and have it read by millions.

But for ordinary people, or even for extraordinary people with minority views, the only way of answering back is to walk about with a placard and hope the press or television cameras will take a picture. Compared with the technology available to the mass media the public is still stuck with a communications system that has hardly changed since the Stone Age.

Perhaps this is one explanation for the fact that protest is edging ever closer to violence. Those with minority views – strikers, those who dislike immigrants or are immigrants, oppose the war in Vietnam or want self-government for Cornwall – have precious little access to the community through the mass media.

Minority opinions do find an outlet in books and through relatively small-circulation papers and magazines. But access to the microphone or T.V. camera is very strictly limited – both by the B.B.C. and the commercial T.V. companies.

What broadcasting now lacks is any equivalent to the publishing function. At the moment it is controlled by editors with slots to fill and a few selected minority views get in some of the slots. But three minutes of cross-examination while you are roughed up by a folk hero T.V. interviewer, or a clip of film showing a protest march on the ten o'clock news is no substitute for the right to speak.

The day may well come when independent groups of publishers would be allocated so many hours of broadcasting a month and told to help those who have something to say, to say it clearly and well, to national audiences. Unless we make a move in that direction we shall simply be denying ourselves access to a whole range of ideas – good, bad and indifferent – which we ought, as responsible citizens, to be allowed to know about through the mass media.

The fifth requirement in a participating democracy will be to build up the strength of representative organisations of all kinds so that they can be consulted and as far as possible become self-regulating.

The obvious model here is the professions which have been consulted and have regulated themselves for centuries. In the nineteenth century the trade unions emerged to represent working people and they too have been consulted and are being asked to take on new functions. The stronger the trade unions are the more functions they can assume and the more effective they will be. The government have been pouring money into private industry to rationalise and strengthen it. Now it is being suggested that public money might be put into the trade unions to help them to rationalise and become more efficient and effective.

We shall also have to look again at the role of the pressure group. This phrase still has an unpleasant ring about it. But modern democracy is now largely dependent on the pressure groups who represent real interests and are often a valuable source of ideas for future policy.

The function of government is to spot trouble before it becomes explosive, pick the brains of those who have thought the problems out and evolve from these ideas a series of practical remedies.

The more representative and professional pressure groups can be, the more government can work with them and the more responsibility can be devolved. This is one way in which power can be redistributed.

The sixth requirement for a participating democracy involves the devolution of much more responsibility to regions and localities.

This does not involve the fragmentation of society into mere geographical areas. It means identifying those decisions which ought to be taken in and by an area most affected by those decisions.

It will be an agonising and difficult task to wrench away from Whitehall powers that have been exercised there for centuries. But this sort of surgery is inevitable and the machine that will be left will be all the more efficient for being free of detail it cannot manage, leaving it to concentrate on the immensely complicated job of reaching more scientific decisions on national matters.

The pressures for changes along these lines are as inevitable as was the incoming tide that ultimately engulfed King Canute. These are among the main political issues that ,will be argued about in the 'seventies and beyond. However unwelcome this pressure may be to those who now believe that the parliamentary system of government is, as now constituted, the finest expression of man's constitutional genius, adjustments will have to be made. If they are not, discontent, expressing itself in despairing apathy or violent protest, could engulf us all in bloodshed. It is no good saying that it could never happen here. It could.

Since the Labour Party now works through the parliamentary system, changes in that system will have profound implications for us too. Moreover, like Parliament, the Labour Party is just another political institution. And like Parliament it could become just as obsolete, just as quickly.

The widening gulf between the Labour Party and those who supported it last time could well be an index of the Party's own obsolescence. Party reform now is just as important as the evolution of the parliamentary system. A participating Labour Party will involve just as many changes.

This year we elect a new General Secretary and, working with the National Executive, he will have about two years to reorganise the Party machine at Transport House and throughout the country. It will be a tremendous task. Indeed the whole function and role and character of the Party will inevitably have to change. The keynote here too will need to be participation and involvement exactly as in the case of the parliamentary system itself. For the evolution of the Labour Party is very closely bound up with the evolution of parliamentary democracy. In a world where authoritarianism of the left or right is a very real possibility, the question of whether ordinary people can govern themselves by consent is still on trial — as it always has been and always will be. Beyond parliamentary democracy as we know it we shall have to find a new popular democracy to replace it.

Politics in a Technological Age*

This interview published in the New Scientist *deals with the machinery of government rather than its political objectives and content.*

How has science influenced politics?

The idea of authority has become obsolete. We must turn to other disciplines to search for guidance on institutional procedures — to cybernetics for the control of systems management, perhaps to molecular biology for a model of the body politic, and thirdly to the theologian-psychologist, like the Bishop of Woolwich, who is saying something about Man's relationship with his fellow men. Science has made authority out of date in the sense that authority is a matter of somebody telling somebody else to do something. Surely we should be trying to create a system (which will still include a Prime Minister, a Cabinet, and a Parliament) which is more self-regulating. We should aim for a consensus, within which people accept the fact of certain

*Interview published in two parts on June 6 and June 13, 1968 by the *New Scientist, *London, the weekly review of Science and Technology. Reprinted by kind permission of the publishers.

decisions being taken at certain levels, because whatever system we evolve is seen to be logical.

Are you suggesting that a government provided with enough accurate information should automatically be capable of reaching and implementing correct political decisions?

Not entirely, but technology should allow us to achieve the effects we desire. What those goals should be must remain a political decision. For example, even if you had a government that wanted unemployment (and there are people — and obviously I wouldn't agree with them — who think our system will only work if there are a lot of people unemployed), then it could program a system to give you the number of unemployed you want. On the other hand you could program the system to produce a pattern of full employment coupled with slightly lower living standards and greater efficiency or indeed with any other objective you chose. The machines won't decide, but they will ensure that decisions taken are actually implemented.

In your Llandudno speech you insisted that people should be given more information about government's activities. How could this be done?

The point I was really trying to get at is that power and knowledge are inseparable, and that one of the ways power has been retained in the hands of those who hold it is that knowledge of the manner in which power is exercised has been confined to a very small number of people immediately surrounding the men who wield it. The whole question of secrecy must now be regarded as a major political issue. Quite significant changes are occurring already. There is the Ombudsman, who can go into a government department and say "I want to see the papers". Secondly there is the select committee procedure which is already proving singularly effective. Ministers and civil servants are now being cross-examined in detail. The balance of knowledge is now moving steadily toward the legislature, and this strengthening of Parliament means that ministers will have to justify themselves, and so it increases participation. Thirdly, I mentioned the televising of Parliament, which I think has a part to play. Once people get into the habit of asking "why shouldn't we know?", then I believe you'll find quite a number of other changes will occur.

Are there any other ways in which you think the public could be kept more continually aware of the machinery of government?

Yes. I've been Minister for 3½ years, and during that time I've taken a lot of decisions. At no time in that 3½ years have the BBC or Independent Television companies come to me and said "What are you doing? What decisions are you currently taking?" They've always confined themselves to what *they* regard as topical issues. For instance, if there's been a sonic bang, they'll come along and discuss it. But when *is* a thing topical? Is it topical when it's a *fait accompli* and there's a row about it, or is it topical when it's being decided?

Take the telephone directory affair. This change has probably been thought about in the Post Office for the past 10 years. I believe it passed across my desk at one stage. But the public only got to hear about it as a decision. If the mass media don't go to the people who exercise power and give them the opportunity – indeed, impose upon them the *duty* – to discuss the problems they are currently considering then all comment on political decisions will be too late to have any influence. The mass media should listen a little more, and interrogate a little more, and publish a little more information, and perhaps editorialize a little less.

Look at metrication, which we're now considering. The idea came to government as a proposal from industry. The government accepted it, and set up a committee which is just about to report. We shall have to reach decisions now whose effects will be felt in the '70s. Then a lot of small engineering firms who have lacked either the time, the money, the energy, or the managerial skill to prepare for the changes involved, will find that their products are obsolete, and a lot of people will lose their jobs because of steps being taken now. It's the duty of the mass media to make it clear that something which seems dull and unimportant has implications which could drastically affect people's lives. *Now's* the time the mass media should be trying to bring out all the facts, instead of waiting until everything's been decided, and then coming out with one of those famous exposés – those posthumous examinations of "why it all went wrong".

But this does mean that the mass media have got to be much better equipped to do their job of reporting. The sort of expertise which papers like *New Scientist* and *New Society* and the *Financial Times* have built up has now to be reflected in the mass media as well.

How can modern technology help a government increase its insight into the nature of the problems it is called upon to handle?

The point about this really is that the publishing of information, and the conveying of information by individuals and by non-government organisations is now also a major political issue – just as much as the question of secrecy on the official side. The reluctance of an individual, or of a firm, to reveal what he or she or it does can be an obstacle to rational government.

In the past when the government has asked for information, people have tended to say "Why should you know?", and this is a view still supported by some newspapers, on the grounds that it amounts to an invasion of privacy. If this attitude prevails, then of course government can never have the information essential for sound planning. This applies particularly in the fields of social and economic policy. The National Plan of 1966 was, I think, based on the figures of the 1958 census. This sort of thing means that economic policy is extremely hard to operate rationally, because the Chancellor of the Exchequer just doesn't have access to enough up-to-date information. I feel a bit of public education and support are required here. People have got to be persuaded that if they want governments to respond to their needs, then they themselves must be willing to make the necessary information available — indeed, they should insist that it's brought to government's attention.

Would you welcome legislation which made the feeding in to the central authority of a great deal more information a legal obligation?

This has to to be handled intelligently. The companies legislation has provided for the supply of more information about firms to the government. And there is a census coming up. Then, I hope, individuals will be prepared to say more about themselves than they have traditionally regarded as proper. We may, gradually, move to the point at which it is accepted as a really perfectly normal thing to have all sorts of personal details recorded centrally. This will probably have to be accepted as part of the process of being a citizen in a society where you would expect the government to take account of the fact that you have lost your leg, that your wife is a spastic, that you have four children, and that one of them is mentally defective. Or, in the case of a company, that its turnover is so much, that it employs so many disabled people, that the pattern of its labour force is thus, and that it requires so many graduate engineers. Thus a personalized approach to social, industrial and economic policies would be possible and would enable the politicians to produce the results which they intend.

I don't deny that information of this sort, wrongly used, could lead to a police state. This raises the question of the constitutional safeguards we should require to make such a situation acceptable — a problem we have so far never really thought about.

Your reference to the need people feel for taking a more active part in decision-making seems to have been the element in the Llandudno speech which evoked the fiercest response from critics. You were said to have advocated the replacement of the ballot box by push-button, electronic referenda. Were you in fact suggesting this?

No. What I said about the referenda was in fact this — that a single cross on the ballot paper once every five years is simply not enough. The choosing between Mr. A and Mr. B in a constituency should not represent the limits of a person's contribution to political thinking.

Particularly since, in many cases, the liberal wing of either the Labour or the Conservative party may well throw up people who in many of their outlooks are very similar. They may happen to fight in the same constituency, and then the voter has a very narrow choice. Both candidates would probably agree on a sensible racial policy, and on capital punishment, and on a good many other things.

Now, we already have public opinion polls. These are not referenda, to the extent that the people whose opinions are canvassed don't carry any responsibility for their answers. But the results are probably fairly accurate. All politicians study them, and it's absolutely right that they should. Could this sort of reference to public opinion be carried further? The immediate problem here is that so many issues are so complicated. If you made the question of raising or lowering taxes the subject of a referendum, almost everybody would opt for lower taxation. If you asked whether people did or didn't want better hospitals, they'd say they did. People aren't in a position to assess the consequences of decisions upon highly complicated, collective issues, and I don't think a referendum would be appropriate in such cases. But there are some issues which might be suitable.

It's been claimed that you'd never produce any liberal legislation if the public had its way, and I've thought about this very carefully in respect of capital punishment which I'm very much against, although the polls have always shown a majority in its favour. But I argue like this: over 40 years, on every free vote, the House of Commons has always voted for the abolition of capital punishment. Why is this? I believe it's because the people who have the responsibility of deciding whether a man lives or dies disapprove of hanging because it is brutalizing, because of the risk of error, and so on. The public has never been asked to be responsible for this decision. My guess is that a first referendum on this issue would give similar results to the public opinion polls, but the next time a man was hanged, everyone who had voted would be sitting there at their breakfast tables feeling a sense of responsibility. And whenever there was one of those cases involving doubt, the argument about hanging would be released in every household. I've no reason to believe that ordinary people, after they'd reflected on the question, in the full light of their own responsibility, wouldn't reach the same conclusions as the House of Commons. I couldn't accept the view that the public at large is more ignorant, or less responsible, than Members of Parliament.

The technical means for undertaking referenda without disrupting people's daily routines are going to be available quite soon. Homes will be connected to central points for the supply of colour television programmes, telephone channels, and for the monitoring of their electricity meters. There will be a two-way link — in and out. Almost

211

certainly market research people will use it. When people suddenly wake up to the fact that they have an instrument for answering back in their hands, don't you think they'll want to use it? I think they will. Then we're going to have to decide whether to let them.

Would you feel bound to act on the results of a referendum? Suppose, for example, 80 per cent of the people voted for the reintroduction of capital punishment, would you feel able to go against that?

There's one way a referendum could be made to play a part within our present system. When both Houses have passed a bill, it goes to Royal Assent, but as you know, nowadays Royal Assent is a formality. Supposing that in certain cases a bill went to popular assent. It would be debated and considered in Parliament, but throughout the whole proceedings the public would know that in the end it would have the last word. If such a system was applied to legislation on such matters as divorce or abortion, the sense of involvement would be considerable. And because the bill's final fate did depend upon popular assent, this would focus the attention of the House much more on what the public thought — and vice versa. I think it would be up to the government to decide when an issue should be out to the people — but having made that decision, then the government must be prepared to abide by the result.

I'm really talking about something that could happen within the next 10 or 15 years. I'm not suggesting that a referendum is the answer to any of our current problems.

You suggested at Llandudno that bodies which at present have no opportunity for putting their views before the public, except by demonstrating and waving placards, could perhaps have radio and television time set aside for them. How could this be done?

I used to have discussions with the BBC about programmes concerning the work of the United Nations. At that time the UN had a TV series describing its work week by week. This was shown on a number of American stations and other stations abroad, and I used to ask the BBC why it didn't screen them. I was told that viewers would be more interested by the sight of a BBC correspondent reporting on the activities of the UN, (inevitably from the British point of view) pictured against the background of the UN building, and that this was being done week after week. But in fact the British public was being denied a view of the UN as the UN saw itself. Instead it was getting a picture of the UN through the eyes of a British editor. We already have a model for the manner in which information can be presented by its originators, and without passing through an editorial filter. There are the party political broadcasts. They aren't popular, but it has been recognized that the political parties have the right to address the nation from time to time on what they think is important. The BBC puts its facilities at our disposal and makes producers available, exactly as a publisher would. But it is not responsible for what we say. Then there are the Reith Lectures. You don't get Robin Day to talk to Professor Galbraith. You say to Galbraith "We think you have something to say, and over the course of a few weeks we will help you to say it".

There are many groups like the Road Research Laboratory, the British Medical Association, the Consumers' Association and trade unions – minority opinions which have a right to an airing. They would doubtless have a minority audience appeal, but I think the mass media owe us the opportunity of access to the views of such people. Perhaps a programme would attract no more than a quarter of a million viewers – but that is vastly bigger than the circulation of the great majority of serious books.

Are you satisfied with the degree to which scientists and engineers are playing a part in the running of the nation's business?

Well, my general criticism of scientists and engineers is that they are far too limited in their interests. Too many of them (not all of them) regard themselves as being specialists, and they simply don't think of the broader consequences of their special activities. They sometimes grumble when they're not consulted – but then, who really wants to consult a man who is a self-condemned specialist? When you talk to a man who's invented a new process, you don't just want to hear about the process – you want to know what he thinks this will do to the shape of the industry and to the pattern of employment in the places where his process is likely to be used.

We should get an awful lot more out of the scientific community if its members learned to interrelate their special understandings with the other aspects of the contemporary scene. Mind you, I don't believe that just because a man is a scientist or an engineer, he should automatically command a position of authority. He has to work to get his views accepted – just like anybody else. At the moment far too few scientists and technologists feel the need for any such effort. As a result the community is losing access to the thinking of a lot of people who are highly skilled in thinking but who just don't think broadly enough.

At the other extreme you have the opinion-formers – the editors and the people who run the mass media – who are painfully ignorant of the technological changes which are going on. And this is where *New Scientist* plays such a notable role. It bridges this gap. But it's terrifying to me to read all the articles written by liberal arts graduates in the newspapers about, say, computers – "computers are taking over", and so on. Most people haven't, still, the first ideas, not only how they

213

work, but what they are doing. This is a very frightening and peculiarly British characteristic, which I believe is a product of our educational system.

Going back to the scientists, I can't believe that it's more difficult for them to appreciate the political implications of their work, than it is for the politicians to attempt – as they must – an assessment of the impact science and technology are having on society.

Over the past two years I've been intensely interested to find the double standard of reporting in the Press about my department. The specialist press, for example, *New Scientist*, has written about us in a highly intelligent fashion, but usually without a political content. It has never for example seen our ship-building policy as having any relationship to development areas. It has just written about ship building. The ship-building programme has not been seen as a part of the process of modernizing British industry. On the other hand the Lobby Correspondents – who are the political journalists – have written very little about us at all, because they have thought of us as a department of gadgeteers. They have never seen that the importance of technology for Britain lies in its power to improve our economic performance.

Have you a message for the scientists and technologists of this country?

Yes. Have the courage, even the effrontery to think and talk about the wider questions that go beyond the field in which they are specialists. As a Minister of Technology without engineering or scientific training, I have had to try to do exactly this. The experience has changed my view of society. Similarly, the engineer and scientist broadening his vision to encompass the politics he is himself reshaping could well change his view, not least of his own role. That would be the best thing that could possibly happen for all of us.

The Barrier of Secrecy*

This article in Tribune *considered the effect of the Official Secrets Act in isolating Labour Ministers from Labour MP's. It recommended a far greater identification of back-bench government supporters with the work of departments. Since then the appointment of political advisers to Labour Ministers has been accepted, though they are not MP's.*

Now that we are halfway through this Parliament, the time has come for serious thinking about future policy. This policy if it is to be any good, has got to be hammered out *in public.* The issues on which we want to fight can only be made public issues by actually encouraging a national debate on them.

Ministers must be able to take part in that debate. The views which I put forward recently on the need for a popular democracy were my own personal views, and were accepted as being compatible with the principle of collective responsibility. Cabinet responsibility relates to what a Cabinet has done, is doing or is seriously thinking of doing. It does not limit the right to think aloud about long-term future policy. That is a right we all have in the party whether we are Ministers or ward secretaries.

If it is important to increase participation in government, it must be equally important to make participation real, inside the Parliamentary Labour Party. How can we harness the enormous reserves of talent, ability and idealism which exists among Labour MPs to the causes we have elected to serve?

There they are — about 350 of them — from all three wings of the movement, every part of the country, from a cross-section of different occupations and representing every shade of party opinion. Do we make full use of them? Of course we don't.

Take first the Ministers who are MP's — about 90 of them — working away in their Departments. These Ministries are huge and the problems with which they have to deal are immensely complex.

How can Labour MP's be used to help exercise the power which the party was elected to exercise? And how can Ministers be kept more closely in touch with party opinion, with those outside who have something to contribute, and with the nation as a whole? A real participating democracy requires these things to be done.

At the moment many back-bench Labour MPs feel that their talents are not used to the full. Only those who have been Government backbenchers can really know the frustrations which are involved. However much you want to help to make the Government succeed there is relatively little you can do. The organisers of Government

*Article in *Tribune,* June 14, 1968. Reprinted by kind permission of *Tribune.*

business in the Commons need your support in the lobbies, but it is hard to find other ways of tapping your ideas.

All sorts of solutions have been attempted. There are specialist groups of Labour MP's studying problems. They invite Ministers to speak to them and listen to their views. Now we have the very useful Parliamentary Specialist Select Committees; and there is always Question Time. But this is just not enough.

Why cannot all Labour MPs be more directly engaged in the work of Ministries? The question is worth posing because it highlights the main obstacle to the participation of Labour MPs in the business of government.

That obstacle is secrecy. The tight, close veil of secrecy which surrounds all government business divides Labour MPs into two groups – Ministers who know and backbenchers who don't. Knowledge is power and without inside knowledge Government supporters are left in the cold.

What would happen if you broke down that barrier of secrecy and let every Minister recruit from the back benches a team of six or seven MPs, with desks in his Department and access to departmental papers? I am not suggesting that they should be paid anything, other than their present Parliamentary salary, or that they should share in collective Ministerial responsibility. That would not be wise or practicable.

But they would be available to advise the Minister, to progress chase for him, to maintain his links with the outside world of advice, to think ahead, to work with Transport House on future policy. They could also set up a political network linking Ministers to each other to run in parallel with the superbly efficient official network that links Departments to each other. They could speak authoritatively in the country about the work of the Department and think aloud about how that work might develop. They would be absolutely invaluable. The political pulse in every Department would quicken and the huge and efficient Civil Service machine would be energised and activated in a way that is now quite impossible.

Ex-Ministers, whose talents all too often now go to waste when they retire would be available to help too, and, freed from the responsibilities of office, would be able to draw on their experience to propose fundamental reforms which, when they were in office, they did not have enough time to think out or carry through. Labour Peers could also be used in exactly the same way and brought into the Departments with all their knowledge and experience.

If such a scheme has so many apparent merits, what are the difficulties and dangers? First, it would be argued that the independence of backbench MPs would be undermined. But this would only be true if collective Cabinet responsibility were wrongly extended

216

to them. If no more were expected of them than is now expected from a Parliamentary Private Secretary, no problem would arise.

Secondly, it will be said that the power of patronage would be dangerously increased. But Ministers would each pick their own team and such patronage would be spread among 25 Departmental Ministers – and would not involve any salary. Those who took it on would just work a bit harder.

Thirdly, it might be said that this is a subtle plan to stop backbench revolts against unpopular Government policies. Insofar as any backbench revolts now stem from the ignorance of the facts (in which backbenchers are now kept by the present system) the wider spread of knowledge would diminish them. And insofar as sheer frustration drives MPs into revolt, this might diminish too. But for revolts that stem from genuine disagreements, it would make no difference. Ministers would be collectively responsible, but their MP teams would enjoy exactly the freedom which now belongs to them, under the new Parliamentary Labour Party code of conduct.

Some backbenchers might not join these Ministerial teams, either because no Minister invited them to join, or because they decided not to accept an invitation to do so.

A reform of this kind would increase the effective participation of Ministers by sharing some of their load of work with others and would increase the participation of backbenchers by allowing them to take part in a way that is just not now possible. But it would also have very important secondary effects. Parliamentary candidatures would be sought much more eagerly by a whole host of people who, although their talent is needed in Parliament, are not now attracted by the thought of life on the back benches. And because the competition would be keener, the quality would rise.

This proposal is in some ways a modest one. It could be argued that it amounts to no more than that every Minister should be allowed to appoint a number of Parliamentary Private Secretaries instead of one as is now customary; and that Parliamentary Private Secretaries should be allowed the same access to departmental documents as is now extended to Civil Service Private Secretaries – principals, assistant principals and executive officers – ending the present inequality of access.

But if it were done the balance of power in government would shift. The effectiveness of Ministers would rise and the role of backbenchers would increase. The machinery of government would move more rapidly in response to the political impulse that each new Parliament brings to Whitehall fresh from the polls. A Labour Government, able to call on all this ability and enthusiasm, might then have a far better chance of doing those things it was elected to do.

These are just my personal reflections committing no one but myself.

But more participation in Parliament should be one of the issues on which we need further debate, as we begin the task of preparing our next election manifesto.

Liberating the Lobby*

This article reviewing a book on the work of lobby correspondents extended the argument about government secrecy to cover the role of Parliamentary commentators.

GUIDANCE TO MINISTERS ABOUT RELATIONS WITH THE PRESS

'On the record'

For use as an attributable quotation.

'Not for attribution'

The material given is freely usable, but source of the information must be protected. This means protected for all time and not just until the source is accidentally or deliberately revealed by one newspaper.

'Not to be used'

This means that the information given is for the personal background benefit of the correspondents concerned and is not for publication in any form. Correspondents should be allowed to pass on this information to their Editors, but in a strictly confidential context and only when it is really necessary.

One of the most closely guarded secrets in the British system of Government is the exact nature of the relationship between politicians and the small select group of correspondents who write about them. This relationship which rotates around what is called the Lobby consists of a complex pattern of contacts with its own rules linking two groups each needing the other. Indeed, the very fact of their mutual dependence sets its own limits on what each wishes to disclose.

Ministers and MPs need the Lobby to release information about what they are doing and why and when and how in the hope that this will help them to achieve their objectives. The Lobby correspondents

*Article in *The Sunday Times*, September 6, 1970. Reprinted by kind permission of *The Sunday Times*.

interpret what is happening in Westminster to the wider public, assess the achievements, failures and motives of the politicians. The whole process is stabilised and sustained by the rock-solid cement of common interest.

Jeremy Tunstall, in his new book,[1] has begun to open up the system for public examination. It is a first-rate piece of reporting in the Bagehot tradition, written by an academic with the help of a grant. He describes the history of the Lobby and discloses the findings of a survey he undertook of its leading members, how they work and what their relations are with their editors, Fleet Street colleagues, civil servants and the politicians. He even achieves his own scoop by publishing, for the first time, the Lobby rules. The least I can do is to reciprocate by publishing the guidance given to Ministers.

If there is one weakness it is that the whole picture is presented through the eyes of the Lobby, leaving out the view of the system as it appears to the politician and even more importantly to those for whom the Lobby are writing.

If a global view is taken it would better reflect the nature of the political system it reports, and of which it forms an integral part, and would in its turn throw a lot more light on the working of parliamentary government itself.

In one sense the Lobby and the politician are allies and both are perhaps to blame for sharing the same obsession with secrecy – though the Lobby is a great deal more successful in maintaining it. Both would defend secrecy on the grounds of convenience, because it helps to lubricate necessary indiscretions and because, in their hearts both sides suspect – I think wrongly – that the public wouldn't really understand it if they knew too much about what was going on behind the scenes.

Secondly, both the Lobby and the politician tend to concentrate their attention too much on to the parliamentary arena to the exclusion of some of the new realities of modern politics which lie outside. In other words might not the very idea of the Lobby – that is the ante-chamber to the national debating chamber – be rather an old-fashioned concept artificially restricting the major political commentators of each generation from reporting the new realities with which they are superbly well equipped to deal?

One such new reality is the huge Government Machine scattered round in Whitehall and manned by men of enormous ability, power and influence whose names are just not known to the public at all. Ministers spend most of their working lives listening to them, arguing with them, persuading or being persuaded; and the civil servants themselves, conscious of their roles as custodians of a continuing tradition of

---

1. *The Westminster Lobby Correspondents*, by Jeremy Tunstall, published by Routledge and Kegan Paul.

policy, are engaged together inter-departmentally in a similarly intimate relationship analysing problems, processing information, presenting and evaluating alternatives.

This is the very stuff of Government but very little is known about it. The secretiveness of successive Governments is partly to blame but the newspapers must share some of the responsibility for restricting their political correspondents too tightly to Parliament, leaving the specialist correspondent to cover the rest, thus missing out on some of the most interesting political stories. If the real workings of Government were revealed politics might look less like the old-fashioned gladiatorial contest – which it so often appears to be – and more like the complex interaction of factors operating within a system that it is. I remember that the major story of the gas centrifuge (which has transformed methods of enriching uranium) was covered in great detail by the science correspondents completely non-politically. It had to wait for nearly a year before it was seen to be what it really was – a diplomatic and political development of great significance.

We tried to get round the problem of fragmentation when I was Minister of Technology by holding some experimental seminars to which we invited all the correspondents from a single newspaper, instead of the usual Press Conference with the correspondents specialising in one field from all the newspapers. It was very interesting to hear the argument about policy breaking out on the other side of the table as the Air correspondent began debating with the City correspondent about the viability of some aero-space project or the Lobby correspondent disagreeing with his colleague covering science about the desirability of some new development. Thus, for the first time, the very same inter-connections which were creating policy within Mintech were seen as a whole by journalists who had previously looked at them segmentally to see whether or not they fell within the area of their specialised responsibility.

This same argument for breaking down the barriers of specialisation in journalism applies even more widely. Whereas the Lobby will follow MPs to their annual party conferences, or travel with the Prime Minister to an important Summit they are not there when Henry Ford comes to talk about his future investment policy to build motor cars or when a group of shop stewards meet in a components factory to reach a decision that will stop all motor car production.

In the space of a single generation the politicians have been stretched – almost to breaking point – by the need to study and work over an area that may range from an international conference on wave-length allocations to a street demonstration that blocks a new motorway; from the problems of world-wide economic management to the political implications of a new scientific discovery.

The sheer necessity of extending themselves has led to all sorts of institutional improvisations by politicians to help them to cope with their expanded responsibilities. The mass media have been slower to adapt their own machinery for reporting what has happened. For wherever politicians now have to go to work the political correspondents should be allowed and encouraged to follow them. If politics sometimes looks narrow and stylised it is partly because politicians and the Lobby alike are finding the problems of adaptation so difficult.

Perhaps we need a Lobby Liberation Movement to free some of Britain's most distinguished journalists from the restrictions under which they suffer so that they can follow the whole story of the nation's affairs more easily than can be done from the cramped accomodation offered to them by the Serjeant-at-Arms.

The Politician Today*

This speech was delivered to an international conference of political consultants – advertising and public relations firms which run political campaigns – in December 1970.

It attempted a job specification for a politician in a democracy in which the public are increasingly concerned with issues and are disenchanted with the hero worship that political PR techniques are directed to sustain. It also argued the case for a strategy of change from below, and the necessity for the Labour Party to reconstruct itself to make this possible.

The new citizen of today is not prepared to leave it to Them – in Government – any more than he is in the Church, in Industry, in the Trade Unions, in the Universities, or in local communities. Strange as it may seem, responsibility can only be exercised by those who are given responsibility, and the only discipline that people will accept is the discipline which they impose upon themselves. They see politics more and more in terms of issues and less and less in terms of selecting a "hero-king" who will lead them out of the wilderness and into the promised land . . . .

I do not, therefore, believe that any amount of public relations effort, designed to package a modern political hero to be presented to the public as a saviour, will really greatly help . . . .

*Extract from a speech to the Third Annual Conference of the International Association of Political Consultants at the Royal Garden Hotel, London, December 15, 1970.

. . . Instead of seeing politics as a perpetual climb up the ladder of power, culminating in the exercise of ministerial authority, I see the role of a politician in quite a new scenario.

First he must be a representative, maintaining contact not just with his party colleagues but with the thousands of organisations that have come into being as an expression of the human response to the pressures on us all from technical and industrial change.

Second, he must be an advisor, helping people to realise their full potential and analysing and connecting the issues which concern them so that society does not fragment and disintegrate into the pushing and shoving of rival interests.

Third, he must be an educator who explains what is happening — and why — so that people are not frightened because they do not understand and thus fall into protest or apathy or demand that others be disciplined to protect their own interests.

Fourth, a politician is a legislator and an administrator — working in partnership to lubricate the processes of change by altering the ground rules and controlling the bureaucracies and humanising the actual business of running a modern state.

Fifth, a politician must recognise that the only real instrument that he has for changing a society is the instrument of persuasion and that is winning the hearts and minds of his fellow countrymen that matters more even than winning elections or winning votes in Parliament or staging, and then winning, confrontations between "goodies" and "baddies" at home or abroad.

Looking back over a hundred years of British Parliamentary democracy and seeing why great changes occur, I have become convinced that these were not the products of enlightened leaders but of the pressure of people from below, who have worked through the agency of political leaders, whose greatest quality may well have been their realism.

We would never have had the vote in Britain for men — and certainly not for women — if it had not been demanded and conceded.

We should never have had state education, the welfare state, the National Health Service, or many of the other civilised developments of which we are proud if the demands for these things had not bubbled up from below.

And the present vigorous campaigns against pollution, for a better quality of life and for a greater respect for ecology, were not thought up by inspired ministers or far-sighted civil servants. They came from the people and we are now conceding what they want.

The danger of parliamentary democracy — if it is presented as if it were nothing more than the achievement of an elected monarchy — is that it retains the arrogance of the benevolent despot and seeks to cloak the elected M.P. with something of the Divine Right once reserved for royal personages. At its worst, it still keeps the citizen at arm's length from the business of decision-making and bullies him into believing that the ballot box is the last word in participation.

However attractive this idea may be, it won't do because it won't work any more. The game is up and we have to think the whole thing out again.

I have certainly not come here with a crystal ball with which to help me peer into the future of democratic politics. Certainly the crystal balls which were used in the last election were well and truly smashed when the results were announced.

But if, as I believe, the policies of the present Government fail to solve the problems which confront us, people will not turn back to Labour unless we have thought through this change which I have been trying to describe, and set the political process into a wider perspective that takes account of the bigger role which the people themselves want to play.

We shall have to extend our representative function so as to bring ourselves into a more creative relationship with many organisations that stand outside our membership but are working for objectives that are compatible with our own.

We shall have to offer ourselves in our new consultant role showing people how it can be done rather than seeking to convince them that if they vote for us their problems are over.

We shall have to accelerate the processes of change so that we are not encumbered by the institutional baggage carried from the past, and we shall have to recognise the role of persuasion as the main instrument of change.

The future of democracy is sometimes thought to be in the balance with some pessimists predicting either a return to authoritarianism or a soft squishy slide into anarchy or perhaps both, in either order, the one succeeding the other.

No democrat can be other than a statutory optimist, believing that it is possible for people to govern themselves and survive the stresses that now mount so dangerously. But if this statutory optimism is not to be mere day-dreaming, it must involve reconnecting the political system to the immensely powerful new centres of human energy that now exist.

The future will not be made by the scientists, the ambitious politicians – with or without the help of political consultants – or by the introduction of modern managerial methods into the great departments of state.

It will be made by the people themselves and shaped by the structure of values to which they subscribe. Anyone who wishes to contribute to that future has therefore got to get into that dialogue and listen and learn and argue and convert. There is no short cut.

All these things were happening, just under the surface, while the last Labour Government was at work. But we were so busy with the business of government that we somehow disconnected ourselves, pulled the plugs out and then were a little surprised to find that our batteries weren't being recharged.

We didn't lose because people didn't know what we had done, but because we seemed to have crossed to the other side of the we/they frontier and we didn't find time to explain what was happening. People did get frightened.

They were frightened of long-haired students and black-faced immigrants and workers on strike and foreigners and decimalisation and metrication and they looked for the nice, safe, familiar traditional characteristics that were so skilfully offered to them by Mr. Heath and his colleagues.

But we would be foolish to suppose that people will be for ever satisfied with that particular brand of pendulum politics, swinging alternative teams in and out of office. More people want to get in on the act and I see it as our business so to reconstruct the Labour Party that a Labour Government will never *rule* again but will try to create the conditions under which it is able to act as the natural partner of a people, who really mean something more than we thought they did, when they ask for self-government.

Controlling Science*

This lecture was delivered at a Collegium at Northwestern University in Chicago on April 13 1971.

It attempts an analysis of the effects of technical change in centralising and decentralising power at one and the same time and seeks to identify some of the demands now coming from below: for sufficiency; greater equality; educational reform; and democratic control.

It ends by calls for a redistribution of political power to spread responsibility in an effort to restore human control over the huge organisations that technical change has created, and which now tend to dominate us.

The structure of government within the nation state, as now organized, is unlikely to survive in its present form. It evolved in

*Paper given to a Northwestern University Symposium on "The Control of Science for Civil Needs" and reproduced in the *Bulletin of the Atomic Scientists,* December, 1971.

response to circumstances very different from those that now exist and, as is evident, it is proving itself incapable of coping adequately with the amount of power that mankind now has at its disposal. It is both too small to exercise really effective human control over the destiny of its own citizens in a tiny and dangerous world; and it is too big and too clumsy an instrument to deal with the rapidly changing and diverse needs and values of people in the communities where they live and work.

This is the inescapable conclusion to which one is driven by even the most superficial examination of the impact of the technological revolution through which we are passing.

This process of political obsolescence has been going on for a long time; and it began to accelerate with the development of weapons systems that extended the range of warfare beyond the heavy artillery and relatively light and slow aircraft which were in use up until World War II. With the advent of nuclear weapons and intercontinental missiles, the nation state was forced to surrender its basic claim on the allegiance of its people – namely, that it served as a necessary and effective instrument for defending its citizens against assaults from the outside. Modern weapons led to the move towards the bloc system of defence which represents, even for the senior partners in each bloc, a permanent erosion of their national independence and sovereignty. And it was recognized at about the same time that the ultimate logic of modern weaponry required the establishment of some world organisation like the United Nations, with the implication that one day it would develop into an embryonic world government, however long it took to reach that state. Meanwhile the paralysis of the super-powers when they try to use their military arsenals is only too apparent.

But it is not only the emergence of external forces that have brought into question the credentials of the nation state. Technology has had an equally dramatic impact on the lives of the citizens, in both less developed and highly developed societies. Their experience of modern life, amplified by the mass media, rendered more intelligible by improved education and made progressively more vulnerable and fragile by the interdependence that is inseparable from economic development, has led to demands being pressed from below which the modern state with a centralized power structure may be incapable of meeting quickly enough to avert intolerable strain, and possibly violent upheaval. Thus the second claim of the nation state that it can effectively protect a society against the risk of internal disorder or disintegration is also in doubt. Looking around the world the stresses in many countries can be seen to be dangerously above the safety level.

Nor is it only in terms of military or civil insecurity that the nation state has found itself on the defensive. Industrial development –

especially by the multi-national corporations — far exceeds the scale of operation of industry a generation ago, and the power of these new companies, not to mention their rate of growth, now exceeds that of many nation states. Governments of even quite advanced societies can no longer, therefore, claim to be wholly effective in safeguarding the interests of their citizens against possibly harmful decisions taken by these firms.

Moreover instantaneous world-wide communications available on more and more television channels means that the nation state can no longer guarantee to erect on its frontiers effective censorship that filters out unacceptable foreign ideas and preserves the sort of broad identity of views, culture and outlook that could be said to represent its way of life as embodied in the consensus on which its society worked.

The death-throes of the self-contained nation may last for a very long time, but the process of transformation in the constitutional structure of society is as inevitable for the nation state as it is for any firm which finds technological change destroying its old management structure and requiring it to adapt itself accordingly.

The emergence of international managements controlling military and industrial power has now virtually ousted the shareholder or stockholder as a centre of power and has simultaneously stimulated greater demand for popular power.

In this process the role of science in society has come to occupy a central ground of argument between the new bureaucracies that see it as an agent for promoting their own aims and purposes, and people who increasingly see science both as a threat to their survival and, if properly used, as one of the key instruments for solving the problems that press on them most directly. Thus science has been drawn out of the academic atmosphere from which it drew its inspiration and original funding, and into the vortex of political controversy.

Science as an instrument for political domination has given birth to the military-industrial complex which is immensely powerful in both the communist and noncommunist worlds. Enormous sums of money are made available from general taxation to develop new weapons systems which it is claimed will preserve a favourable power balance for those nations that are ready to pay the bill and spare the necessary qualified manpower.

But meanwhile, from below, more and more voices are being raised to divert these same resources to meet the needs of development and to improve living conditions. It is not just modern war with its inevitable killing that is becoming unacceptable, but the growing conviction that war-making absorbs money and skill on such a scale that, were it to be turned to constructive purposes, the causes of many conflicts that lead to war might be eliminated.

The same tug of war is evident in civil industrial developments. The bureaucracies which govern large firms (sometimes supported by governments) are forever seeking to maximize their return on capital invested by using science to make more sophisticated products and by employing complex techniques of persuasion to create a demand for them; at the same time, the public is beginning to question the whole process. First, they are concerned with the side effects that may follow from the unchecked economic growth that has up to now been regarded as an unmixed blessing. Second, they are beginning to wonder whether there are not other needs to be met than those which express themselves through market forces. The conflict between private and public transport in major cities is one example, and the whole structure of educational provision with its tremendous concentration on graduate and post-graduate work is another.

National governments are caught between these two formidable forces which are pulling in opposite directions. They know — because it is their business to know — that large and efficient managements will be required if the delicate balance in *any* world system is to be maintained. To this extent they are necessarily in close and continuing contact with the big organizations concerned.

At the same time, especially in societies where the vote has been granted, national politicians are painfully aware of the pressures coming from their electorates conveying, however, imperfectly, the problems and aspirations of ordinary citizens.

National governments are thus the fuse box connecting two conflicting realities. A great deal of current passes through that fuse box, and the heat is intense. If it blows, there could be a total blackout and a total breakdown. President Truman once said: "If you don't like the heat, get out of the kitchen." But somebody has to stay in the kitchen at least until we can find a cooler way to cook.

Until recent years the centralized bureaucracies seemed to be having it all their own way. They generated technology, and controlled the use to which technology was put. The public was so astonished by the new scientific miracles and felt so humble in the presence of the experts in science and technology who master-minded these achievements that they hardly questioned the purposes to which this power was being put. Henry Ford was seen as a man who had put technology at the service of man. Military scientists were seen as key figures through whom security could be achieved and our enemies vanquished. Technical decisions were uncritically accepted as lying outside the capabilities of ordinary people to question and they stood back while the experts decided. Thus it was that President Kennedy's historic decision to put an American on the Moon by 1970, or the Anglo-French Treaty to build the supersonic airliner, were accepted without public debate. Both these ventures were

227

seen as glorious examples of man's freedom deriving from his new-found power to control nature.

But once freedom — in this case scientific freedom — had been won, people started to question how that freedom should be used. It may take a highly skilled chemist to develop a contraceptive pill or a brilliant engineer to develop a new system of communication. But the use to which either is put involves the application of a scale of values which it is entirely within the capability of everybody and anybody to apply for himself. The problems of the control of technology in a scientifically permissive society can therefore be seen to be no more complex than any other value judgment which democratic societies now accept and that electors and voters are qualified to take.

Indeed, there is now growing evidence that more and more people are quite independently coming to the same conclusion and this is expressing itself in more forceful demands from below. These demands are not new ones, but what is significant about them is that for the first time the technology capable of satisfying them now exists.

Take first the demand for sufficiency from those who are still experiencing poverty — both the poor in developed societies and the even greater number of poor in societies that have not developed. These people are different from their forefathers in that they know that other people have escaped from poverty and that the technology that made escape possible is available to them. It is one thing to be poor when there is no choice, but it is another to accept what may appear to be an unnecessary poverty. This is the cause of the revolution of rising expectations in both developing and developed socieites. As living standards rise expectations seem to keep well ahead of them and produce the curious phenomenon of levels of personal dissatisfaction rising in parallel with affluence.

The demand for greater equality is also gathering force, similarly fanned by the mass media. This is not merely a demand for greater economic equality, but also for racial and sexual equality which sees in discrimination an entrenchment of unacceptable privilege and a perpetuation of a more fundamental oppression. The use of resources including scientific resources to secure greater equality is highly relevant, especially in the educational field.

The worldwide demand for educational reform touches directly on the control of science. More and more people are becoming sceptical of the established objective of education to educate elites, including scientific elites. Even if looked at from a purely practical point of view it would appear that the main barriers to human advance lie more in our failure to apply well-established techniques than in our tardiness in evolving new ones. For example, millions more lives could be saved by raising the general level of simple health services than by pouring millions of pounds or dollars into perfecting heart transplants or other sophisticated surgical operations. There is even a curious convergence of view between a community which doesn't quite know how to employ the many PhDs emerging from graduate schools, heavy with honours but short of experience, and the students who everywhere are discontented because their studies are so academic and appear to lack "relevance." This feeling is shared on both sides of the Iron Curtain and there are more similarities between modern thinking on this in China and the United States than there are between the old-school academic establishments in both these countries and the communities they are supposed to serve. Educational bureacuracies are already finding themselves on the firing line along with the military-industrial complex as this pressure begins to build up.

The demand for greater popular power — or participation as it now tends to be called — follows from the demands described above. Where the franchise has not yet been won, it is being demanded; and where it has been achieved, there is a mounting pressure for further democratisation of decision-making.

This pressure is not really new at all. It is as old as political philosophy itself, out what is new is that it is being extended far beyond the simple demands of the Founding Fathers of the American Republic or the French Revolution, or the modest advocates of universal adult suffrage. More and more people are coming to suspect that democracy has slipped through their fingers while they were busy watching science proving its apparently limitless capability.

Now, all of a sudden, people have awakened to the fact that science and technology are just the latest expression of power and that those who control them have become the new bosses, exactly as the feudal landlords who owned the land, or the capitalist pioneers who owned the factories, became the bosses of earlier generations. Ordinary people will not now be satisfied until they have got their hands on this power and have turned it to meet their needs.

This may sound like a very revolutionary doctrine, and so indeed it is. But once we understand what is happening, it is no more frightening than the demand for power that emerged in the past as a popular clamour for political democracy.

What we lack are the institutions capable of realizing that demand in today's world, and making it effective. It must necessarily lead to the strengthening of international and supranational institutions big enough to encompass the totality of man's needs as he gradually learns that brotherhood has moved from a moral aspiration to an essential prerequisite of survival. We are mainly short on imagination bold enough to extend our sense of responsibility to embrace the area of our common interest. This imaginative leap is difficult for the old and the middle-aged, but it comes quite naturally to the young. Their view of the Spaceship Earth with its people living closely together will in time replace the distortions of Mercator's flat projection showing every country highly coloured within its political frontiers – just as Galileo's view of the universe replaced the flat concept of the Ptolemaic astronomers.

Nationally, the demand will express itself in more subtle ways. The pressure for open government which reveals the choices before they are made will intensify. Decisions affecting the use of science and technology, whether by governments, corporations or universities, will become increasingly the subject of critical scrutiny, as has been shown most vividly by the recent economic and environmental debates and decisions on the development of the supersonic transport. People may still argue as to whether the decision was right or wrong, but no one can doubt that it was taken openly and that the decisive pressure came from below in sufficient strength to overturn the wishes of an Administration and the aerospace industry, both of which wanted to go ahead.

Similarly, the environmental pressures that have built up over recent years can be seen as having a political significance greater even than the actual cause which the environmentalists espoused. They can be seen as a direct political demand under the classification of technology assessment aimed at securing a proper consideration of the consequences of all decisions before they are reached, so that the side effects can be taken into account at the time of the basic decision. This is a move to better and more democratic decision-making and if it can be made a permanent feature of political life, it will be far more important even than the improvement of the environment. It may, in fact, serve to check the wildest environmentalists who are now pressing for unrealistic policies which could have unexpected industrial and human side effects.

But the pressure for democratisation will not stop there. It is bound to extend to the democratisation of industrial power, through workers' control, educational power and the power of the mass media which, by their control of information output, can play a decisive part in shaping society.

We are presently so conscious of the centralizing forces that derive from technological change and of the huge new and powerful bureaucracies that they have created that many people tend to be despondent, to believe that ordinary human influences are quite powerless and the cause of democracy is irretrievably lost as man surrenders to the new power centres. The emergence of countervailing power from the grass roots is less easy to recognize. It is dispersed so widely, its exercise is so uncertain, and the time scale of its successes is so long that many people do not believe it really exists. At the moment it may be only a potential power, but its potentiality is far greater than most people realize. We have not yet learned to organize ourselves to use the power that has fallen into our hands because we are not fully aware of it and because it requires us to think about our system of government in quite a different way.

The study of civics or political institutions as most of us learned about them at school, or through the mass media, always focuses upon the formal structure of the nation state. We are told how accountability has been secured by freedom of speech and the vote. But even this interpretation stresses what our leaders do and say. Policy and changes of policy are presented to us as coming from the top.

But is that really how our political system works? I greatly doubt it. There is an interpretation of political change under which one can argue that it is change from below that has been and is really significant and can, over a period, be decisive. Certainly, the demand for the vote was a demand that came from the grass roots and was reluctantly conceded by the political leaders of the time. The demand for human rights or racial equality has never been particularly acceptable to those in authority in societies which denied these rights. The groundswell demand for free trade unions or socialised education or socialised medicine in a welfare state was not thought up in the corridors of power. They bubbled up in the community, lapping around the foundations of the establishment until they acquired sufficient momentum to swamp the opposition in Congress or Parliament. By this means, too, the environmentalists captured the White House and Number 10 Downing Street, making it clear that they would no longer tolerate the barbarities of technology. The new movement for women's rights has also gathered force outside the system and is already making progress within it against the entrenchment of male privilege.

It is arguable from this that the historic function of the politician is to capitulate, and that the good politician capitulates only to forces that he has helped to create by education and argument and by his encouragement of those who are trying to extend the area of human responsibility.

Indeed, the task of statesmanship today requires leaders to be more than bureaucratic administrators of vast governmental machines. For anyone who looks around him and, even more, anyone who looks ahead should see one fact staring him in the face. The amount of power that the technological revolution has created far exceeds the capability of even the most inspired, dedicated or brilliant leaders to control unaided.

In June 1940, when the seemingly unconquerable German Army stood poised on the French Coast ready to attack Britain, Winston

Churchill pledged himself to carry on the struggle "until, in God's good time, the new world with all its power and might steps forth to the rescue and liberation of the old." That is exactly the position confronting the statesman of today as he observes the massive and menacing power of technology which encompasses us. He must carry on the struggle until, in God's good time, the people with all their power and might step forth to the rescue and liberation of mankind.

Only a massive dispersal of power conveying responsibility beyond and within the nation state to those upon whose wise exercise of it our survival depends can possibly redress the balance in favour of the people in their battle to gain control of the machine. To pretend otherwise would be an illusion — an illusion we can ill afford to nourish.

The Civil Service and Political Advisers*

This article, published in the Times *in July 1973, was based on a memorandum submitted a few weeks earlier to the National Executive Committee of the Labour Party advocating more open government, and the appointment of political advisers. The advisers have now been appointed but the curtain of secrecy is still proving hard to lift.*

The question of secrecy in government has now at last become a major political issue. For too long ministers and civil servants have justified the cloak of secrecy with which they have surrounded themselves by reference to some supposedly unchallengeable assertion that the national interest requires it.

At long last this habit of protective security is being challenged. There is a growing public recognition that democracy itself cannot function unless the people are allowed to know a great deal more about what goes on inside government, even to the point of knowing when ministers disagree on important issues coming up for decision.

But the problem goes deeper than that. Ministers themselves are at present severely handicapped by the traditions of secrecy that operate within Whitehall, which prevent them from maintaining the close connexions they need, both with their colleagues and the public, if they are to do their job properly.

*Article in the *Times,* July 11, 1973. Reprinted by kind permission of Times Newspapers Limited.

The workings of the Civil Service and the growing pressure in the Labour Party for political advisers for ministers is closely connected with this issue.

The Civil Service half consciously uses the Official Secrets Acts to maintain itself as a two-way filter between ministers and the outside world. Most policy recommendations, even when they derive from ministerial directives, reach ministers through the (publicly anonymous) Civil Service, and much of what ministers want to convey to the outside world emerges through the (publicly anonymous) agency of their civil servants.

Ministers have no staff specifically charged with the development and maintenance of the political links they need to have with those who work outside Whitehall, or even their own ministerial colleagues. The network of ministerial and official committees under the Cabinet Office, which is supposed to facilitate the smooth running of government business, also acts in such a way as to hinder the political, and strengthen the departmental view at every stage.

To take one example: the Cabinet Office tightly controls the number of sets of Cabinet papers which are made available to Cabinet Ministers. These papers may arrive as late as 48 hours before the Cabinet meeting at which they are to be discussed. Usually only two sets are provided — with instructions that they are not to be copied. One set will go to the Permanent Secretary to arrange the departmental briefing. Thus only one other set is available for the minister's own use. This makes it unnecessarily difficult to arrange for other comments to be sought even from fellow ministers.

The problem extends to ministerial committees. Each minister will be fully acquainted with the political importance of the recommendations expressed in his own papers because he will have written or commissioned them. But on proposals put forward by his ministerial colleagues his own "official" brief mainly consists of references to whatever marginal side-effect these proposals will have on the departmental interests of his own civil servants. Since he may not be personally acquainted with these side-effects, he and all other ministers with a marginal interest are tempted to accept the official view, and if it is negative, to oppose what his ministerial colleague proposes. Thus the weight of official advice sometimes prevails when it should not.

There is no ministerial or political network comparable to the Civil Service network — through which ministers can brief each other, politically, in advance of the committees at which papers are to be discussed.

These are some of the defects in our machinery of government which must be remedied if ministers are to be able to maintain real contact with each other, real contact with backbench MPs and are to have adequate consultation with the world outside — including those advisers who may have helped in Opposition to develop the various policies, upon which the party was elected.

The problem is essentially one of isolation rather than of sabotage or obstruction by the Civil Service. It would certainly not be helped by adopting the American system of appointing political sympathizers to senior Civil Service posts. Nor would it be wise to seek a solution solely by expanding the Prime Minister's office to make it — as in the White House — a centre of independent advice for him alone. This would inevitably weaken deparmental ministers at the expense of the Prime Minister's "cabinet".

What is required is the open acceptance — with proper safeguards — of a new category of political advisers who would be appointed to serve an incoming government, and each of the departmental ministers, and would go out of office with them. Such advisers would have no executive power within the department and no civil servant would be expected to take orders from them.

To provide some accountability to Parliament, these advisers might be paid out of a separate vote in the estimates and their names could be reported, on appointment, to the House of Commons by whom they would be theoretically removable.

These advisers would have access to papers and information the Minister thought necessary, would not be subject to the restrictions on political work that apply to civil servants, and would only be limited by a much liberalized Official Secrets Act. Each minister within his own department — especially in the economic or industrial fields — would need both a political adviser, and a trade union adviser, as well as an economic adviser, all properly serviced. Parliamentary Private Secretaries could play a much more active role within such an advisory group.

These changes, minor as they may appear to anyone not familiar with Whitehall, would strengthen the political impulse within Government without disturbing the sound and practical administration of the Civil Service. A Labour Government, particularly, needs to have closer links with the Labour movement which, by definition, presses its needs from outside the establishment.

That is why reforms designed to reduce unnecessary barriers of secrecy, and to provide better methods for developing and extending contact between a Labour Government and the community it seeks to serve, must now be seen as a central policy issue.

X

The Fuel Crisis
and
The Three-Day Week

The Energy Crisis*

The Financial Times *Conference in December 1973 provided an opportunity to develop the relevance of Labour's new industrial policy against the new and threatening energy crisis which will require a massive programme of national investment.*

The real credit for forecasting what would happen in the present oil crisis must go to the authors of a report published in December 1967 — exactly six years ago this month.

I should like to quote a few words from this report.

"We believe that government policy of increasing dependence on oil is fraught with danger . . .

We think that the assumptions relating to oil prices in the future are based on completely baseless and illogical reasoning, and certainly not related to the reality of the new developing situation in the Middle East . . .

Our privileged position in the Middle East has largely been obtained and retained by power, and unlike the government we think that situation is changing and will continue to change. We do not think it necessary to be political theoreticians to estimate that the people of the Middle East, who, like ourselves, are anxious to assure and improve standards of living, will in fact demand just that. This eventually can change the whole relationship of oil prices with other fuels, and long-term represents a critical economic factor in the costing of the nation's fuel."

The report I have just quoted was published by the National Union of Mineworkers — Kent Area — and signed by Jack Dunn, its Area General Secretary, now classified as a militant.

I quote these words because at the time they were written almost the entire establishment in the civil service, industry, the CEGB, Parliament, the academic world and Fleet Street were taking a

*Speech at the Conference on the North and Celtic Seas organised by the *Financial Times, Petroleum Times* and British Airways at the Royal Lancaster Hotel, London, December 5, 1973.

completely different view and were united in being proved wrong. The miners were right then, and no-one listened to them.

There is a lesson for us in that.

Now, at this very moment, the major industrial powers in the world – the USA, Japan and Western Europe – are all seriously affected by the situation the miners predicted.

But for Britain the oil crisis poses a special problem because it comes on top of a deteriorating economic situation after a generation of economic difficulty with which we are only too familiar.

During those years something went wrong. I believe that what went wrong can be simply and non-controversially stated, as a national failure to meet essential needs because we allowed less necessary objectives to take priority.

In economic terms we neglected essential industrial investment; in social terms we ignored pressing human problems like poverty, poor housing, regional unemployment and inequality. And we wasted energy of all kinds and in all forms.

Now it is the energy shortage that has caught up with us, accelerated all our other problems, and has created within a few weeks a completely new and different situation with which we have to grapple.

This energy crisis has, as its very first result, hit us, an economy ill-prepared to cope with further increases in world prices of any kind and heavily dependent on exports to live. Even without the shortage of oil, the effect on our balance of payments of the higher oil prices would be very grave. But the oil supplies we need are not guaranteed even at higher prices. We, and many other industrial countries, face a cut back in production, and world trade, a serious risk of more unemployment accompanied by inflation that will reach new peaks as the new oil costs work their way through the economy.

The present rate of economic growth, which is already slowing down, could be cut back to zero, either because our factories cannot produce, with oil supplies limited to the September delivery rate or because the Government has to introduce new economic measures.

If that happens and we have another 'Stop' it will be a bigger, firmer and more serious 'Stop' than we have had in any other postwar economic crisis.

Indeed, if the dislocation, world-wide, is greater than that there is the possibility of a severe recession or depression, and the whole economic global industrial, social and political environment will change.

We, in Britain must therefore now concentrate on essentials, and postpone, or give up, inessentials. Once we are clear in our minds that this is what we shall have to do a lot of other things will become clear too.

We must be clear that any Government in this country, of whatever party, must put Britain's national interest above every other consideration — in our relations with foreign companies or the E.E.C.

Conflicts of interest are already beginning to emerge, even in the short term.

It would, for example, be quite wrong for this country to put the interests of its Common Market partners above our own industrial and economic needs at this time.

I am *not* referring to the special difficulties of Holland, deriving from her sympathies in the Middle East, which most people in Britain understand.

I am referring to the Government's present policy of permitting the continuing export of oil and oil products to Common Market countries generally, at a moment when the shortage here could endanger our own position. Trade must be in the mutual interest of both partners. Since the British people were never consulted as to whether they wished to join the Common Market there is no 'European patriotism' to which the Government have any right to appeal.

Similarly, there is a clear potential conflict of interest between the British Government and the oil companies that now operate here, and others that are engaged in the North and Celtic Sea exploration.

Charles Wilson of General Motors once said that "What is good for General Motors is good for the United States." Many Americans did not share that view even as stated. But it is even clearer that what is good for the international oil companies is not at all necessarily good for the countries where they sell their oil, or for the peoples in countries from which they obtain it, or hope to obtain it as in our case.

This is why I welcome the Fuel and Electricity (Control) Bill, now before Parliament. It enables the Secretary of State to control the production, supply, acquisition, and use of petroleum and any other substance derived from petroleum and any other substance used as fuel and the production, supply and use of electricity.

The Minister will get the power to require the keeping of records and the furnishing of information by any undertaking.

The Bill also provides for direct Ministerial control of all prices, a power now taken away from the Price Commission.

This is not a temporary legislation, though it needs to be extended year by year if it is to remain in force.

I have no complaint at the drastic nature of these powers. Indeed we shall insist these powers are used to safeguard the national interest against anyone — even the EEC Commission — or any multi-national oil company, whose policy might conflict with our national interests.

When we are discussing problems of sheer industrial survival — as we are — there is no sensible alternative.

Similarly, when we come to the question which principally concerns this Conference — namely the North and Celtic Sea development — the same clear expression of our national interest must be dominant.

The British Government must decide the rate of exploitation, the price at which the oil is acquired, the use to which it is put, and the markets to which it is distributed — always in the U.K. interest. When these arguments were first put forward we were told that such a strong national policy might frighten away the oil companies. It would require a great deal more than that to frighten away anyone from an oilfield these days.

It must be the Government, and not the oil companies, that dictate the nature and pattern of development — and its speed, always in the interests of Britain.

It must be the British Government, and not the EEC, which decides who gets our oil. Indeed, the whole case for entry into the Common Market looks very different now that we know that Britain is sitting on the richest oil and coal reserves in Europe and has a highly mechanized coal industry, also the best in Europe with scope for considerable future development.

In interpreting the national interest we must see British policy for the North and Celtic Seas as part of an integrated fuel policy.

Never again can we go back to the illusion that market forces will somehow allocate fuels rationally without government having any part to play, beyond noting trends in demand, and trends in prices, and being guided by these factors, into accepting as inevitable, policies for distribution and use that flow from them.

The Government has a duty to take a very broad view of United Kingdom energy requirements, and, if we are to make sense of our North Sea decisions we have got to see them as part of the whole picture.

Perhaps we should be grateful that we didn't discover our offshore oil earlier, and waste it earlier, for the North and Celtic Sea reserves are so valuable as to make all the gold in Fort Knox look like a few savings certificates locked up in a sub-Post Office safe.

We must look afresh at the economics of all energy sources, and re-examine the uses to which oil is put. Long term, oil may be too valuable to burn wastefully and we should certainly give priority to its other uses as a feedstock for the chemical and allied industries.

We can now look again at the possibility of producing oil from coal if we are ready to put in the necessary capital investment to do it.

In short I am arguing that all energy decisions are now political decisions. That point does not now need to be stressed, after the recent policy decisions of the Arab states.

Indeed Britain's post-war decision to go for a major nuclear power policy at an enormous public expenditure of men and money for research and development years ago, was equally political.

I am not here seeking to spell out, in detail, what a nationally integrated fuel policy should be.

But it is obvious that it will have a far greater place for the coal industry than successive Governments since the war thought possible.

Uneconomic pits will become economic again, and North Sea coal exploration — together with the development of new seams like the Selby seam — indicate the need for a new corporate strategy for the Coal Board which will also require large public investment.

In the shorter term it must mean a greater coal burn at dual-fired power stations, and the commissioning of new coal-burning stations, and changes in the CEGB order of use so that oil stations are brought in last instead of leaving the coal-burning stations to do the power peak-lopping.

It means the more rapid development of fluidised bed combustion of coal on which a great deal of research has now begun. And other technologies will have to be advanced as well.

On the nuclear side, it is obvious that we must proceed as rapidly as we can. Britain has an unrivalled capacity and experience in this field with Magnox Stations at work, AGR stations coming into service, the Steam Generating Heavy Water reactor, with a big export potential, that still unaccountably awaits a domestic order, and with the high temperature and fast breeder reactors coming along.

In these circumstances it would be intolerable if the Government were to decide to switch from these British reactors, and buy the American light water reactor which is now being pressed upon us.

I might add that it is equally intolerable that the hundreds of millions of pounds of research and development paid for by the taxpayer, should have gone into the private National Nuclear Corporation, exchanged for a mere 15% public holding. The Select Committee has already criticised that and rightly so.

As to the North Sea, we must determine the extraction rate to meet our own needs. We all want the oil landed as quickly as possible but after that we must be free to determine how quickly and how it is used.

We must here consider the speed with which we can develop the associated oil technologies in Britain and create the industrial base able to sustain them without undue dependence upon foreign companies or imports.

I am not saying that we should only buy our pipes from the British Steel Corporation. But there was a serious failure of long-term planning somewhere which allowed huge piles of Japanese pipes to be landed in the North East within a mile or two of a B.S.C. pipe plant, that was scheduled for run down and closure.

I am not saying that we do not need American know-how and

expertise acquired from their own off-shore experience. But I am questioning whether it was right or necessary to accept that American engineering firms should have majority holdings (with British civil engineering contractors as junior partners) in an arrangement under which the Americans learned from our quite different and difficult North Sea conditions the engineering requirements of deep sea exploration, not available to them before, and will be able to export these technologies to other parts of the world, and make most of the money out of our experience.

My impression on a recent visit to the North East and Scotland confirmed my worst fears. The atmosphere of uncontrolled gold rush is unmistakeable in a scramble for quick profits.

There is no long-term British capability being systematically developed, as it should be, out of this whole operation. The Government seem to have too little knowledge of what is happening. The scale of their thinking about their role in assisting British firms to get contracts is totally inadequate.

It is for these reasons that the Labour Party has put forward its proposals for a National Hydrocarbons Corporation to develop the necessary British public sector capability. We will require at least a 50% public participation in future exploration and will insist on a tax structure that really benefits our economy.

A large public investment and extended public ownership will be required. There will also have to be a very big programme of public investment in the equally important areas of energy conservation and use.

We must have higher standards of building insulation, and more district heating, and find other ways of cutting back inessential energy demands.

We have to look again at our transport system and consciously shift the emphasis, wherever this is possible, from private transport to public transport, from road freight to rail freight and, on the railways from diesel oil use to electrification with all its associated environmental advantages.

The scale of this investment taken together is absolutely massive and it too will require the development of an industrial capability able to provide the necessary equipment. Fortunately it can also help us tackle the difficult employment problems we may have to face.

It would be absurd to contemplate a situation in which we were buying foreign equipment, and technology, to undertake our big investment programme of fuel development and fuel saving, during the very same years that we shall be importing oil at the inflated prices which now rule and which are likely to rise still higher.

Our balance of payments just could not sustain this double burden, without crushing the British economy.

Later, we hope that the gains from our own oil resources will begin to accrue, but we have got to get through the next few years on the basis of a planned programme of essential investment here, that will make a heavy demand on our capacity.

It is for these reasons that the Labour Party seriously argues for a national policy controlled and executed through an expanded public sector.

This will be all the more necessary if the short-term employment position is as difficult as I fear it may be.

If for example engineering factories and skills now locked up, for example, in the motor car industry are threatened by the oil shortage, there is no hope whatever − outside the public sector − of converting these resources rapidly to meet the needs of the investment programme in fuel equipment, conservation equipment, and transport equipment, which we would need urgently.

Similarly the national energy research effort which must be expanded should logically be based on the wide range of skills of the Atomic Energy Authority within the public sector linked to public sector industrial expansion.

It is difficult to understand − let alone convey − the sheer magnitude of the task of industrial transformation and renewal that the United Kingdom will have to undertake if it is to emerge from what I fear will be hard years ahead, into a new era of balanced economic development, which we must aim to resume when this task is completed later this decade.

There will be those attending this Conference who will be critical of the proposals the Labour Party has made for an extended public sector to undertake this task. I hope they will see our arguments against this background, for it was against this background that we prepared our policy.

It is a policy designed to put the interests of the British people first − not in a narrow, nationalistic way − but because no other objective could possibly justify us in seeking the co-operation of our people in the difficult years that lie ahead. The North Sea is a new heritage that belongs to us all in Britain.

It is also a programme contemplating such a scale of investment, to be undertaken so quickly, that it can no more be left to the market economy, distorted as it is by multi-national oil interests, or the confused thinking of the EEC, than one could leave a major rearmament programme to be met by the chance of competing business interests.

Britain's sudden confrontation with reality should not alarm us. Affluence unevenly distributed appeals principally to selfish interests, and fragments our society, and divides the people who live in it.

The British are always at their best when they are told the truth about the problems they have to face, know what they have to do, and are invited to get on with it.

The best election address I ever read was never used in an election. It was Churchill's famous phrase 'All I have to offer you is blood, toil sweat and tears'.

We are not talking about blood because we live under the new umbrella of the detente. If there is sensible international co-operation we shall get through without a repetition of those terrible 19th century wars for raw materials.

But there will be toil, there could be tears, and there is certainly going to be sweat.

As in the war we must go for essentials, not only industrial and economic essentials, but human and social essentials too.

The gross and unjustified inequalities that disfigure our society are no more acceptable than the unplanned features of an economic system that has let us down.

If we keep our nerve, and are steady, no one is going to be frightened of toil, tears and sweat if it means *equal* toil, *equal* tears and *equal* sweat.

Get that right — as we can — and we shall learn in the next few years that the real undiscovered resources that this country commands are not locked up under the sea bed. They are available here and now for immediate use — the immense resource and capacity of our own people.

We need those human resources now, and it is the first task of statesmanship to release those resources at once.

Monitoring the Crisis*

The campaign against the three-day week or National Lockout imposed by Mr. Heath before Christmas 1973 was launched in an exchange of letters with the Prime Minister at the turn of the year.

His replies failed to stem the growing public doubts as to the necessity of these draconian measures except as an act of mobilization for a long "war" against the miners which most people did not want. One weapon that proved most useful against the government's propaganda barrage was the institution of a Labour monitoring service which tapped the knowledge of the Labour movement and produced the most valuable information. This is the memorandum which launched it.

Labour and the Three-Day Week

For the duration of the present industrial situation the Labour Party will be mounting special monitoring and information services.

The Monitoring service will consist of questionnaires sent out by Transport House to Labour groups on local authorities, Constituency Labour Parties, affiliated trade unions, Labour MPs and candidates who will be notified by the General Secretary in his newsletter.

A similar notice will be issued by the Chief Whip to Labour MPs for use in their own constituency.

These questionnaires may be reproduced for further circulation by Labour parties, Labour councillors and Unions for completion by a wider group of people.

As the information comes in it will be made the basis for questions to Ministers, parliamentary action, and where appropriate, for policy purposes.

The Information Service which the party intends to establish will be issued in the form of press bulletins released by the Director of Information of the Labour Party and will go out as often as is necessary.

This regular information bulletin will contain material that has come through the monitoring service, together with statements by the Labour Party, the Parliamentary Labour Party and appropriate committees.

Labour Monitoring Service

Draft questions to be circulated by the Labour Party to Labour Groups on local authorities, Constituency Labour Parties, affiliated trades unions, Labour MPs and candidates, for use by them and those to whom further copies of these questions may be circulated by them.

*Statement issued on Labour Party Monitoring and Information Services during the 3-day week, December 31, 1973.

These replies will be studied by the Party and Front Bench spokesmen and where necessary will be referred to the National Executive Committee and the Energy Committee of the Shadow Cabinet.

Where appropriate, the information gathered in this way will be made available to the press and will form the basis of questions to Ministers.

Questions

1. Do you have any information about coal or oil production, imports, exports, movements or stocks?

2. What is the fuel position where you work, in terms of stocks, use or shortages?

3. How many workers at your place of work have been
    (a) put on short time;
    (b) laid off;
    (c) declared redundant?

4. What do you estimate to be the overall loss of incomes at your place of work?

5. What do you estimate to be the loss of production, or exports, each week in your firm or plant?

6. What transport difficulties are you experiencing?

7. What difficulties are being experienced by local authorities in providing essential services in your area, especially for the old and the sick?

8. What difficulties are there in dealing with local offices of the Department of Employment and the Department of Health and Social Security?

9. What increases in prices are taking place?

10. Have you any other information on the situation which you would like to make available?

Note:

Please provide all the information you can and also seek the facts from:

1. Local authority offices
2. Local firms — both management and trade union representatives
3. Local trade union branches
4. Local community groups
5. Individual contacts

Please give the exact source of all information with names, telephone numbers etc., to allow further enquiries to be made.

Labour Monitoring Service – Questions to Ministers

The following questions are being put to the Prime Minister and other Ministers arising out of information conveyed to the Labour Party as a result of the earlier monitoring system:

1. Will the Government now take immediate action to protect those people who cannot afford mortgage and hire purchase repayments because of the cut in wages which they will suffer due to the three-day week, by deferring all such payments due and prohibiting repossession or eviction?

2. What action is the Government taking to inform the people that they are now entitled, if they experience a fall in their wages, to receive rent rebates, free school meals for their children and family income supplements and to tell them how these benefits can be claimed?

3. Will the Government now suspend the three waiting days imposed under the 1971 Act so as to allow those workers who lose working days to claim unemployment benefit for them?

4. What additional discretionary powers are to be given to Managers of local Social Security Offices to allow them to respond immediately to cases of hardship and severe need attributable to the Government's measures?

5. Will the Government offer any help to firms with export contracts containing guaranteed delivery dates by under-writing their losses or penalty payments, or re-negotiating the dates of delivery on a government-to-government basis?

6. Will the Industry Act be available to help firms to sustain production, exports and investment especially in the regions?

7. Will the Government provide assistance for firms – especially small firms – facing bankruptcy as a direct result of the three-day week?

8. Will the Government make an Order legislating for a moratorium for business firms unable to pay rent, taxation and meet bank repayments due to cash flow difficulties created by the three-day week?

9. Will the Government arrange for the Central Statistical Office to make available, directly to the public, a daily report on coal and oil stocks, and all other relevant information including the mounting cost in lost production, exports and public expenditure so that the public may have this information from a neutral and reliable source?

Why the Three-Day Week?*

The day after Parliament resumed in January 1974 there was a debate on the three-day week, which provided an opportunity from the Opposition front bench of deploying the arguments against the Government. This became in the event an occasion for warning against the essential threats to democracy implicit in continuing with the Conservative Government's policies.

. . . The Opposition's view may be summarised briefly. It is to invite the Government to take the TUC proposal very seriously; to allow the National Coal Board and the National Union of Mineworkers the right to negotiate freely and to reach a settlement at which normal working could be resumed; to set aside the Pay Board — which has been a major complication in the situation — entirely from the mining dispute; to let the Secretary of State himself decide, as Parliament intended he should in any case where the national interest required Ministers to take responsibility; and finally to call off the three-day week.

One of the subjects for special emphasis today has been the three-day week. I think that many of my hon. Friends and most people outside who have experienced it, will agree that anyone who had doubts about the Government's real motives for the three-day week will have had those doubts wholly dispelled after hearing the Prime Minister yesterday.

The Prime Minister's attempt to justify the three-day week was not concerned, as one would expect, were it a genuine proposal, with husbanding the nation's fuel resources and protecting the people at a moment of shortage. It was an act of mobilisation for a long war against the miners.

We in this House have a duty on behalf of our constituents and on behalf of the country — and right hon. and hon. Members on both sides have tried to discharge it — to draw attention to the very high cost of the three-day week. I have asked the Prime Minister for the Government's estimate of the cost of the three-day week. No estimate is forthcoming officially from the Government. Some indication has been given by the National Economic Development Office, but in practice there is no one here tonight who disputes that the three-day week will have a grave effect on production, on exports and on investment.

For those working in industry it means a savage and direct cut in their wages. There will be inevitable bankruptcies among small businessmen — and we bear in mind that the Conservative Party has so

*Extract from speech in the debate on the "Three-Day Working Week" in the House of Commons, January 10, 1974.

often boasted to be their special friends in Government and in Parliament. It will mean higher unemployment in terms not only of lay-offs in the short run but of higher unemployment for a longer period if the bankruptcies mount to the level to which they may mount and, if the grave damage to the steel industry about which many of my hon. Friends spoke in the debate has the effect that we fear. It will also have a very serious effect upon the morale of the nation when people realise, as they are now coming to realise, that this was part of the mobilisation of psychological warfare against the miners by the Government. That is what the people believe, and I will give the House the reasons why they believe it.

First they believe it because the Government have throughout suppressed key figures — no one more than the Secretary of State for Trade and Industry now, thank goodness, stripped of the responsibilities which he discharged so poorly for the nation's energy resources. The Government have suppressed the coal figures. The Government have suppressed the oil figures. The Government have ordered public authorities set up by Parliament not to answer questions put to them by Members of Parliament, which is a complete denial of the duty of a public authority to tell the public how it is discharging its statutory responsibilities.

The Government have implied that 7 million tons is the minimum stock without telling the public that in the past four years stocks have been below 7 million tons for no fewer than 16 weeks, thus implying that we were on the point of crisis. The Government have pretended that the CEGB ordered the three-day week when the CEGB was operating on the basis of oil supplies that had been cut to 75 per cent. of what they were last winter, an understandable policy following the Rothschild Think Tank's analysis of the need for a stronger coal industry, but not making sense when the Government were faced either with the restoration of 100 per cent. oil supplies or putting the nation on a three-day week.

In his pre-Christmas speech the Prime Minister made great play with the effect of the ASLEF dispute upon coal deliveries from the coal mines to the power stations, although the British Railways Board has made it clear that there has not been the slightest delay in the delivery of coal from the pits to the power stations. Were there time, I could give the House the information that is pouring in from power stations and pits all over the country, giving the lie to the scares that the Cabinet has systematically tried to use to justify its policy.

The fact is that the Government cut oil to the power stations and then ordered the restoration of some of that oil. Because they did not control the multi-national oil companies, or have any real power over them, they were unable to get the restoration of the oil to see us through the winter. There was no consultation with the CBI or the TUC. Could anyone seriously believe that management or labour would have opted for a three-day week on this basis, which gives entertainment priority over exports, domestic use of all kinds priority over production, and pleasure motoring priority over oil for power stations? It does not make sense as a management decision.

The right hon. Member the Secretary of State for Trade and Industry said in the new year that the oil problem did not exist, that our only problem was the coal crisis. At that time, he was trying characteristically to get cheap political popularity by saying there would be no petrol rationing. The right hon. Gentleman knows better than most that the three-day week will bankrupt Britain long before the coal runs out.

The Government have done nothing to protect the housewives working a seven-day week on a three-day pay packet. They have done nothing to lift the three-day waiting rule. They have done nothing about family allowances during the crisis. They have given no special help to industry. They have done nothing whatever that one would expect both the CBI and the TUC to require of them to try to see us through this difficulty with the minimum damage to our fundamental strength.

The people do not believe the reasons that the Prime Minister has given. They see this as part of the Prime Minister's obsessive campaign against the miners. They see now the explanation of why the mini-Budget before Christmas contained no tax increases — because the Chancellor of the Exchequer found a way of getting more money out of the pockets of working people by the wage cut than he did and should have done by some redistribution of wealth.

I would only say that watching the Prime Minister I am reminded of his predecessor, Sir Anthony Eden at the time of Suez obsessively pursuing a policy which would lead to the destruction of a basic national interest and backed up by a group of party supporters hypnotised by his strength into neglecting their duty to defend the country they were elected to represent. It would have taken this Prime Minister to get a ban on overtime by Spitfire pilots during the Battle of Britain — and I believe he could have done that given half a chance.

Perhaps the Prime Minister should think of what Harold Macmillan or Churchill would have done. He might indeed at least use the phrase which equally applies to the miners — "never was so much been owed by so many to so few". There have been 15,000 deaths from pneumoconiosis in the mining industry in the last 15 years, and if the Conservative Party had recognised in its public speeches the debt this country owes to the miners one quarter of their problems would be solved.

Now we come to the Government's reasons for rejecting the miners' claim. First, stage 3 must be upheld. Stage 3 was destroyed by the escalation of oil prices. The outdated calculations upon which it was based are known to all. The Government have themselves directly violated stage 3 by announcing through the Chancellor that there would be substantial increases in coal and electricity prices which were not provided for in the Pay and Prices Code. Ministers have said, which is not true, that stage 3 has the force of law. Stage 3 never had the force of law. It was an advisory document to the Pay Board. And ít was for the Pay Board to consider it. The law came in only if there were a settlement on which the Pay Board imposed an order to desist and then there would be a prosecution only under the fiat of the Attorney-General. The law has never been a part of this situation. Ministers have sought to imply that we are upholding our constitution against a lot of law-breakers. The Secretary of State for Employment knows full well that Parliament has given him the power to set aside any Pay Board ruling, and that is what he should do.

Another argument is that the settlement is unfair to other workers. That is a most interesting argument. We have heard tonight from many people who have described how private industry has got round stage 3 by regrading, fiddling, sacking and re-engaging, and by reorganising its structure. It is the public sector, with higher standards of management morality, which has observed stage 3 and if anybody thinks that the ordinary workers who have not the organised strength of the miners have a friend in the Government they do not understand what is going on now among the shop workers, the hospital workers or those who lack the muscle of the miners.

We are also told that the offer is generous. The figure of 16½ per cent. has been quoted. Now 16½ per cent. is a good offer for someone on £10,000 a year and the man who reads his *Daily Telegraph* and hears the figure of 16½ per cent. might well calculate that he would do well. The plain truth is – and it has never been denied – that after taxation, national insurance and the rise in prices the Government offer is worth 60p a week for the miners, compared to what they were earning a year ago. When I hear talk about ransom and blackmail, I must say that I have never heard of a blackmailer being prepared to settle for 60p a week.

These arguments are getting through to the public. The fact is that people understand the miners' case. It will not do to pretend that it is all due to the Communists because, candidly, if the Government believed that, they would have used their own legislation to have a ballot of the miners to establish straight away whether the miners support their executive members or not. I should like to meet the Conservative who inquires whether the coal he burns in his hearth has been dug by a Communist, or whether the train in which he travels as a commuter is driven by a Communist, before we listen to the sort of talk we have had today, which is a warning to the nation what it must expect when the General Election comes.

It is also slightly odd that the Communist Party shared with the Prime Minister in 1970 one thing in common – opposition to a statutory wages policy – and when the Prime Minister has abandoned his manifesto and the Communist Party still believes in it, that is said to be an undermining of the British constitution. Ministers must find a rather better argument than that.

People in this country now know, even more than they did before the oil price increase, that we need the coal. They see the miners fighting the same battles as they fight, because the miners have to face higher prices and higher rents and have all the difficulties that have been intensified in the past 12 months.

My hon. Friend the Member for Oldham, West (Mr. Meacher) is good and accurate with a slide rule and he has produced figures – which have never been challenged – to show that real living standards fell last year while trading profits went up by 16 per cent, dividend and interest payments by 28 per cent, and net asset value of property companies by 20 per cent. There has been massive redistribution of wealth and income but it has been in the wrong direction.

I wish to say a word to Ministers as well as to editors and television interviewers about the way in which they treat the miners on television and in the Press. It sickens many people – I am one of them – that when there is a mining disaster and a man is lying trapped in water in a dark underground roadway for days, and newspapers show photographs of grief-stricken widows in a mining village, the miners are the heroes of Britain, but when they put in a wage claim which not a single hon. Member of the House would accept as a basis for his own living wage, they are described as Communists and blackmailers holding the country to ransom.

Ministers, editors and television interviewers get incomes far in excess of those which the miners could ever dream of getting. Ministers, editors and television interviewers get incomes which are secretly arrived at. Their incomes are never discussed on television as to whether they are justified, or whether the person concerned should get the sum proposed. These people are the last who should misrepresent the miners of this country and try to hold them up to public abuse.

If there is a new element entering into the whole argument of incomes policy it is simply this: we have come to the end of the road when the rich and the powerful can expect to get a hearing from working people as they ask them to restrain their incomes in order to preserve the pattern of wealth and property which the rich and powerful use so much to their own advantage.

It is time that we had a new look at the incomes policy question. I put this to the Secretary of State because his mind is bent mainly on this problem. Successive Governments have tried and failed with policies which bore some resemblance to the one which the present Government first thought of introducing. But we must now try to look at this problem from the point of view of those whose consent is essential if any such policy is to work.

I have a word to say here to those commentators and editors who look through every speech and every manifesto for a sentence containing a reference to a tough incomes policy as somehow a test of credibility or of statesmanship. In effect, all that these pompous editorialists and commentators are saying is that they want us here, across the Floor of the House, to agree to tight wage control as the basis for future policy, whichever Government be in power. When we are told that this is the time for straight talking, for plain speaking, for doses of reality and for moments of truth, let us perform our representative function and say to those who put that to us that they must now learn the hard truth, listen to some straight talking and have a dose of reality.

For tight wage control by law will not work, and by consent will never be achieved unless we are able to make a change in our whole approach to the sort of society we have. [*Hon. Members:* "Ah".] Obviously, what those hon. Members who shouted "Ah" meant was that this House is inextricably linked in its existence and its democratic practice with one form of distribution of wealth and income, and that the people cannot use Parliament democratically to change the distribution of wealth and income. But of course it is just that change that we must have.

Unless and until there is a major social reform to make our society fairer and more nearly equal, workers will not co-operate in wage control where they have bargaining power and if they have the strength to resist. And they are right. They remember what the Prime Minister did to the postmen when he had the big stick, and they know what he has done to the lower-paid workers. When the Government have the power, they use it to keep living standards down.

It is time that the Government, all right hon. and hon. Members and people in Press and television listened more to what the trade union movement is trying to say to us about the problems of an incomes policy. It is no use saying that, unless the trade union movement can overnight convert itself into a corporation which can be accountable for the behaviour of all its members, nothing it says is a bankable guarantee or is worth examining.

The trade union leader, with less backing than a Minister — for he does not have the Statute Book at his disposal — has to operate by consent. He has to listen to his members. It is not too much to ask that Ministers should listen to what the trade unions say. The Secretary of State had the reputation, no doubt justly, in Ireland of being one to listen. If he has listened, he will have learned that during his Government's period in power the trade union movement has put forward highly constructive proposals about how, given that most trade unionists do not share the present Government's political philosophy, something could be done to create an atmosphere in which co-operation would be possible.

What have the trade unions asked for? They have asked for fairer Budgets so that an incomes policy did not just mean wage control without some re-examination of the distribution of wealth and income at the top. They have asked for food subsidies, which would make a great difference to many millions of families. They have asked for a rent freeze. They have asked for higher pensions — which gives the lie to the argument that the trade union movement is concerned only with its own members' wage claims, for it was the TUC which played a notable part in triggering off and continuing the campaign for a higher pension. They have asked for an end to property speculation. They have asked for the repeal of the Industrial Relations Act, for it to be put on ice, as Stormont was put on ice by the right hon. Gentleman when he assumed his earlier responsibilities.

All these proposals that the trade union movement has put forward represent the beginnings of a basis of co-operation on which something might be achieved. They are all embodied in the programme which the Labour Party will put before the public at the General Election, but they have all also come forward to the present Government in proposals from the TUC. No one thinks that he will get 100 per cent. acceptance of anything in a voluntary society, but if the Government and Fleet Street expect TUC leaders to sign on the dotted line to prop up an unfair society, let me tell them that it will not happen. If they did sign on the dotted line, it would mean nothing whatsoever; if it did mean something, it would not be just to use the trade union movement to underpin a society so fundamentally unfair in its distribution of rewards.

The basic democratic proposition that the Opposition have put to the House in the last two days is very simple to state. It is that the only policy that will work in our society is a policy that is accepted. The only policy that will be accepted is one that is fair, and a fair policy requires programmes of social reform extending widely over the field of domestic policies. Working people now want that reform to be carried through by Parliament and not by revolution.

What is the alternative to doing it this way? If we reject voluntarism — which has, as a matter of fact, an even older history than democracy

— and social justice, we are driven inevitably to authoritarian solutions. The Industrial Relations Act took away the power of the unions because trade union democracy was not compatible with Government policy. The Housing Finance Act took away the democratic responsibilities of local Labour councillors because they would not raise the rents of the people they represented. The Pay Board, which is not accountable to the electors — its members have never been elected and are not accountable to Parliament — is another part of this authoritarian structure.

Now the emergency powers, then the three-day working week, then compulsory overtime — for that is what the Government wish the miners to accept — then tonight some speakers, a little ahead of their time, calling for the proscription of political parties that challenge this view. The Prime Minister is moving to 1984 10 years ahead of schedule, and he is doing it with a nightmare of centralised control, under the control not of the Left but of the Right.

I do not believe for a moment that the problems confronting this country are insoluble within the framework of the parliamentary system for which our forefathers fought and won. We do not want a British Stalin or a tinpot Mussolini lecturing us from Lancaster House. The paradox that confronts the House is that in this country today moderate people want radical change. Moderate people want a fair society, when our society is now not fair. They want justice in areas where injustice has been preserved. They want more democracy and not less democracy. They want a sharing of the power and an enfranchisement of the community, of industrial workers, of tenants, and of the regions, and not the corporate ideas which are being put before us by the Government.

We cannot hope that a coalition of Ministers and editors, and all those in society who enjoy the power, can any longer expect to lecture working people to make the sacrifices that are required.

To this extent this is the end of an era, as my right hon. Friend the Member for East Ham, North (Mr. Prentice) said. It is not just about the balance of payments, inflation, energy or growth. What are now being questioned are the values of a society which have, in a sense, been tested and found wanting, and whether we can any longer have the House of Commons being told that miners earning £30 a week, or a little more, can be described as selfish, greedy blackmailers, and expect the public to believe that.

At this moment the affairs of the country are in the hands of a man who knows so little about those he was elected to serve, and has so little faith in their capacity, save under the pressure of punishment, to rise to the occasion that he misses three important and what should be non-controversial points.

We cannot expect responsibility unless as a House we are prepared to share power. We cannot expect social justice unless as a House we legislate to dispense justice. We cannot save democracy unless we practise democracy. We cannot win the trust of the people of this country unless we show to the people, and those who create its wealth, the trust and respect that they deserve.

Challenging the Class Structure*

This speech delivered on January 27, 1974 just before Parliament was dissolved provided an opportunity to link the election issues to the class structure of our society and the master illusion of British politics that denied the existence of those divisions. It identified the main task of the Labour Party to defend working people and their families and the trade unions, and warned of the dangers that a corporate state might emerge if Mr. Heath succeeded. It also listed six establishment tests by which all political leaders were to be judged which constituted the essentials of Conservative thinking, and ended with a quotation from Clause Four, whose relevance was now so obvious.

The crisis situation which is developing in Britain as a result of the Prime Minister's decision to seek a confrontation with the miners is quite different from anything that has happened within the life-time of most of us.

The next few days, while the miners' ballot is taking place, and before the result is known, offer us all an opportunity to analyse the elements of this crisis and to reflect upon it, before events take charge. Let us start with the dispute itself.

The National Executive Committee of the Labour Party unanimously passed a resolution, last Wednesday, deploring the government's summary rejection of every attempt to solve the miners' dispute, pointed to the suffering imposed by the unnecessary three-day week and expressed "its full support for the efforts of the TUC to bring about a settlement of the mining dispute, and calls upon the British people to back the mine workers in their efforts to achieve a fair and honourable settlement of their claim and a sound basis for the future of the coal industry".

The following day, after the decision to proceed to a ballot had been announced, Labour's Shadow Cabinet unanimously approved a

*Speech at a conference jointly sponsored by the London Cooperative Party Education and Political Committees and the London Federation of Trade Councils at the New Ambassadors Hotel, London, January 27, 1974.

statement which made it clear that the country and the miners wanted a settlement; and appealed to the Prime Minister to abandon his provocative and negative posture, and to permit active negotiation with the NUM and the TUC in order to bring about a settlement by conciliation, negotiation and compromise.

We are also agreed that it is not for others to seek to instruct the miners as to how they should vote in the democratic machinery of their own ballot. The miners know what is at stake.

So do other workers whose living standards are being eroded by the Government's phase three which ministers claim is essential to its counter-inflation policy.

Working people are becoming aware of the consequences of Mr. Heath's counter-inflation policy which is deliberately designed to bring about a substantial redistribution of wealth and income in favour of Capital at the expense of Labour.

It is, indeed, obvious to everyone that even the developing discussion about pay relativities is being confined to the relationship between the wages of higher and lower-paid workers — without dealing, at all, with the wide and growing gap between the richest people on the one hand, and working people as a whole, on the other.

This is why, in the long run, Mr. Heath cannot win. There is no immutable law of economics or nature — no "Iron Law of Wages" — which requires working people to be treated as a separate class allowed only to compete amongst themselves about who is to get most from a fixed proportion of the national income allocated to them in wages by those with wealth and power who regard the differential between themselves and working people as a whole as being naturally exempted from public discussion.

It is the absurd injustice of this system that has begun the first serious public questioning that has taken place in this country, about the total distribution of wealth and income, for very many years.

In short our class structure is at last being publicly examined. Questions of class have not been properly discussed for over a generation.

Yet the reality of class privilege, and class deprivation, remained and was understood and accepted by all classes even if only as an undiscussed and undiscussable fact of life, reflected in the type of housing people had, the wages they received, the educational opportunities afforded to their children, extending right throughout their working life to the two nations in old age.

When historians come to write about this period of British history Mr. Heath will certainly be credited with having awakened people, who had never thought about class before, to what class means, and how it relates to their own experience. This will greatly increase support for the unions and the Labour Party and it explains why the people are rallying to the miners now.

The Conservative party has already become uneasily aware of the dangers for it of Mr. Heath's own action in awakening class consciousness by his policy of confrontation.

The very existence of the Conservative party, the alliance of forces that make it up and its appeal to workers in an election, depends upon the denial of the existence of class divisions in British society.

The Conservative version of national unity rests upon the creation of an illusion that the rich are kind and that if only working people would be restrained we could all raise our living standards together in an unending bonanza of capitalist growth fuelled by some "necessary" inequalities to provide the profits, mainly needed for investment.

That is the master illusion of British politics.

If we cling to that illusion we shall condemn ourselves to a continuation of the present sterile stalemate in British politics. Destroy that master illusion and the democratic reform of our savagely unjust society becomes possible.

This is why the Labour Party in its manifesto argues for "a fundamental and irreversible shift in the balance of wealth and power in favour of working people and their families" through the ballot box and parliamentary democracy which our forefathers fought for and won.

Labour's main task in the next few weeks is to defend those whose living standards are under attack; and to protect our basic democratic rights.

For it is clear that Mr. Heath has decided that the preservation of the existing pattern of power and privilege must be maintained, and he has shown himself ready to do so even if it means dismantling the traditional democratic structure of the Trade Unions, local authorities, and Parliament itself – and attacking the democratic traditions within the Labour Party itself.

The legislation on industrial relations, rents and the Common Market was passed for that purpose.

The Conservative party, and their allies, including the mass media, are prepared to sacrifice even free enterprise itself in order to preserve the pattern of power and wealth that corresponds with their class interests.

This is why they are moving towards an industrial system with some features drawn from corporate states.

This is also why the Establishment has developed six acid tests by which all political Leaders are to be judged, before they can be supported by Editors, and television and radio commentators.

These tests are as follows:

1. Uncritical support for British membership of the Common Market.
2. Full backing for the Industrial Relations Act.
3. Belief in a statutory wages policy.
4. Opposition to the links binding the Trade Unions to the Labour Party.
5. Hostility to the democratic role of the Labour Conference in the policy-making of the party.
6. Denial of the existence of class as a factor in British politics.

Loyalty to these six principles is now seen as essential for survival by those who control our society.

It is exactly these principles which stand in the path of working people as they seek to safeguard their interests.

It is against this background that the Labour movement must now – this very week – take up its historic task again.

It is for us to tell the nation clearly that we are committed to the political, social and economic emancipation of the people, and more particularly of those who depend directly upon their own exertions by hand or by brain for the means of life.

XI

Labour Party Democracy

The Labour Government and the Labour Party*

This letter to my constituents written in February 1968 was one of a whole series of speeches made that year to analyse what had gone wrong with the Labour Government delivered by me as a politician instead of as a Minister.

At the time it was seen as a firm declaration of the importance of the role of the Party at a moment when it was wholly overshadowed by the work of the Government.

...I have been trying to analyse these anxieties. They can be grouped together into three distinct kinds. I do not share them myself, nor I believe do most of the Party. But those who do are sufficiently numerous to be taken seriously.

First: Taking the most extreme case first, there are some of our supporters who are always ready to believe the worst of Labour Governments and who, in their hearts, suspect that they will all ultimately sell out to their enemies. This fear is not, I think, widely shared. It is certainly quite distinct from the criticisms that are made about specific items of policy. But within a Party covering as broad conspectus as we do, it would be surprising that there were not some members of the rank and file who feel this way.

Second: Another group are made up of those who believe that the Government has, in the course of its work, willingly or unwillingly compromised too much with enemy forces. These forces are variously described as including the gnomes of Zurich, Tory leaders in the City or industry, or the conservative establishment in this country. This group attribute specific items of policy with which they disagree to these compromises and their suspicions therefore go beyond the limits that the disagreements themselves would justify. They fear that the Government has lost interest in the Party, is ignoring or even trampling over it. They say we are out of touch with ordinary people or else have chosen to ignore how ordinary people feel.

*Extract from a letter to Bristol South-East Constituency Labour Party, February 22, 1968.

Third: The last group of critics, discouraged by the persistence of our economic difficulties, appear to have convinced themselves that the Government has been blown off course. These include those who were, and remain very sympathetic with what we were elected to do; retain faith in our continuing desire to do it; but fear that we have been driven from one remedy to another and have not followed a clear and identifiable line of policy. They are beginning to doubt whether the Government has now got a clear vision of the sort of society it wants to create, or is just preoccupied with tactics designed to keep itself in power until things improve.

Almost all the criticisms that are now levelled against the Government by party members derive from one or other of these three causes, or when examined, lead back to doubts of the kind I have described.

I have spelled out these doubts clearly for two reasons: First, because it may help those who have them to know that members of the Government understand that they exist. No one should think that any of us delude ourselves about that. Indeed, it would be quite impossible for Ministers, who are M.P.s, to get very much out of touch with what their supporters think, in a Party whose members are accustomed to speak their minds.

The other reason for spelling them out is that when hidden anxieties are brought into the light of day many of them can be seen to be unjustified.

Most, if not all of them, can be attributed to one basic uncertainty — an uncertainty about the role of the Party at a time when a Labour Government is in power.

At the grass-roots level the Labour Party is made up of people, each of whom, individually, joined it and work for it, as a means of getting the things that each of us personally want to see done, done. Each of us therefore has personal criteria by which we judge the actions of the Government. To this extent we are quite different from the majority of active Conservative Party members. Their philosophy encourages them to believe that their prime duty is to sustain a Tory Leader and a Tory Government in power and to defend them against their enemies. Our view is different.

There is an additional factor, which complicates the situation. After years in opposition, the Labour Party found the transition to power difficult. Once a Labour Government was elected, some party members behaved as if they felt that their leaders had got completely swallowed up in the Government. They sometimes seemed to think that the Party has been almost de-capitated, by 'giving up' its top twenty to the Cabinet, leaving no one free from ministerial responsibility to articulate the aspirations and anxieties of those ordinary people who constitute

260

our Party of conscience and reform.

What matters is not whether this fear is justified – but whether it exists. There is ample evidence that it does and the question is – How can it be resolved?

What is, and ought to be, the role of the Party and its leaders while Labour is in power?

It is perhaps easiest to start by defining the formal position. In our Parliamentary democracy a government derives its authority from its majority in the House of Commons, and the House of Commons its authority from the electorate as a whole. A Labour Government has therefore responsibilities to, and for, those who voted against it, as well as those who voted for it, and for those who didn't vote at all.

The difficulty for some party members lies in reconciling this formal position, with their own inner conception of the Labour Government as being, in a special sense, the agent of the Party. For every party member knows that without the work done in the constituencies, guided by the National Executive Committee and Conference, there would be no Labour Government at all. Thus, on this analysis the Party is everything, and the Government is just one of its manifestations.

This apparent contradiction has, in practice, been resolved by the establishment of certain clear conventions. The election manifesto is jointly agreed between the National Executive Committee and the parliamentary leadership. But the implementation of the manifesto is the responsibility of the Cabinet alone. The Party Conference and the National Executive Committee retain their freedom of action, even when Labour is in power, but they cannot and do not seek to dictate to a Cabinet what it should do.

In practice, Labour Cabinets are very close to Party opinion. They are after all made up of Labour M.P.s whose constituency work keeps them, as individuals, in very close touch with the rank and file and with ordinary voters. They are, indeed, in far closer contact with ordinary people than most journalists and others, who so often accuse them of having got out of touch. No Labour Cabinet Minister is unaware of the human consequences of the decisions reached in the Cabinet, nor are they likely to overlook the political consequences of taking the sort of unpopular decisions we have had to take.

Thus, many of the fears which I have described have no real foundation. But the problem is still real enough to make it well worth considering what more the Party itself should do, so as to play its special part more effectively while the Labour Government is in power.

There are now five clear tasks which the Party should set itself, and which only the Party can perform. They are all wholly compatible with the independent role of the Labour Government as I have described it, but they are all necessary for the health and development of the Party as a continuing political entity that will outlive individual Ministers and the life of the Government itself.

First, it is the task of the Party to represent to the Government, more effectively than is now done, the views and anxieties of party members.

This dialogue between Party Leaders and Government Leaders — if you can really disentangle them — is essential both for the health of the Party, and for the health of the Government. The debates at Annual Conference provide one occassion when this dialogue can occur. It continues at the meetings of the National Executive Committee, and its sub-Committees, at each of which Executive Members who are not Ministers meet with Executive Members who are. That, incidentally, is one reason why it is a good thing to have Ministers on the Executive. If they were not there would be no dialogue of this kind at all.

What we need to create are more opportunities for dialogue. We have got to build up the idea of a Party leadership, performing a distinct role as such. The debates that ensue, so long as they do not involve personal attacks, or systematic attempts to defeat the Government in the Commons, are altogether healthy and desirable. They would almost certainly strengthen the Government in what it wants to do.

Second, it is the task of the Party to connect together the different items of Government policy, both as they occur, and retrospectively, into clear themes to give greater coherence to all that is being done. Ministers who are tied down by departmental responsibilities, and are involved in delicate negotiations cannot always, or easily, find the time and opportunity to do this. It is a communications job that needs to be done. And it is for the Party to undertake it as part of its internal political education and campaigning for public support. Had this been done more effectively over the last 3½ years the major themes in the manifesto would have been seen to have been implemented. And most, if not all, of the fears of those who thought we were drifting would have been set at rest. This is a job that a Labour Government, as such, finds it almost impossible to do. The Party is uniquely qualified to do it.

If it is not done effectively during the remaining years of this Parliament the task of fighting the next election, on the record of the Government, will become infinitely more difficult. You cannot produce a framework within which our achievements can be understood and get it accepted, all during the campaign itself. Only if people understand what is happening and why, while it is happening, will the unity of the Government's policy be apparent when it seeks re-election.

Third, it is the task of the Party to look ahead, identify the problems that are on the horizon and evolve policies to meet them at local,

262

national and international levels. Here again the Party is better placed than Ministers for this job. Ministers have an important part to play, and must be drawn into the task of future policy-making, so that their experience and special knowledge is available. But it is only in a Party environment that this experience can be related to the major themes which will be emerging. Moreover, though departments can and should do forward planning, and prepare and publish statistical forecasts, they are not the right or proper place in which to plan the policy of the Labour Party. Nor are they the most congenial location in which to attempt it.

There is not much time to lose. The policy upon which the next election will be fought by Labour has got to be relevant for the first half of the '70's. It has still got to look sensible retrospectively, when it has become the record on which the election of 1975 will be fought. And that election will be decided by voters who, by then, will be thinking about 1980. These forward policies will need to be clear by the end of next year, if we are to allow 12 months to campaign for them before polling day. That means that they have got to be evolved by the Executive and put before Conferences this year and next. A great deal of work is going on. But, there is no time to lose.

Fourth, it is the task of the Party to strengthen its organisation in anticipation of the General Election. The recent Enquiry into Party Organisation is going well and a number of important changes are likely to emerge as a result. But, even when these changes have been agreed, we shall still have the job of carrying them into effect, in the constituencies and at Transport House. It will be a very big job to do all this and it has all to be carried on simultaneously with the tasks that are described above, with which it is intimately connected.

Organisation cannot be tackled in a vacuum. At best it is a way of harnessing the energy and enthusiasm of ordinary people who want to help and want to know how to help. Thus, unless we are able to raise the morale of the Party, its Staff and its Membership, the organisational improvements cannot be fully effective.

No one who cares about the Party can be in any doubt about the magnitude of the task which lies ahead for it in the next election. Tremendous forces will be marshalled against us. There will be huge financial resources at the disposal of the Tory Party for its propaganda. Organisation will be the decisive factor in a sufficient number of marginal constituencies to tip the balance. And we do not yet know how many constituencies will be marginal.

Fifth, it is the task of the Party to protect itself and the Government against those who want to destroy it during the critical eighteen-month period which lies ahead. The Tories and their friends in the City, industry and the press have just begun to realise that if the Government gets through the immediate aftermath of devaluation, its political prospects, which now look so bleak, will be transformed. These people know, better than most, that there is likely to be a large balance of payments surplus next year, and that thereafter, the cuts in defence and overseas military expenditure will improve the position still further. They also know that the measures already taken to improve our industrial competitiveness are beginning to pay off and will do so even more quickly from now on.

That is why the period just ahead is one of such serious potential political danger. For, if the Tories and their friends want to destroy us they have got to do it very quickly indeed — probably in the next few weeks or months.

There is now some evidence building up to suggest that they may well attempt this. The Party must be ready to prevent it if they do.

I have spelled all this out because it is only when one looks at the situation from a Party point of view that the opportunities and the dangers become apparent. The opportunities that would be open to a strong Party over the next few years are immense. The immediate dangers ought not to be ignored.

It is for this reason that loyalty to the Party at this moment is so important. For in pursuit of sincere opposition to specific policies, which individual members of the Party may find repugnant, a crisis of the kind that our enemies are waiting for, could be created.

I have written at length, because I thought it would be helpful if we all had these considerations in mind, when we meet together at our forthcoming Annual General Meeting.

A New Style of Politics*

This speech delivered to the Young Fabians in November 1968 opened up the role of direct action and community politics, the need for a renewed study of Marx and other socialist philosophers to strengthen our analysis of the situation, the importance of open government, the need for democratic decentralisation of power, and the importance of self-criticism within the movement.

. . . Since individual action cannot achieve a great deal, more and more people are banding themselves together to get things done, outside the

*Extract from a speech at a meeting organised by the Young Fabians, November 5, 1968.

party system. In the nineteenth century the main mass organisations that developed — and those were pretty primitive — were political parties. But these organisations do not command complete loyalty today. In any case their sheer size, and the comprehensive nature of their interests, prevent them from dealing completely satisfactorily with individual issues.

They are therefore being supplemented by the development of thousands of pressure groups, which grew up to deal with specific issues and usually draw their support from people of all political affiliations. It would be more accurate to describe these group as Action Groups, for many of them have a life and purpose of their own that extends beyond the exercise of pressure on political parties.

Into this category one must now re-classify the C.B.I., T.U.C.; the new nationalist parties which are single-issue groups; trade associations, individual trade unions and other national organisations based upon the special interests of different groups from chartered accountants to pensioners. To this one must add the consumers' movement, tenants' associations, Shelter, the Black Power movement, the student Left, the Free Universities, the play school movement, the campaign against poverty, the comprehensive schools' committee, the United Nations Association, the W.V.S., and thousands more. Each of these Action Groups is now syphoning off more and more political effort into this sort of direct action.

Even inside the political parties we are now coming to accept more readily that there are stable Action Groups, complete with their own leaders, systematically campaigning to push the loose party coalition, of which they form a small component, in the direction in which they want it to go. The Socialist Chartists, the Monday Club and the Liberal Red Guards are all in this category.

This phenomenon of a myriad of political Action Groups is not really new. What is new is the realisation that they have now become an integral part of a new-style parliamentary democracy, and may, in the process, be undermining the monolithic character of the parties, and in part supplanting them.

Political scientists have always been slow to recognise new trends.

It was not until quite recently that they discovered the importance of political parties, which at one time did not even feature in constitutional text books.

We have now got to accept that political Action Groups are in fact a very powerful factor in our system of government and that unless the political parties find some way of linking up constructively with them, they could undermine the party system, without being able to replace it.

This is certainly not a plea for a wishy-washy consensus politics to mask the sharp clashes and conflicts between parties. Quite the reverse. It is an attempt to restate these inevitable clashes and conflicts in contemporary society, in terms of the multitude of individual issues through which they are expressed, instead of trying to bludgeon us into believing that every political argument of any merit can be compressed, absorbed and dealt with, by two major parties, each with its turn in office, according to the swing of the pendulum.

A political party is by definition challenged by the growth of any new power centres emerging from among the ranks of the electorate as a whole. But the Labour Party should welcome them just because it came into being to make political democracy more meaningful and widespread in economic and social terms. It has got to find a new role for itself and see how best it can serve the people of the country in new circumstances.

The proposals which I am listing should be seen as indicating the direction in which we might move, in our effort to find that new role. The basic formula of the party is right but its methods of operation may well have to change, and indeed are changing in the direction I want to indicate.

First: Labour should broaden the basis of its policy-making

If the new Action Groups, each specialising on particular issues, are to be meaningfully linked to the processes of national political decision-making, the Labour Party must make a conscious effort to establish contact with them. The Party must be modest enough to accept the fact that, with its own necessarily broad responsibilities covering the whole field, it cannot possibly expect to have within itself all the expertise necessary to evolve its own policies unaided. The Party must consciously go out to these groups which are studying contemporary issues, whether those groups or the people who compose them are politically sympathetic or not, and deliberately seek to learn from them.

Obviously the Party must reserve to itself the ultimate right to accept or reject the recommendations that it receives from the Action Groups. It will only incorporate in its election programme those policy items which it finds compatible with its outlook, practicable to implement and sufficiently urgent to command priority. But it will recognise that only in this way can it reconnect itself with the new centres of political initiative which are springing up around it.

To suppose that the vitality of contemporary democratic politics is synonymous with the state of health of the major parties is to miss the significance of what is happening. The argument about broadcasting that is now raging is in part an argument about whether these Action Groups should be given more direct access to the public, as a whole, through broadcasting. While this is denied, the public will continue to be deprived of news and views it is entitled to have.

Second: Labour should offer a continuing and connecting analysis of events

In recent years it has become fashionable to decry both political ideology and religious doctrine. Both words are regularly used as terms of abuse. No doubt there are dangers in an uncritical adherence to old philosophies, distilled from the experience of earlier generations which, if blindly followed in new circumstances, can be irrelevant, dangerous and stupid.

But as we saw in the 1950's political parties wedded to pragmatism may find themselves so absorbed in dealing with the symptoms that they miss the causes of our political malaise, trying remedy after remedy on a suck-it-and-see basis.

All political parties of the Left require both a moral inspiration and a bag of analytical tools to help them to diagnose the causes of current discontent and to identify the character of the power struggle which lies behind important political controversies. The Labour Party is fortunate in having such a rich heritage of both Christian and Socialist thinking upon which to draw. And since socialism, including Fabian Socialism, was intended to introduce a more scientific method into political analysis it is less likely than most political philosophies to be outdated by events.

A really scientific analysis of underlying trends is not synonymous with the advocacy of policies appropriate for dealing with nineteenth century capitalism. It requires the continuing study of the experience of all types of modern society — capitalist, communist and social democratic — from which lessons for the future can be drawn. Karl Marx, Robert Owen, and all the nineteenth century socialist thinkers, taught us much that was of value. Some of what Marx said was wrong, is unacceptable, or out of date. He has however been unfairly held responsible for the horrors perpetrated by Stalin and others, in his name, long after his death. But it is high time that Marx and others were studied again within the democratic socialist movement. They still have something important to say to us, about the nature of society. Moreover the appeal of a socialism that is both internationalist and libertarian is likely to grow.

If the Labour Party is to re-emphasize the role of ideology, it has got to do so in an intelligent and liberal way. It must not be made the occasion for arid controversies nor must discussions about it be conducted like medieval disputations. It must be used analytically to explain and connect together what might otherwise appear to be the unrelated issues of contemporary national and international politics, with which the Action Groups are concerned.

Third: Labour should evolve a thematic approach to election Campaigns

One of the major causes of disillusionment with politics in recent years has stemmed from the fact that election campaigns have been reported on as if they were auctions in which rival candidates seek to outbid each other in promises to the electors. This charge directed against the Labour Party has no foundation. A study of recent Labour election manifestos reveals many clear warnings that the implementation of all the pledges given would depend upon economic circumstances which might well not be within the control of the government.

The Labour Party has much to gain by continuing to present its programme much more in terms of its priorities, the outlook which inspires them, and the themes which it thinks important. That is not to say that policies should not be worked out, in detail, ready for implementation, when the victory is gained. But what ought to be stressed even more is the way in which a Labour Government would approach the sort of issues — many of which simply cannot be predicted — that are likely to confront it during its period in office.

Fourth: Labour should explode the myth of Government omnipotence

Most people now realise that the power of any government is seriously circumscribed by national and international factors over which it has virtually no control. We have had enough evidence, in recent years, of what a Middle Eastern war, an international monetary crisis, or a London dock strike, can do to our economy. But these are only the tip of the iceberg. The fact that freedom of national action is often extremely limited must become much more widely understood. It may be embarrassing to constituency political activists, who would naturally like to claim that their Party can solve all problems, to have to learn to make more modest claims. But if they decline to do so, and gain support by encouraging the idea that they are capable of doing more than can be done, they must not be surprised to find that the greater the expectations they have raised, the greater the risk of disappointment.

Fifth: Labour should press for more open Government

When authoritarian government was both possible, and acceptable, huge barriers of secrecy divided the government from the governed. The governing elite did not want to share its thinking with the masses, and the masses, satisfied by the simplicity of their loyalties, did not want to know the facts. Thus almost everyone was apparently satisfied. There are obviously many issues with which governments deal — military, financial and economic — which the national interest required to be protected by the tightest security procedures. But that is not to say that everything with which a government deals is, or ought to be, secret. The theme of open government ought to be a dominant one for any Party on the Left. Privilege and elitist power are both nourished by secrecy. Exposed to the bright searchlight of public enquiry they crumble into dust. If the Labour Party could continue the policy the Government has already begun, of pressing for more open government, and achieve just that and nothing else, it would release the very forces of change which it now has so much difficulty in mobilising in support of its policies.

Sixth: Labour should seek to sub-contract more of the work of Government to others

If policy is to be drawn, as I have suggested, from a far wider base than has hitherto occurred, it may well be that much more of the functions that government is executing can also be transferred back to the people, organised as they are, in existing or newly-created institutions. The responsibility for overall policy, and for the deployment of resources of men and money, must necessarily remain a function of a central government after assessing the rival claims for priority. But when these overall decisions have been made, the execution of a great deal of policy could well be handed back for others to implement. We see this already in local government and may soon see more of it in regional government too. We have developed it in the nationalised industries, through new organisations like N.R.D.C., I.R.C., and the Shipbuilding Industry Board all manned by industrialists. We would like to see the Trade Union movement willing and able to play a larger part in respect of incomes policy, and one could visualise circumstances in which they assumed far greater responsibilities, by processes of self-regulation of a kind that the medical and legal professions have enjoyed for centuries. Some Action Groups would be capable of discharging these responsibilities.

Indeed the whole theme of self-regulation, which is completely in line with modern scientific management techniques, must become one of major importance. If the development of policy could really be decentralised, and so could much of its implementation, government, freed from those details with which they are ill-equipped to deal, could concentrate more on the task of thinking more deeply about the direction and purpose of society and how national aspirations could be realised.

Seventh: Labour should seek to raise the level of political controversy

Parliamentary democracy is a substitute for civil war. It would be surprising if this did not sometimes lead to fierce, bitter and personal conflict. There are some evil ideas about. But there are probably far fewer villains than one might think from listening to some political debates. There may well be foolish, incompetent and wrong-headed politicians, but few, if any, of our opponents are as bad as we sometimes make them out. Personal bickering usually obscures the issues, irritates the uncommitted and even fails to satisfy the faithful. It is time we recognised this fact, and tried to encourage a higher level of argument that does greater justice to the maturity of the audiences to which it is addressed. If we did so we should get a better hearing. And we shall need a hearing if everything that has to be said is to stand any chance of being accepted.

Eighth: Labour should stimulate and welcome self-criticism

There is nothing that irritates the public more than the apparent self-righteousness of politicians. When they are not attacking their opponents they seem always to be vigorously defending themselves. It is not hard to understand why this should happen. Every politician is understandably sensitive about the violent and unfair things which are said about him by his opponents. To remedy this state of affairs, and to restore the balance, he uses such skill as he possesses in debate to rebut all the charges made against him. Unfortunately this policy of robust and indiscriminating self-defence goes far too far, and amounts to a virtual assertion of infallibility which simply cannot be sustained, and which people will not accept.

Political parties have much to gain from recognising that they too make mistakes and from being a little readier to say so. Self-criticism is only difficult for the weak, and a Party that is strong and intends to remain so, has nothing to fear from devoting some of its critical faculties to a balanced assessment of its own record, from time to time, in order to improve its future performance. That is exactly why the mid-term manifesto was published during the Blackpool conference.

These then are the directions in which I think the Labour Party is moving and should be moving still faster in the next few years. The nature of political activity is in the middle of a profound process of change. Greater complexity of issues, greater inter-dependence of people, the rapid breakdown of authoritarianism and the growing maturity of the people who make up the community, are among some of the factors combining to create a completely new situation, calling for a new style in politics.

If the Labour Party can broaden its policy base, provide a consistent analysis, present its themes clearly and raise the level of political argument, it can offer leadership to a new generation in a society where power is going to become more diffused than it has ever been. It can lead back into the system of peaceful political change, those forces and ideas, which now prefer to live outside that system. If left completely outside, some of those forces could seriously damage the system, possibly by violence, or more likely by just withdrawing their support from it.

The level of latent violence and apathy in a society is a good measure of the effectiveness of its political system. If it rises too high the warning lights will flash and some of them are winking ominously even today. In the immensely difficult and dangerous period of history through which we are passing, we have got to have institutions that are capable of chanelling the energy generated by discontent into constructive effort directed to remove its causes. If that cannot be done it would not just be the Labour Party which would be destroyed, but the whole system of self-government we have painfully built up over the centuries, which would suffer.

We cannot sensibly ask young people today to confine their entire political effort to work within the Labour Party – still less to seek to subcontract their social responsibilities to us to discharge. Everyone has the right and duty to reach his own conclusions about the nature of society and how it should evolve – in short to be his own one-man party. Everyone also has a right and duty, by non-violent action, to work for changes through any Action Groups to which he finds himself attracted.

These two aspects of personal political activity may well absorb the overwhelming majority of his time, effort and loyalty. But the Labour Party's appeal to the new voter must lay claim to at least a small part of it. We must seek to convince him that the creation of the environment in which he can give his best, does require the maintenance in power of a party of conscience and reform, inspired by a purpose, guided by a systematic analysis and drawing its support from a mass movement. If we can harness the new generation, on this basis, to this aim, the Labour Party can play a significant role in the transformation of Britain, and in contributing its own influence to help humanity to meet the terrifying problems which confront it, here and now.

Developing the Party's Objectives*

In this message to the Party issued as the new Chairman on October 15, 1971, I set out five objectives for the year ahead. The uniting of the political and industrial work was seen as central. That year we established the Trade Union/Labour Party Liaison Committee which has met every month since. The end of consensus politics was recorded; the need for a new policy to shift the balance of power and the urgency of working for a greater party democracy were emphasised.

To follow Mik will not be easy. Anyone who sat under his chairmanship on the Executive or watched him preside over three great Party Conferences will know why. His leadership since our defeat in June last year has helped carry us successfully through a very difficult period and set us on the way forward. We are all in his debt.

The Chairman of the Labour Party draws his strength from the apparent weaknesses of his position. He is only there for a year and he has no administrative responsibilities. But just because he is both temporary and powerless, he can speak with greater freedom to and for the movement, listening to what it is saying and helping it to identify the main objectives.

Our objectives this coming year have already begun to emerge and we shall be much more effective if we concentrate on them consciously.

First: We must fight unemployment.

When they came to power, the Tories decided to attack the unions with the oldest weapon of all — the dole queue. Now as the figures move towards the million mark — if in real terms they are not already well above it — ordinary people are beginning to fight back.

This battle cannot be won in Parliamentary debates alone. We have all learned from the UCS and others how important it is that workers stick together and refuse to be bullied.

Success requires the welding together of members of all the unions involved, working with their national officials and planning as for a political campaign.

This is the way to bring the industrial and political wings together in the workshops and constituencies in Britain.

Second: We must campaign for a General Election.

Party Conference has overwhelmingly voted against Heath's attempt to drag Britain into the Common Market without any form of public consent. On this issue Labour speaks for Britain. What is at stake is a high constitutional and democratic principle commanding support well beyond the ranks of the Labour Party.

*"The Thoughts of Chairman Benn", *Labour Weekly*, October 15, 1971. Reprinted by kind permission of *Labour Weekly*.

Heath has even destroyed the faith of some "Europeans" by his contempt for the public. As in the campaign against unemployment, we must work outside as well as inside Parliament this winter so that those who have been brainwashed into believing that they can do nothing realise this is not so.

If a decision as important as this is taken without the approval of the nation, Parliamentary democracy will be undermined.

Third: We must broaden the base of Party support.

The campaign against unemployment and the Common Market will both strengthen us. We must see that this leads to much closer links between the trade unions and constitutency parties up and down the country.

We want more vigorous young men and women trade unionists as Labour candidates and more political education in the factories, so that the lessons Heath is teaching us can be fully understood.

We must also join with those others working on a host of social welfare issues in progressive pressure groups who will ultimately need a Labour Government if their efforts to fight poverty and injustice are to succeed. From these groups, as from the unions, we must aim to recruit more individual members.

Fourth: We must intensify our work on future policy.

The Tories have already shattered the post-war consensus in British politics. Now it has gone, many members of the Party have learned how fragile were some of the gains we had made.

This has turned our minds to the need for more radical policies. Most of the speeches at Conference brought this out and the one policy document presented by the Executive on economic strategy reflected this same belief.

If we are serious about our democratic socialism, we shall require to do more detailed work drawing on the expertise available from outside as well as inside the movement and presenting it for Conference to decide. To succeed, our policy must command wide support of the trade union movement.

More than that we must generate the will among a majority of people first to demand new policies and then to sustain us as we carry them through.

Even with Labour in opposition we must try to force changes in Government policy and by doing so educate a new generation to see the necessity for a real change in the power structure. Everywhere democracy seems to be slipping through our fingers as more and more power is concentrated into fewer hands.

This problem has created something of a crisis of identity, as most people come to think that they don't count any more.

The best way of overcoming it is to encourage people to see political progress as something that they must work for themselves all the time and not just at elections.

Fifth: We must strengthen Party democracy.

If we are to be taken seriously in our desire to revitalise British democracy, we must first prove it by revitalising Party democracy.

Cynicism and pessimism breed on the belief that whatever we do, no one will take any notice. The Party was founded as an instrument to give ordinary people a chance to shape their future by putting their own MPs into Parliament to carry through the changes they wanted to see made.

Sixty-five years later we find that although we have achieved a lot, the basic balance of power in society has not been shifted. Serious problems, which Britain is quite rich enough to deal with, remain unsolved.

This is why Conference matters. However imperfectly some of their specific proposals may seem, it is through Conference decisions that the instincts and aspirations of the movement have been expressed.

And, looking back over the last few years, the instincts of Conference have often been shown to be surer than the most measured judgment of the Parliamentary leadership on many key issues.

On Vietnam, on prescription charges, on the British presence East of Suez, on industrial relations, and even the timing of devaluation, rank and file members can now be seen to have had a pretty good idea of what needed to be done.

How then, can we see to it that these instincts get turned into clear political objectives to guide a future Labour Government? The need for more Party democracy isn't a mechanistic or constitutional issue. It is a major political question that we have got to debate inside the movement this very year.

The leadership of the Party at all levels has got to be more accountable for what it does. This is the only way we can develop democratic responsibility.

These are five tasks on which I believe the movement wants us to concentrate our efforts this coming year. It will be a year marked by a massive constitutional struggle, a continuing industrial battle, both of which will be going on at the same time as we strengthen our organisation, work out future policy and criticise ourselves.

There is something else we need to do as well. We must tear down the barriers of secrecy that still conceal so much of the thinking and working of the Party leadership from its members in the country.

People cannot shape the policies that affect them unless they know what is going on.

The Labour Party nationally and locally has in the past sometimes seemed obsessed with secrecy. The time has come to open up our work.

How better to do it than be seeing that *Labour Weekly* is free to write about it for everyone to read?

Democratic Politics*

In this Fabian Autumn lecture, delivered in 1971, I took the opportunity to set out my views in depth on the future of the Labour Party and democratic socialism united to the trade union movement, and to attack outdated concepts of Parliamentarianism which excluded the role of change from below.

. . . I am optimistic because I believe that the Labour Movement has far more power than it realises. The trouble is that we don't use it properly and worse still, we haven't started to think how to use it effectively.

Until we realize the full extent of our past failures and our present weakness, I do not believe we shall seek to deploy that unused strength to change our society.

There are three main theories about what has gone wrong, and I want to examine each of them in turn before coming on to my own analysis. Let me put them in the form of questions.

Have we failed because Socialism itself is out of date?

Some people argue that what people want now is a responsible and humane administration and the development of a mixed economy distributing the fruits of economic growth more fairly, rather than radical change. It is said that if we adopt the policies advocated by the Left we shall be kept out of power; and that what we need is more research to produce detailed policies which will win back public confidence in our capacity to run a modified capitalism.

It is certainly true that we must be responsible and humane and practical. But my impression is that the people, when they are confronted by the problems thrown up by modern society, demand more radical collective action, not less, and what we lack is not the means but the will to face the powerful forces in society that would be threatened if that change was carried through.

*Extract from the Fabian Autumn Lecture, November 3, 1971.

Have we failed because Labour has been betrayed by its leaders?

There are others who say that our basic problem stems from the fact that the Party has been betrayed by its leaders throughout its history, and that if these successive acts of treachery had not occurred we would have built Socialism long ago. It is argued that these men have got to the top by making promises, both to the Party and to the public, and then, when they get there, they have cynically let us down.

It is certainly true that political achievement measured against promise is often disappointing. It is also true, almost by definition, that anyone who gets to the top by means of the status quo is bound to see, in the status quo, advantages that are not so apparent to those who do less well out of it.

But this analysis implies that Socialism can be created simply by change at the very top. The danger of believing that is that it encourages an endless search for new hero figures. What we really need is a search for new sources of public strength to achieve Socialism.

Have we failed because people are selfish?

There are those who say that many of our problems are insoluble since people are so selfish and so ignorant that they are virtually ungovernable. There are some who have for this reason lost faith in the democratic process altogether. They are looking for a strong Government which will take over and do things. Appeals of this kind come from the extreme right and the extreme Left in the political spectrum.

It is true that the problems are difficult and some seem insoluble, and many people do not appear to want to assume responsibility. But the development in recent years of pressure groups like Oxfam and Shelter and the Child Poverty Action Group should remind us that the public are becoming more rather than less aware of their responsibilities.

But this raises the question of whether you can possibly expect responsibility to be exercised if you do not first give responsibility. Even more fundamentally, it forces us to ask how we can give responsibility, except to people who are already demanding it.

This brings me straight to the major theme I want to develop in this lecture. It is very simple, very old, but, for all that, very radical. It is this: we shall never change society unless we start to do it ourselves by directly challenging the unaccountable power now exercised over us, and prepare to exercise it responsibly ourselves, exactly as our forefathers did in demanding the vote in the nineteenth century.

Technical change has certainly led to the creation of enormous power groupings. Not only are governments bigger and more powerful, but so are local governments, which will be far bigger and more remote when they have been reorganized, corporations, universities, public authorities, and the mass media. These are the unaccountable powers that seem to oppress us, make us feel so helpless, and almost threaten our sense of personal identity.

But we sometimes forget that the bigger these organizations are the more fragile they are, the more vulnerable to dislocation, the more sensitive to public disapproval, and the more anxious they themselves are about their own elephantine paralysis of decision-making.

If we try to face them alone with a philosophy of individualism, we are lost before we start. But if we gather together in collective effort, we can win some surprising victories.

The workers at UCS, and now in other factories too, are important because they are trying to do just that and are a small but significant contemporary example. The victory of the American people over the Pentagon on the question of the Vietnam war that forces Nixon to campaign for re-election by visiting Mao Tse-Tung is even more dramatic.

Indeed in much of the world it has been the apparently weak who have banded themselves together resolutely with clear objectives who have done best against the lumbering monoliths with their modern management methods, computerised decision-making systems and over-sophisticated technology. Ralph Nader's successes should prove that.

Everywhere today, people, possessed of better education and more knowledge than ever before in history, sense that this is true. There are literally thousands of voluntary groups now engaged in the battle of ideas. If the people have so much potential power, why do those who enjoy privileges seem to be able to hold on to them so easily?

The awful truth is this: that it is outdated concepts of Parliamentary democracy accepted by too many political leaders in Parliament and on Local Authorities, which have been a major obstacle to the full use of that winning combination of popular power.

This is not a criticism of Parliamentary democracy itself which could work better if it could harness that power. What I am saying is that Parliamentary democracy will never achieve Socialism unless it does succeed in doing so. For too many modern political leaders have inherited an arisocratic view of parliament and their role in it.

They even assert the 'divine right of Parliament', as has happened over the Common Market, which is just as unacceptable as the 'divine right of kings', a doctrine fought and defeated 300 years ago. We didn't struggle for all those years to win the franchise just for the right to elect benevolent despots to govern us.

This is not a personal criticism of individual Labour leaders who are

277

genuinely doing their best according to their idea of how Parliamentary government works.

It is a criticism of that completely obsolete philosophy of Parliamentary government uncritically accepted by so many people which holds us back. This philosophy explains why political leaders often seem to be telling the people two things: *first* — "There is nothing you have to do except vote for us"; and *second* — "If you do vote for us, we can solve your problems."

Both these statements are absolutely and demonstrably false. There is a great deal that ordinary people can and must do besides voting, and there is practically nothing that political leaders can do unless the people work with them in parallel and in partnership.

The credibility gap in British politics stems far more from the persistent exposition of this archaic theory of democracy from political platforms, the mass media and in schools and universities than from any individual failures of individual political leaders.

It does not arise mainly from excessive promises made in particular policy fields. It arises from a wholly incredible claim made for the whole system which cannot achieve what it claims just because it focusses too exclusively on Parliament and virtually ignores the people's role in social change.

We won't solve this problem by always seeming to look for new candidates for office with charisma and impatient to take over the reins of power ready to work miracles of achievement single-handed. All such men are destined to fail until we have exposed the whole fraudulent philosophy that is really to blame. This is what is so depressing about the way American Presidential campaigns are conducted, selling candidates as if they were super-human whilst cynically accepting that they are disposable.

This is not an appeal for violent revolution or even systematic and sustained civil disobedience. In Britain we don't need them. It is an appeal for a strategy of change from below to make the Parliamentary system serve the people instead of serving the vanity of Parliamentarians: an appeal for popular democracy. Indeed the greatest achievements of the Left came about this way.

Historically, when democratic pressures from below were strong enough, the system worked just because the people on top accepted them. This is how the British people won free trade unionism, got the vote, the Welfare State and the Health Service, and why we are tackling the environment and thinking afresh about women's rights.

This being so, why should it be regarded as so unacceptable when Parliamentarians interpret their representative function as meaning that they should accept these pressures and respond to them?

So long as political leaders are reluctant to admit to what really happens, they will effectively keep their own supporters, whom they need to change society peacefully, in a state of semi-demobilisation, implying that there is nothing much they can do outside Parliament. In short, the historic role of democracy is to allow the people to have their way. A real leader will actually welcome the chance to give way to the forces that he has encouraged and mobilised by a process of education and persuasion. Legislation is thus the last process in a campaign for change. It is the role of Parliament as a forum, and the role of a political leader as an adviser or teacher, that we must see to be the most important.

Those who find it disturbing that an aristocratic and authoritarian view of democracy is no longer acceptable, workable or credible, should note an important new development.

Just as the massed ranks of the citizenry appear to have mutinied against their officer class and it looks as if discipline has utterly broken down, another very remarkable change can be seen taking place. The very people who are no longer prepared to be shouted at through a megaphone, and told what to do, are crowding round the back door asking their leaders for advice.

They are looking for advisers to help them. But often they aren't finding them, because their leaders are dressed up like generals, geared only to giving orders instead of acting more modestly as advisers. And, since politicians are so reluctant to assume that modest role, people search elsewhere for leadership.

In the process of political advance we must therefore start at the bottom and work back towards the top, or what it would be more accurate now to call the centre of the system.

The people must be helped to understand that they will make little progress unless they are more politically self-reliant and are prepared to organize with others, nearest to them where they work and where they live, to achieve what they want. An individualist philosophy tenuously linked to an aristocratic political leadership will get them nowhere.

This is not a wishy-washy appeal for 'participation' as a moral duty or 'job enrichment' as a management technique, or 'involvement' as a Dale Carnegie philosophy of life. It means telling the people the truth: if you don't organize with others to change your life situation, the only change we can guarantee you is the 'in' and 'out' of alternative parties in power.

Democratic change starts with a struggle at the bottom and ends with a peaceful Parliamentary victory at the top. That is what I want to call Popular Democracy.

Three arguments are used against this idea of popular democracy.

Some people say the public don't want to change things. Of course, if they don't, things won't change. But they do want change. One of

279

the reasons that they don't even try to get it is that so many political leaders tell them that a ballot paper each quinquennium is their only weapon, and the people rightly find this view lacks credibility, but know no other way.

Some people say that the public are not intelligent enough to do it themselves. What does that argument mean? It means that those leaders who use it, are saying that they are much cleverer than the electors, and are really trying to use their 'brains' not to communicate and persuade, but to conceal behind a phoney smoke screen of phoney complexity, so as to hang on to power.

Some people say that the public, if given more power, would start hanging and flogging, and deporting immigrants, and behaving like savages, and assert that an emotional instability of the public is a barrier to popular democracy, and that it is only the 'civilised' M.P.s who protect us from this terrible anarchy. This is a grave condemnation of the whole idea of democracy and it flies in the face of all historical experience. Any study of the past will show that ordinary people have been responsible for far less savagery than can be laid at the door of political leaders of all complexions in the exercise of their power, even in pursuit of quite honourable ends. If the polls imply that they are, it is often because, deprived of power they are driven to simple solutions in protest at their exclusion.

What I am, therefore, seeking is a different analysis of political change that recognises some new realities and consigns the old outworn interpretations to the dustbin.

Major political reforms usually occur when people want them, go out to get them, and some Leadership exists to connect together all that is happening, so that each part reinforces the rest, and the whole creates the confidence that success can be achieved. Belief in the possibility of success is an essential ingredient.

The Labour Party was created to perform this function. Such achievements as it has to its credit have stemmed from a convergence of all these factors. But more recently progressive pressures have mainly developed outside the party.

Gravest of all the party, when in power, alienated the most important pressure group of all from it — the British Trade Union Movement. We now need their energy and they now need our Leadership, if we are to succeed.

Our object must be to stress the role the people can play, more consciously. We must stimulate everyone to demand a greater share of power and responsibility.

I now turn to the party itself. Our internal democracy is also riddled with the same aristocratic ideas as deface our national democracy. What has happened over the Common Market has pinpointed both the weaknesses of Parliament and the weaknesses of the Labour Party at one and the same moment. This is what is so deeply worrying.

We must therefore start with Party democracy and start a debate to see how we can make it real.

The problem of achieving greater party democracy is now the central internal problem facing the Movement. It is not just a question of considering constitutional amendments — though constitutional amendments might well follow from the debate at a later stage.

It is not a question of re-opening old arguments about the relationship of conference decisions to the Parliamentary Labour Party which have been clearly explained and are fully understood within the party. It is not just about the merits or demerits of the block vote — although the debate must deal with the relations between the Party and the Conference and the political work of the Unions.

It is not just about organisation, although the vitality of our Party organisation ultimately depends upon the morale and motivation of those who have to make it work. It involves all these things and it does so by making Party democracy a major *political* theme which we must come to see as being just as important as what policies a future Labour Government may one day pursue, and as an essential preliminary to the process of getting those policies right, and seeing that they are really carried through when the electorate choose us again.

Why have such a debate? Will it be unnecessary and divisive? Must it involve bitter personal controversy?

Not at all. Properly conducted it can actually help us to get away from personalities, and as it proceeds even the fierce argument it stirs may help us to arrive at a new understanding about our own role as a Party.

Many of our problems and difficulties stem from the fact that we have never had this debate except in the context of particular political arguments. In the past, the line-up in the Party has reflected the particular issue we were then discussing, rather than the problems of party democracy that it has highlighted.

While the Common Market issue highlights this problem this year, I hope that the debate about Party democracy can maintain its impetus and vitality alongside, and separately from it.

The connection between party democracy and the pace of social change may be closer than we think. Year after year Conference and back-bench MPs have urged more radical policies; and yet measured by the demands that these contained the performance has been disappointing. Conference decisions, however imperfectly they may be drafted, and however impracticable some of their specific proposals may be, are at the present the only means by which the instincts and aspirations of the movement as a whole can be expressed.

There are serious defects in the system of debate and decision which lie behind conference decisions. We should see them not as pieces of party legislation precise enough for enactment as they stand or enforcement in the courts. They are broad political objectives formulated by the mass membership to guide the Parliamentary leadership. The problem is that many of these objectives have not been realised.

This is why any debate on party democracy requires us to look at the different views expressed by the National Party at Conference and the Parliamentary Leadership in the Commons.

Looking back over the years of the last Labour Government there were a number of occasions when the rank-and-file Party and Trade Union members and Conference found themselves in conflict with the Labour Government.

Let me give five examples:-

First: From 1964 to 1966 the Party instinctively disliked the idea of restricting economic growth to preserve the value of the pound. The Government, on the other hand, with access to its inside information, thought it best to delay devaluation and put the balance of payments before growth.

Second: The movement generally wanted to see an immediate end to the East of Suez policy; so as to hasten defence cuts and release resources for use at home. The Cabinet, however, only reached its decision to end Asian military commitments after devaluation, and the process of withdrawal was not completed by the time we left office.

Third: The movement instinctively disliked what it took to be the Government's implied support for the American policy in Vietnam, and wanted a clear declaration of opposition to it. Ministers, however, argued that private representations were more effective and resisted appeals to speak out openly against the war.

Fourth: The rank and file greatly resented the prescription charges reimposed in the devaluation cuts, and were not convinced by Ministerial arguments that these were an essential ingredient of the economic success we sought.

Fifth: The Labour Cabinet's industrial relations policy is still too close for it to be necessary to remind ourselves that the movement as a whole did not accept the way the Government approached the problem.

I must emphasize at this stage in this argument that I fully accept the collective responsibility that I personally shared, and still share with all my former ministerial colleagues for *all* the policies that I have described and am not seeking to escape from any part of that responsibility. What I am saying is that with the benefit of hindsight it is likely that the movement had a surer instinct on these issues than the Cabinet.

I have not said this to reopen old wounds, but to encourage us to ask ourselves whether, and why it was that, the instinct of the Party may have proved better than the majority view of good and loyal Party members who happened to have been Cabinet Ministers.

If the judgement of the Labour Movement on major policy was as, or more often, right than that of Labour Cabinets with their access to the sheltered advice of their civil servants, how can we make the movement more effective – in setting the political objectives which are to be implemented by a future Labour Government? The only possible way to do so is by treating Conference decisions with greater respect – not on narrow and legalistic constitutional grounds – but because of their wisdom.

At the moment there is a blockage in the system which prevents this from happening. To be precise, there are two blockages: one is the blockage in Party democracy and the other is the far greater blockage in Parliamentary democracy which I have described.

For at the heart of our presently accepted theory of party democracy too, you will find embedded the doctrine that elected leaders advised by experts must by definition be more likely to be right than the Party as a whole. This doctrine which those who favour entry into EEC obviously deeply believe is at the very best a half-truth, at worst a fundamental misconception of the whole nature of party democracy, and must be wholly unacceptable within the Labour Movement.

We must therefore try to make the representative system work more democratically inside the Labour Party, by making Labour Leaders more accountable for what they do. Every elected person has a healthy respect for his constituents who put him there, and can remove him, thus ensuring his accountability. But how much power in the Labour Party is really accountable?

The fact is that those who exercise power in the Labour Party are not as accountable as they could be or should be.

Some people think that this is a very good thing. They almost imply that democratic pressures are by definit'on improper, and divert elected representatives from performing their duty as laid down by Edmund Burke two hundred years ago.

Back-bench pressure on a cabinet is automatically assumed to be something that a cabinet should resist. A conference resolution is seen as a threat to the independence of Parliament, and the relations between an M.P. and his constituency party are scrutinized for any hint of victimisation.

This idea is so deeply rooted in the aristocratic philosophy of politics that it is time we examined it more critically. For if democratic pressures are improper then how do you achieve any accountability of power within the party, and if you don't want accountability to democratic pressures what about the other pressures to which representatives are subjected?

The strength of undemocratic pressures are enormous. Cabinets are subjected to foreign pressures on major questions of economic policy, industrial pressures from large corporations, pressures from the mass media which are accountable to no-one — to name but a few.

The case for positively stimulating democratic pressures is in part to act as a countervailing power to prevent representatives from being dominated from other sources.

There is another reason too. These outside "non-accountable power centres" which press on representatives are the very same as those which press on the citizen himself. He can do nothing about them and he must necessarily want his democratic influence to be strengthened since it is the only tenuous link he has with real power in Parliament through his political party or trade union.

It is certainly arguable that if we could have found a way of making democratic pressures within the Labour Party more effective we could have accelerated the pace of social change.

These are the considerations we should have in mind as we approach the debate on party democracy.

We should resist the temptation to propose some obvious ways in which the democratic pressures within the Labour Party could be considerably reinforced.

I have heard it argued that the leader of the Labour Party should be ratified by conference after he has been elected by Labour MPs.

It has sometimes been suggested that when Labour is in power the Cabinet should be elected by back-bench MPs just as the Shadow Cabinet is elected by them when we are in opposition.

Similarly some people have urged that there should be a system of primary elections on the American model in which all registered party supporters could join in the process of selecting their candidate.

But it would be a great mistake to start this debate by looking for precise solutions to problems of democratic responsibility that have not yet been properly analysed and considered.

I am therefore not recommending any more than that we begin this process of analysis.

Take for example the role of back-bench MPs when Labour is in power.

Here are men with a great experience who are cast in the role of the governed even when their party has assumed the role of government.

They are of course shut out by the Official Secrets Act from knowing what factors are influencing their ministerial colleagues.

These ministers are appointed by the Prime Minister and when they address back-benchers they are not speaking to their constituents, as opposition spokesmen are when the party is out of office.

A Labour Prime Minister, unlike a Leader of the Opposition, is himself only confirmed in his office as leader at the beginning of each Parliament and not elected session by session.

Ought we to be looking for ways and means of making a Labour Government more accountable here?

Take a Labour leader himself and his relations with conference. He, and the deputy leader, are the only two men who sit on the National Executive Committee on the platform at Conference who never meet their constituents there at all. Unlike every other member of the N.E.C., each of whom is elected by a section of the Conference, these two men are only addressing a mass rally when they speak.

Is this something that requires further study and if so, how could one create a link that expressed itself in a creative way?

Take the MP in a safe Labour seat who may serve in Parliament for years on the basis of his victory at a single selection conference by a narrow majority. Where is the thread of accountability here to his political colleagues as distinct from his accountability to his registered Parliamentary electors?

Before anyone thought of tampering with the present system all its implications would have to be considered very carefully but that is no reason for not asking the question.

Similar questions should certainly be asked in respect of the leaders of Labour groups on local authorities, the Chairman of committees in Labour-held councils and even Labour councillors themselves, and these questions will be a great deal more relevant to the massive new local government bodies created when the reorganisation of local government goes through.

The same question should certainly be asked about the representative system within the trade union movement in respect of the big political decisions in which they participate at annual conference.

Insofar as the block vote reflects the real power of organised Labour which is the heart of the Labour Party it is right and proper that it should be recognised.

But it is also quite reasonable for those within the Trade Unions who are taking up the theme of party democracy to want to see that those who exercise this massive voting power should be accountable to their own members for the use they make of it.

Indeed the more seriously we are to take conference decisions the more interested we must be in the way those decisions are reached.

I must emphasize that I am trying to start a debate and not suggest what the solutions should be. I have deliberately chosen some of the most sensitive issues in the hope that this debate will not get bogged down in detail.

I suspect that support for strengthening party democracy is not confined to one section of the party or one wing of the movement but is more widespread than we had imagined.

Most of us know that this issue is closely linked with the problems of apathy and pessimism and is far more relevant than sterile personality clashes from which the party suffered in the past.

It is also a much better way of handling our differences than could ever be achieved by trying to use disciplinary methods to secure agreement. The party has always gained from having men of principle within it who have fought hard for what they deeply believe. No-one wants to coerce those who have so much to offer.

One of the most difficult and important questions that we shall have to face relates to the relations between the Party and the Trade Union Movement.

The whole tradition of Parliament, and indeed its composition and its idea of leadership are different from those that have emerged in the Trade Unions over the years.

Parliament, on both sides, is made up of people most of whose incomes have been individually determined, rather than collectively agreed. MPs are operating within an institution that is more used to giving orders and working on their own initiative unlike Trade Union members, who spend their lives in an authoritarian working environment and have their income collectively agreed after tough bargaining. Like any organisation that was created from below the traditions of T.U. leadership stem from a desire by people to have their representatives accountable to them in contrast to the Burkean traditions which guide MPs.

Therefore the problems of getting a good working relationship between the Parliamentary and Trade Union wings of the Party involve discussing differences that are almost cultural in character. This should not deter us from trying.

Certainly Labour MPs would find it easier if they recognised more publicly the enormous role of the Trade Unions in safeguarding the interests of their members, that go well beyond wages and working conditions and involve pressing for legislative changes on Governments of all Parties and are more effective than oppositions or back-benches alone can be.

Similarly Trade Unions who are properly concerned with the interests of their own members have now got so much power in society that their responsibilities have grown too. These must necessarily encourage them to take a sympathetic attitude towards a Labour Government, which has to face very difficult problems – not least the outer reality of looking after the interests of Britain in a world where many of the key decisions are necessarily taken elsewhere.

This relationship also needs to be deepened.

At the top there should be far closer contact to allow discussion of common problems upon which the success of future Labour Governments depend.

And in the constituencies there would be everything to be said for trying to involve Trade Union members in political work on a more systematic basis, and for seeking to do more political education in the factories and workshops and offices.

In this way a relationship which has sometimes been tense and difficult could be improved and made beneficial not just to the two sides but to the nation as a whole.

The public as a whole will become very interested if they think we are ready to criticise ourselves and really want to make ourselves and British politics more democratic. They listen to us much more seriously when we criticise the Government, and ask them, as people, to play a larger part in changing our society.

And that is our larger long-term Socialist purpose: to democratise British life. Democracy is the life blood of our socialism, and distinguishes it sharply from the dictatorship we have seen in communist societies.

We shall be a far more effective instrument to do that if first we have considered the same questions internally in the Party. Indeed we must if we are to be credible and effective in democratising Britain by mobilising all the energy of our own people to change society for themselves, in partnership with us.

But we cannot do that unless people know more accurately what is going on. The essential pre-conditions of success is that this debate must be conducted in the open.

The aristocratic view of politics that now dominates Parliament and from which the party is not altogether free thrives on the maintenance of secrecy.

Since it is an integral part of my argument that a change in our national and party democracy must begin from below, those who work below must first be allowed to know exactly what is happening at the top.

Having argued strongly for self-reliance as the basis of all do-it-yourself social reform, I have had to consider what the chairman of the party can best do, to help the party to reform itself. Perhaps the best answer to that question is to try to make the chairman himself more accountable by reporting as accurately and faithfully to the

287

movement, exactly what is happening within the national and parliamentary leadership.

The truth is more likely to unite than to divide the party – by helping it to see its way forward to a new and broader interpretation of modern popular democratic socialism. Whether this is right or wrong will depend on whether the themes developed in this Lecture command general support within the movement.

These then are my reasons for urging a period of intense public discussion about the nature of Parliamentary democracy – in which I passionately believe – and the nature of Party Democracy where there are important problems to be faced.

If it is thought they are too difficult, or too dangerous or too divisive to embark on this debate I fear that we shall miss a great opportunity.

Moreover I suspect that if we don't face the issues we shall make it easier for people to drive wedges between differing groups within the Parliamentary Labour Party; between the PLP and the Party nationally; between the Party and the Unions; and between the Movement and the Public at large.

If this were to have the effect of weakening people's confidence in the Party or in the capacity of Parliament to meet their rapidly changing needs the trend to the right would continue.

Our best safeguard against this is the development within the movement of closer links between the Leadership, the Party and the people.

If this can be constructed more democratically, and in a way that allows people to be responsible by giving them more responsibility, then we shall have the organic strength to resist the swing to the right and resume the advance towards democratic socialism.

It is therefore for National, as well as Party, reasons that the debate should begin, and I believe that when it does we might be surprised to find how welcome it will be.

Unity with the Unions*

These fraternal greetings from the Chairman of the Party at the Trade Union Congress in Brighton in September 1972 called for a joint programme of industrial and political action to meet the challenge posed by the Conservative Government, and to prepare for a Labour Government with which the Unions would help shape policy up to and including Cabinet level.

My fraternal greetings will be short and simple.

Four years after the Labour Government and the TUC clashed directly over Industrial Relations; two years after the defeat of that Labour Government, we now have to start again, stop blaming one another, and work out a joint programme of industrial and political action to meet the needs of the people we represent.

For the last two years, we have been defending fundamental, industrial, political and democratic rights against the most direct attack that has been made on them for more than fifty years.

The unions are in the front line of that battle and you have won some notable successes.

We must not underestimate the difficulties.

This Government is backed by all the richest and most powerful economic interests in Britain, using expensive and successful propaganda campaigns to promote those interests.

We have also to contend with the mass media which are, in the main, ignorant about, and hostile to, the working people.

Even television does not seem to be interested in them before their problems become explosive, and it forgets them again as soon as the immediate crisis seems to be over.

We shall never make progress if we are not all constantly reminded of the unemployment, poverty, inequality, injustice, class, sex and race discrimination that still scar our society, and that the Labour Movement has failed to eliminate in over a century of our industrial and political work.

The mere defeat of this Government and the election of another Labour Government will not therefore, of itself, transform our society overnight, or automatically, into a fair, democratic and humane community.

If we mean to do better we should first take a hard look at our own experience.

The last Labour Government — in which I was proud to serve — faced and surmounted appalling economic difficulties, and carried through a formidable programme of socialist reforms.

*Fraternal greetings of the Labour Party to the Trades Union Congress at Brighton, September 5, 1972.

It also made some mistakes.

One of those mistakes was in our approach to industrial relations, and we lost the confidence of many of our own people.

I accept my full collective responsibility for that decision. It is not pleasant to admit you were wrong. But we must if we are to learn from our own experience.

Even so, history will be much more generous about our achievements than were our critics.

It is simply not good enough to blame the Labour Government or the Parliamentary Labour Party entirely for our defeat in 1970

The Trade Union Movement, with all its virtues, must also accept its share of responsibility.

Until very recently, the unions have hardly made any serious effort to explain their work to those who are not union members, even to the wives and families of those who are.

You have allowed yourselves to be presented to the public as if you actively favoured the conservative philosophy of personal acquisitiveness.

The fact that the Trade Union Movement came into being to fight for social justice, as well as higher wages, has just not got across.

If the public opinion polls prove nothing else, they certainly prove that.

Finally, neither the Party nor the TUC has given sufficient support to other movements of legitimate protest and reform led by women, by the old and by the young and by others — who are, in reality engaged in our common struggle.

If we want them to be more interested in us, we must be more interested in them.

We have not yet agreed how we should respond to these challenges.

But these are not new problems.

There is nothing that I can say that has not been said before, at past Congresses, facing far greater difficulties than this Congress faces.

The past experience of the Labour Movement is still our best guide to the future.

Let me try to summarise that experience:

1. There must be a large, strong united Trade Union Movement, with the courage to stand for the rights of its members.

2. The Trade Union Movement must seek its political objectives as an integral part of an organised, democratic, Labour Party in Parliament, with a socialist programme.

3. The Labour MP's we put in power must abide by majority decisions reached through its own democratic procedures, and never forget those who put them there.

4. The Unions and the party must shape policy together, at every level,

– not just in opposition – but even more when Labour is in power up to, and including, Cabinet level.

5. We must gain democratic control over the new, huge and remote centres of irresponsible managerial power created by the latest industrial revolution.

6. We must welcome the growing demand for greater workers' control in industry, so long as it grows organically within the trade union structure and tradition, and is democratically achieved.

7. We must rediscover our internationalism. Capital has always organised itself internationally. Labour has not yet done so, effectively.

8. The Labour Movement must always exercise its power responsibly, and in the public interest.

These are the very same principles upon which our movement is based.

Our whole history tells us how to work together for the transformation of Britain, by our own direct efforts, combining industrial and political action, peacefully, by persuasion, using Parliament as an instrument to serve the people.

It *will* be a slow and difficult process and may take many generations to complete.

Some, even in our Movement, say it cannot be done. Others that it is not worth trying. But there is not short cut to socialism.

When it has been attempted it has often led to a betrayal of the very ideals of freedom that inspired its founders.

The Movement must have faith in its own experience and use it.

This year we have, in fact, begun to do just that, in our Liaison committee.

We have deliberately worked, slowly and carefully, to win back mutual confidence.

We have agreed on the total, unconditional and immediate repeal of the Industrial Relations Act by the next Labour Government, to be replaced by legislation to strengthen free voluntary Trade Unionism.

Next, we shall tackle issues of economic management – to which no-one has yet found an answer – including what is called Incomes Policy.

We shall certainly reject a general freeze, overall statutory restraints, any system which penalises the lower paid, and the whole idea that wages are the sole, or even the principal, cause of inflation.

We shall be talking about the whole question of the distribution of wealth, and income of all kinds and from all sources; about social policy, public ownership; about industrial and regional and employment policies.

In these talks we are bound to discuss the relationship between earnings and production; between incomes in the public and the private

291

sectors; between the higher and the lower paid; and between the level of income at work, and, the scandal of poverty amongst those who have retired.

The lower paid, the unemployed, the poor, the old, the sick and the disabled, *expect* the Labour and Trade Union Movement to use its industrial, and political, strength to compensate for their weakness and to guarantee them the income they need.

Any fool can write a book about these problems. But it takes hard work, and much public debate, to find solutions that are fair and acceptable and that will work.

But you can't expect to leave it to the TUC General Council or the next Labour Cabinet.

If we are serious about making Britain into a country worthy of its people, every single person living here will have to accept his or her share of responsibility. This is more than participation. It is a necessary part of a mature democracy.

There are already signs that more and more people are ready to assume that responsibility, and are demanding radical reforms that prove they are in earnest.

They need us to work with them and for them.

If we are ready to serve the people there is nothing we cannot achieve — together.

Closing the Conference*

This speech was delivered at the end of the 1972 Conference as the chairman's final address.

... What did this conference say? It said, I believe, three things. First of all it said we want the Party to turn towards Socialism in the next government. It said we want Socialist answers to the problems of industry, to the problems of land, to the problems of homes, to the problems of health, to the problems of education, and that unmistakably came from the floor and from the platform.

Secondly, it said we want unity. We want unity between the trade union movement and the political wing. We want unity between the Parliamentary Party and the Party in the country. We cannot at this moment fail to respond to the demands of our own people that we should be able to take up the challenge when next we have the chance.

*Extract from closing speech as Chairman of Labour Party Conference, October 1972.

Comrades, the third thing they said was, we want democracy. We want democracy in industry. We want democracy in education. We want democracy in local government. We want democracy on the Common Market. We want democracy in the trade unions. We want democracy in the Party. I believe that great theme, far from being, as has been presented, some new fashion of participation, is the oldest message working people have ever taught their rulers throughout the history of this country.

Comrades, this week we have spoken for Britain, but more than that, we have demanded the right of the people of this country to speak for themselves. We have demanded that they should have access to the public to speak of the dignity of labour, to raise the problems that concern them in their life and work. To give them the right to govern Britain for themselves, which is what democracy is all about.

Comrades, we have demanded a general election and we have demanded it now. And that is the message that has come out of this conference. By a chance, not of our own making, the opportunity to bring about that election has at this very moment been given to us. It was announced 50 minutes ago that there is to be a by-election in Lincoln. We are told it is to be fought by a Democratic Labour Candidate who is neither democratic nor Labour.

I say nothing of our departed colleague, though a tinge of sadness must mark his going. I say nothing of him because other men have done it before and they have never been able to do any damage to us.

Comrades, the importance of this occasion is that we are for the first time in the history of British politics fighting a political party invented by the press of this country. That is the significance of the Lincoln election. Last Sunday the editor of the *Times* invented a new political party. He sent out his market research people to ask the public "What sort of a party would you like?" – the man, I might add, who has been condemning what is called populism. He sent them out to say "Would you like it a bit to the left? Would you like it a bit to the right?", as if he was designing some soap, detergent or beer. The television companies are now preparing the.most massive campaign in support of the candidate Fleet Street is promoting in the Lincoln election. Television companies, who have ignored working people, distorted what they have said and insulted them in so many of their programmes, have tried to suggest that our people are either apathetic or violent. These people have made the great mistake of coming out of their corner and testing their party in the ballot box.

Comrades, the problems of Fleet Street may be difficult to handle when they are coping with their newspapers. I sometimes wish the trade unionists who work in the mass media, those who are writers and broadcasters and secretaries and printers and lift operators of Thomson

House would remember that they too are members of our working class movement and have a responsibility to see that what is said about us is true.

We have in our history, as I said in my Chairman's Address, comrades, we have taken on kings, we have taken on land owners, we have taken on factory owners, and now in this impending by-election, make no mistake, we are taking on the mass media in the campaign that is just about to begin. I may say too, comrades, that when Fleet Street tests itself in the polling stations the British people will have the opportunity to give their answer in unmistakable terms, for the truth is that the people who are supporting the campaign there are people who have not got the interests of our working people at heart.

Now comrades, we shall not fight this battle with equipment of the same kind or with the same money behind us but if every delegate who is here at this Conference, and those to whom the report back is made, would go quietly to Lincoln to talk to the people and tell them what we have said here, there is no doubt that we shall win, and in the process we shall precipitate the general election that we want.

Comrades, I have had to bring many speakers to a conclusion. Ron, you must give me the red light. But it is a red light for Mr. Heath and for Socialism in Britain and I invite you to join me now in singing the Red Flag.

Conference Democracy*

Tribune *asked for a personal account of my Chairmanship of the 1972 Annual Conference, at which I sought to make the chair a servant rather than the master of the delegates.*

Annual conference is the central policy-making body of the Labour Party. It is mainly through conference that individual party members and affiliated trade union members can really influence Labour MPs or can contribute items for future election manifestos to shape the programme of Labour Governments in office.

The maintenance of democracy within the Labour Party therefore depends upon upholding the role of conference. Without it, the rank and file could become a mere fan club of the Parliamentary leadership, passing resolutions bereft of meaning. Many of the tensions between the last Labour Cabinet and the movement arose over Conference decisions that were set aside.

*Article in *Tribune*, January 19, 1973. Reprinted by kind permission of *Tribune*.

It is not surprising that so many of the press and television commentators and a lot of academics should try to belittle conference by ridiculing its proceedings and downgrading its importance. For if conference really could strengthen its influence within 'the party it would significantly increase the power of working people over government decisions which affect their lives and prospects.

It was with that single object of strengthening the democratic role of conference that, as chairman, I approached my task at Blackpool – and before.

First, I encouraged the presentation of Labour's *Programme for Britain* as a "Green Paper" to go to conference for discussion, and not as a cut and dried programme that had to be accepted or rejected as a whole. The NEC agreed to submit it in this way so that it could be debated alongside resolutions placed on the agenda; to be amended, as it is being, in the light of those resolutions which were passed. This year a comprehensive statement can be laid before the party to which conference has already directly contributed its part.

Secondly, I made it clear – in a speech at Tiverton before the conference began – that the resolutions that were passed "must be accepted by the movement." This phrase, carefully chosen to highlight the gravity of conference decisions, was widely taken by the press as an attack upon the Parliamentary leadership.

It was no such thing. It was to reassure the movement that its decisions really mattered. Without that reassurance, conference might well have been tempted to pass resolutions couched in stronger terms than it really intended because it might fear they would be disregarded. Had it been driven by frustration to do so, it would have restricted unnecessarily the discretion in applying conference policy which the PLP needs and has always had.

Thirdly, I tried to interpret the role of chairman, not as the strong-arm man of the Executive railroading NEC policy through, but as the servant of the delegates as a whole, treating them with respect and consciously helping them to arrive at the decisions which they wanted to reach.

From this principle of chairmanship, every one of the so-called innovations at Blackpool listed below flowed. It involved assuming that conference was just as interested in maintaining an orderly debate as was the platform – an assumption that was wholly justified by what happened that week. We got through all our business and emergency debates too.

Fourthly, I tried to sort out the different grounds on which the reference back of the Conference Arrangements Committee's reports were moved, thus identifying the main issues. Delegates were therefore able to have a clear vote on the first day to guide the Conference

Arrangements Committee — which obligingly altered the timetable to make room for the emergency debates which conference really wanted.

Fifthly, I gave a precise ruling on the exact meaning of an NEC reservation — when it accepts a resolution — thus clarifying a most important aspect of conference procedure. The NEC had fallen into the unsatisfactory practice of accepting resolutions which contained some points with which it did not really agree, by telling the NEC spokesman to enter a "reservation" about this or that phrase in them.

Since conference was usually glad to be told that the resolution was accepted, it tended to ignore the "reservation" and, so the resulting decision became blurred and might be shrugged off later as having been qualified by the platform — even though the mover and seconder and conference had never really been given a chance to say whether or not they accepted the platform reservation.

This was the very point raised on the Monday evening in respect of the NEC reservation about the Housing Finance Act resolution. Conference, given a second chance to vote the following morning on that resolution, voted against the NEC reservation.

In future the NEC, and delegates, will think a lot more carefully about the real meaning of resolutions that they are debating and deciding. That is important.

Sixthly, I treated every point of order seriously and without any automatic prejudice against them before they were made. Many delegates find it very difficult to understand the arrangements about business, and to discover exactly when the debates that concern them will take place and, even more, whether the subjects in which they are most interested will ever be discussed.

By allowing a little more latitude than is usual, many of these points were brought up by delegates at the rostrum and disposed of quickly and without ill-will. Some were not points of order at all, but they were all points of substance, and were accepted as such.

Seventhly, I made myself available informally to meet delegates half an hour to an hour before the conference sessions began in order to hear their points of order or problems and try to sort them out. This chairman's "surgery" or advice bureau was appreciated and it saved the time of conference.

Eighthly, I showed, to anyone who came to consult me, the chairman's notes prepared each day by the staff at Transport House. These notes listed every resolution that was to be debated, together with the amendments and the names of movers, seconders and of the NEC member who was to open or wind up — including the time allowed and the NEC recommendation that was to be made on each resolution and amendment.

With these on his desk, no chairman can fail to do his technical job properly. There is nothing secret about these notes – but by sharing them with anyone who wished to see them, the chairmanship was converted into an information centre at the disposal of the conference as a whole. This is how it ought to be.

Ninthly, I sought and obtained the support of conference for the "Request to speak" cards to be used, so that every delegate who wanted to speak had a direct personal link with the chair.

Some delegates have always written urgent notes asking to be called; and those who knew the chairman personally have always had an unfair advantage. The cards gave the others a chance. It was also a great help to be able to go through the cards and review in advance the whole range of opinions from trade union and constituency and socialist society delegates so as to keep a fair balance as between different views and between age groups and between men and women – especially as there were far too few women elected by their organisations to be delegates.

This system can work only if conference trusts its chairman. But some of the best speeches were made by those who would never have been called without the card system. It also saved a great deal of time as the next speaker to be called was always ready by the rostrum and we had 40 more speakers than the year before as a result, and more women. In addition, in the official report of conference, the names of all those who wanted to speak in the Common Market debate – but were not called – are printed, together with a note, taken from the cards, of the main point which each one wanted to make.

Tenthly, I tried to treat the delegates with the respect due to a body of men and women who bring together a wide experience of life, a high sense of personal responsibility, long service to the movement and deep convictions – rather than as an unruly mob who have to be kept in order, by tough chairmanship.

No chairman watching the faces of those who come to conference or listening to each and every speech made, can fail to be deeply impressed by this Parliament of Labour, which is the only forum where working people, not themselves holding an elected office as an MP or councillor. can actually reach real decisions.

Of course, with such a large assembly of people discussing such complex problems, there is no guarantee that every decision will be. right. Nor can you avoid some confused moments since real democracy is untidy at the edges. But, with all its imperfections, the Labour conference is by far the most democratic in the world.

What of this year's conference? Each successive chairman has his own personal style and Bill Simpson has a very great deal of experience of trade union conferences behind him.

But I naturally hope that some of the changes made at Blackpool

1972 will carry forward to Blackpool 1973 – and beyond.

1. That we shall insist that the role of conference remains central and its decisions are accepted, as constituting the highest policy-making body in the Labour Party.

2. That the resolutions and amendments submitted are worded with the precision appropriate to their importance, and call for practical socialist policies.

3. That the NEC takes its function even more seriously and carefully explains exactly what it is saying to conference about their resolutions – so that no one is in any doubt about its recommendations.

4. That the chairman's prime role is seen to be to help delegates by providing them with all the information they need to get the most out of conference – including general access to the notes he gets to guide him.

5. That the card system for speakers be continued; and perhaps extended so that all the names of those not called can be entered into the printed records of each debate published by the party – to provide a really full account of the work of conference.

These are simple but important ways of entrenching democracy within the Labour Party which, as chairman, I sought to make the keynote of my year. Many other aspects of party democracy need to be considered too.

But a really effective Labour Party conference, mapping out the road to democratic socialism in Britain, offers the best guarantee we can hope for that the Labour Party will serve the interests of the huge majority of workers by hand and brain who brought it into existence and look to it to work for them.

Secrecy and the National Executive*

This article published in Tribune *in June 1973 argued the case for publishing the minutes of the National Executive Committee of the Labour Party to allow Party members to know how the Party was run.*

My motion was defeated by 11-9 at the NEC on June 27th; and the same motion moved for the same reason at the Shadow Cabinet was defeated by 12-1 on the afternoon of the same day.

The debate on party democracy has now acquired a new significance.

One proposal bearing on this was put to the National Executive Committee at its last meeting and will be coming up again for a decision

*Article in *Tribune,* June 15, 1973. Reprinted by kind permission of *Tribune.*

this month. It is extremely simple and straightforward but if accepted, it will have the immediate effect of strengthening the rank-and-file within the movement.

The proposal is this: that whenever a motion or amendment is voted upon by the NEC at any of its meetings, the text should be recorded verbatim in the minutes and so should the names of those executive members voting for, and against, and also those present but not voting.

These recorded votes would then go forward for approval, as part of the minutes in the normal way at the following meeting; and these complete minutes would then be printed along with the NEC report to conference each year. Delegates — and others — would have before them a full record and report of the work — and views — of the NEC and its individual members. Indeed, as soon as the minutes of the previous month's meeting had been approved those minutes would be available for inspection on demand. Copies could even be supplied on request — at cost.

This proposal would have far-reaching effects. It would tear down the rather patchy curtain of secrecy that is supposed to "protect" the NEC from inquisitive people who want to know exactly what the NEC is doing and thinking. At present NEC minutes are supposed to be kept secret for 15 years; until recently there was a 30-year bar before students of party history were allowed to see them at all. The party has, in the past, seemed to be modelling its own practices on those of the Official Secrets Act, which have kept Government documents from the public until those responsible had virtually all retired from office.

In fact the party has moved some way from that rigid position. At the end of 1970, the NEC accepted a recommendation from the Information committee calling for a more open information policy. Some papers prepared for the NEC, which previously had "private and confidential" marked on them, almost as a matter of course, began to be declassified and even circulated as information papers for general use.

Sir Harry Nicholas, when General Secretary, was authorised to brief the press after each NEC meeting to describe the decisions that had been reached together with the background necessary to explain those decisions. It gradually became accepted that when a vote had taken place, the figures for and against (but *never* the names) were also given. This innovation helped to set the record straight, and it reduced the damage done by partial leaks and briefing undertaken by "private enterprise", although this still continues.

But when, at its April meeting this year, the East Surrey party actually wrote to NEC members asking each of them how they had voted on a particular issue over the Housing Finance Act, we were quite properly reminded that the NEC had always declined to reveal, or even

299

record, the names of those who had voted by a show of hands. There never are written ballots except in the case of voting for the appointment of a General Secretary or National Agent and these ballots are secret — and should remain so.

The present proposal arises directly out of the East Surrey request, since it provided an opportunity for the NEC to reconsider its past practice.

Why is it important that a change should be made?

First, because members of the executive are elected bv conference delegates and those delegates are entitled to know how those NEC members actually vote. This embodies a simple principle of democratic accountability comparable to the publication of the division lists showing the voting record of every MP.

Second, because the NEC has moved towards the greater openness described above and this proposal only carries that movement forward to its logical conclusion.

Third, because the reports that appear in the newspapers and on television are still sometimes inaccurate, malicious and misleading and these derive from slanted leaking and briefing that cannot be corrected without making a full and accurate account available.

Fourth, because there is no valid reason why the decisions of the NEC should be kept secret. The NEC is not the Shadow Cabinet with its special Parliamentary responsibilities, still less the Cabinet itself with Government secrets to protect. It is the custodian of conference decisions, accountable to conference, and to nobody else. It has the responsibility for placing policy proposals before conference, and then of seeking to develop, into further policy, the resolutions passed by conference. This is a job it cannot do properly unless conference is allowed to know almost as much about the NEC as the NEC knows about conference.

Fifth, because when a Labour Government is in office, the NEC will assume an even more important role. In the past *Tribune* has always argued that Labour Cabinet Ministers should not serve on the NEC because, with collective Cabinet responsibility to uphold, they were likely to be just a "payroll vote" committed to defend the Cabinet's decision whatever their real view was; and, also, in the process tilting the NEC away from conference decisions when conference and the Cabinet were in conflict, as sometimes happened.

These attempts to remove Cabinet Ministers from the NEC on the grounds of conflicting loyalties were never successful. Perhaps conference sensed the value of providing a forum where a limited dialogue between Cabinet and NEC was possible. Indeed on one famous occasion a senior Labour Cabinet Minister did actually cast his NEC vote against a key item of what was then Cabinet policy. This was supposed to be secret, but it did get out.

The question we should be asking ourselves is why the meetings of the NEC, when such important issues are discussed during the lifetime of a Labour Government, should be secret at all. Surely this is the time when it matters most that they should be public.

No one is suggesting that a Labour Cabinet should be constitutionally accountable to the NEC or conference. It is established in our parliamentary system that all Governments are first accountable to the House of Commons, and ultimately, to the electorate as a whole.

But that being clear, even party members who are elected to Parliament, and appointed to Ministerial posts, are also responsible for the decisions they reach, to everyone, including their party on whose manifesto they were elected.

If NEC minutes, complete with the recorded votes were available this Government-party dialogue would help to stimulate the necessary cross-fertilsation of views that could only be of benefit both to Ministers and the rank and file.

If this is the basic case for a change, what are the arguments against making it? The proposal does create practical difficulties. Will it change the character of the NEC and make it more rigid and formal? Will it tend to drive real discussion back into little caucuses, held before NEC meetings, and thus reduce the scope for compromise? Will it lead to undue pressure being brought on NEC members? Will it harm the party by advertising its disagreements too openly?

Will it make it harder for party leaders to campaign on the hustings for policies they are known, for certain, to have opposed in the NEC?

Will it affect the role of Labour MPs in a way that could damage the party? Would the rank and file and the public understand the reasons for our disagreements if they were made public? Would our opponents be able to exploit our openness to their advantage?

These are real problems that we have got to face frankly. It is no use brushing them aside.

But even so, I do not believe that these fears are really justified. Our differences of emphasis and policy are already widely known and fairly clearly understood.

Indeed, our strength as a party has always lain in our capacity to debate them publicly, and then accept the majority view — even if as individuals we went on trying to change it.

Nor should we underestimate the intelligence of the public or be too ready to assume that they would not understand the importance of what we are discussing and be reassured by knowing that, in these policy discussions, different viewpoints were being put forward and were being resolved by votes, and sometimes changed later by other votes. It is certainly arguable that people will have much more faith in the Labour Party if they know that these debates take place, and how they are settled, than if they are asked to believe that we are all of one mind on all questions; and that there are no minorities at work trying to get a different view accepted, which they know is not true.

These then are some of the considerations, for and against, that will precede the vote on this question at the next NEC. No one has any idea which way that vote will go.

But the matter need not necessarily rest with the NEC whatever it decides. It is a matter that concerns the whole membership of the Labour Party, as much as it concerns members of the NEC, just because what is being discussed is the relationship between the two. If the party as a whole wants to express its view – as well it might – then this could be done by submitting a conference resolution on it and having it voted upon at Blackpool. If the conference were to decide that it wanted the NEC minutes, in the complete form suggested, to be published and included in the NEC Report to future conference, then it has the power to say so and its decision would be final.

Indeed, unlike policy resolutions which would have to wait for implementation for the election of another Labour Government, a decision about the practices of the NEC would take effect immediately.

Thus, this simple proposal acquires an importance out of all proportion to its apparent simplicity. If it is carried it will firmly tilt the balance of power in favour of the rank and file with long-term consequences that could be very significant. It would also constitute an important victory for those who believe that our long campaign to democratise power in Britain has, first, to be won within our own movement.

Index

Aircraft Industry 87

BBC & ITV 15, 37-8, 136-152, 173-5, 205, 208, 212-3, 250
Bristol 95, 100, 151, 177-184, 259

Civil Liberties 153-175
Civil Service 89, 160ff., 215ff., 219, 232ff., 235
Common Market 13, 38, 70, 72, 79-80, 93-134, 165, 237-8, 241, 257, 272-3, 277, 280-1, 283, 297
Computers 42, 53, 64, 162ff., 204
Conservative Party 190ff., 246ff., 256, 260, 263
Cort, Dr. Joseph 153-9

Dockers 35-9

Education 39, 50, 59, 65-6, 91, 146, 192-3, 228-9
Engineering Industry 48ff

Farren, Mick 185-7
Fuel Crisis 89ff., 235-57
Fuller, Buckminster 52

Heath, Edward 26, 36, 38, 83, 87, 97, 103ff., 113ff., 131-3, 164-5, 224, 243, 246ff., 253, 254ff., 272-3, 294
Honours and Titles 100-1, 177-9, 197-9

Incomes Policy 21, 23, 78, 80, 248ff., 252ff., 268, 291, 298
Industrial Relations Act 17, 20, 21, 35ff., 79-80, 90, 143, 164-5, 170 252-3, 257, 291

Labour Party 11, 16ff., 25ff., 33ff., 38, 76ff., 84ff., 99, 100, 115, 117, 130, 135ff., 168ff., 190ff., 201ff., 215ff., 221ff., 232ff., 241, 243ff., 252, 254, 259-300
Labour Party Conference 84ff., 99ff., 113, 130, 133, 171, 261, 272ff., 281ff., 292ff., 294ff
Liberal Party 115, 121
Lincoln 293-4

Mansholt, Dr. E 117-9
Marx, Karl 32, 63, 160, 169, 267
Mass Media 15, 37-8, 66, 88, 135-152, 164, 172ff., 190, 205, 208-9, 212-4, 231, 235, 250ff., 257, 266, 289, 293-5
Mining Industry 30-1, 141-2, 235ff., 246ff
Ministry of Technology 12, 17, 18, 43ff., 48ff., 52ff., 64, 68-9, 81, 95, 220

Motor Car Industry 12ff., 46, 67ff., 86
Multinational Companies 12, 13, 39, 67-76, 79, 81, 85, 99, 186, 226, 237

National Hydrocarbons Corporation 240
National Union of Mineworkers 235, 246ff., 254ff
Nationalisation, extension of, 23ff., 29ff., 80ff., 84ff., 91, 240ff
Nationalised Industries 23, 29ff., 47, 51, 80, 86, 235ff., 246, 268
New Bristol Group 179-182
North Sea Oil 237ff
Nuclear Power 47, 53, 108-9, 238-9

Owen, Robert 32, 169, 267

Parliamentary Democracy 103ff., 113ff., 118-9, 120ff., 130ff., 164ff., 177-9, 201ff., 215ff., 221ff., 232ff., 268, 277ff
Parliamentary Lobby 214, 218ff
Pentonville Five 35-9
Post Office 41ff., 47, 51, 209

Robens, Lord 31, 32, 87
Rolls Royce 24, 30, 47, 86
Referendum 38, 95ff., 100ff., 119ff., 201ff., 210-2

Secrecy 62, 65, 160ff., 203, 209-10, 215ff., 218ff., 232ff., 268-9, 274-5, 284-5, 298ff
Shipbuilding 25ff., 29ff., 37, 214, 268
Slater Walker 78, 82, 84
Socialism 31, 32, 128-9, 165ff., 194, 275ff., 292-4

Technology 12ff., 43ff., 46-7, 48ff., 52ff., 62ff., 70ff., 81, 94-5, 112, 191, 205, 207ff., 224ff
Three-day Week 243-257
Thorpe, Jeremy 106, 121
Tolpuddle 35ff,, 38
Trade Unions 12ff., 16ff., 42, 63, 74, 79, 87, 140, 143ff., 150-1, 164-5, 169ff., 190ff., 206, 243-57, 268, 272ff., 289-92

United Nations 72-3, 94, 212, 225
Upper Clyde Shipbuilders 18, 25ff., 29ff., 33, 37, 51, 277

Wilson, Harold 84, 94
Women 38, 127, 188ff., 231, 273
Workers' Control 11ff., 16ff., 25ff., 29ff., 87, 91, 230, 291

Youth 185-7, 265, 271, 273